KOREAN
MASCULINITIES
AND TRANSCULTURAL CONSUMPTION

TransAsia: Screen Cultures

Edited by Koichi IWABUCHI and Chris BERRY

What is Asia? What does it mean to be Asian? Who thinks they are Asian? How is "Asian-ness" produced? In Asia's transnational public space, many kinds of cross-border connections proliferate, from corporate activities to citizen-to-citizen linkages, all shaped by media — from television series to action films, video piracy, and a variety of subcultures facilitated by internet sites and other computer-based cultures. Films are packaged at international film festivals and marketed by DVD companies as "Asian," while the descendents of migrants increasingly identify themselves as "Asian," then turn to "Asian" screen cultures to find themselves and their roots. As reliance on national frameworks becomes obsolete in many traditional disciplines, this series spotlights groundbreaking research on trans-border, screen-based cultures in Asia.

Other titles in the series:

The Chinese Exotic: Modern Diasporic Femininity, by Olivia Khoo

Cinema at the City's Edge: Film and Urban Networks in East Asia, edited by Yomi Braester and James Tweedie

*Cultural Studies and Cultural Industries in Northeast Asia: What a Difference a Region Make*s, edited by Chris Berry, Nicola Liscutin, and Jonathan D. Mackintosh

East Asian Pop Culture: Analysing the Korean Wave, edited by Chua Beng Huat and Koichi Iwabuchi

Horror to the Extreme: Changing Boundaries in Asian Cinema, edited by Jinhee Choi and Mitsuyo Wada-Marciano

TV Drama in China, edited by Ying Zhu, Michael Keane, and Ruoyun Bai

KOREAN
MASCULINITIES
AND TRANSCULTURAL CONSUMPTION
YONSAMA, RAIN, OLDBOY, K-POP IDOLS

Sun JUNG

香港大學出版社
HONG KONG UNIVERSITY PRESS

Hong Kong University Press
14/F Hing Wai Centre
7 Tin Wan Praya Road
Aberdeen
Hong Kong
www.hkupress.org

Hardback   ISBN 978-988-8028-66-5
Paperback   ISBN 978-988-8028-67-2

British Library Cataloguing-in-Publication Data
A catalogue record for this book is available from the British Library.

Printed and bound by Goodrich International Printing Co. Ltd., Hong Kong, China

To Chung Soon-Chul and Yoo Myung-Ja

Contents

List of Figures

Notes on the Usage of the Korean Language

1. This book uses the "Revised Romanization of Korean," which is the official Korean-language romanization system adopted by South Korea.

2. This system allows for very limited use of the hyphen. For the convenience of non-Korean readers, however, I use the hyphen in this book for some words such as Dae-jang-geum.

3. The names of some Korean authors and stars, such as Kim Kyung-Hyun and Lee Byung-Hun, have been predominantly romanized using the previous McCune-Reischauer romanization system in English-language works. In such cases, this book keeps the conventional romanization of their names.

4. In romanizing Korean names, this book uses the Korean convention of placing the surname before the given name. For example, the name of the Korean director, Park Chan-Wook, is written as such so that "Park," his surname, precedes his given name "Chan-Wook."

5. Unless otherwise stated, all translations from Korean to English are my own.

1

Korean Popular Culture and Transcultural Consumption: Globalized Desires between "Ours and Others"[1]

> For the next step [of *Hallyu*], we shouldn't have that name. Specially, Hal [Han] in *Hallyu* actually means Korea. So, I think from now on, if you really want to take it to the next level, maybe we shouldn't have a name like that ... [Before] it was basically about introducing Korea, Korean songs, Korean dramas. And hopefully I think it can be changed into something like, sharing. You know, mutual understanding through cultural sharing.
>
> — From the public lecture of JYP, a singer and music producer, at the forum "*Hallyu* in Asia: A Dialogue" held at Harvard University on February 16, 2007

South Korean popular culture has circulated globally since the late 1990s. Broadly, its global popularity can be observed in two major cultural phenomena: *Hallyu* (한류, 韓流), which is more evident in the Asian region; and cult fandom of the Korean genre film, which is more evident in the West.[2] The literal translation of *Hallyu* is "Korean Wave" and this term refers to the regional popularity of South Korean cultural products such as cinema, television drama, popular music, and fashion within Asia. The origin of *Hallyu* can be traced back to the success of the South Korean television drama, *What Is Love?* (*Sarang-i Mwogille* 1991).[3] When *What is Love?* was screened in China on CCTV (Chinese Central Television) in June 1997, its audience share was 16.6%, which is the highest record achieved by any foreign drama series to be broadcast in China up to that time (M. J. Lee 2006: 77).[4] Besides the early success of South Korean television drama in China, *Hallyu* also expanded into cinema with the regional success of the blockbuster film *Shiri* (1999) in Asia. In Japan, for example, *Shiri* sold over 1.2 million tickets (S. M. Kim 2001: 121).[5] Following *Shiri*'s success, the films *My Sassy Girl* (*Yeopgijeogin Geunyeo* 2001) and *My Wife Is a Gangster* (*Jopok Manura* 2001) also reached number one at the box office in several Asian countries including Hong Kong and Singapore. In Hong Kong, *My Sassy Girl* stayed at the box office number one spot for two weeks and its total box office revenue was more than US$1.7 million (Korean Film Council 2004). *Hallyu* was also evident in popular music: a South Korean female singer, BoA, became a regional superstar in Asia after all her albums and a number of her singles reached the top of Japan's *Oricon* music chart.[6] However, it was not until April 2003 when the drama *Winter Sonata* (*Gyeoul Yeonga* 2002) was first screened on NHK (*Nippon Hoso Kyokai*/Japan Broadcasting Corporation) that *Hallyu* became the regional popular cultural phenomenon within Asia that it is today.[7] The enormous popularity of *Winter Sonata* in countries such as Japan, Taiwan, Hong Kong, and China created "the *Yonsama* syndrome," which refers to the phenomenal stardom of *Winter Sonata*'s male lead, Bae Yong-Joon (BYJ). A year later, in 2004, another South Korean drama, *Full House* (*Pulhauseu* 2004), was screened in the region, where it also achieved around 50% of the average audience share in countries such as Indonesia, Thailand, the Philippines, and Hong Kong (JYPE 2006; E. J. Lee 2006).[8] The success of *Full House* helped contribute to the regional stardom of *Full House*'s male lead, Rain, who was later selected by *Time* magazine as one of "the world's most influential 100 people" in 2006 (Walsh 2006). Finally, a historical costume drama, *Dae-jang-geum* (2003–2004) has achieved phenomenal popularity in various regions. Since 2004, the drama has been widely broadcast in more than sixty countries around the world, including Taiwan, Hong Kong, China, Japan, Philippines, Singapore, Indonesia, Malaysia, Thailand, India, Iran, all the Arabic countries (through Dubai satellite television), Australia, the U.S., Canada, Russia, Uzbekistan, Turkey, Hungary, Ghana, and Zimbabwe (J. Y. Kim 2008).[9]

In addition to the regional phenomenon of *Hallyu*, the recent Western embrace of the South Korean genre film also exemplifies the global circulation of South Korean popular culture. In 2003, the well-known UK magazine, *New Statesman*, wrote of South Korean genre films: "It was South Korea that emerged as the new home of excitingly extreme Asian cinema, with bizarre export offerings ranging from the acclaimed serial-killer thriller *Memories of Murder*, through the ghostly chiller *A Tale of Two Sisters*, to the revenge-laden comic-book fable *Oldboy*" (Kermode 2004). The popularity of these genre films in the West was first evident in the international film festival circuit where the films were critically acclaimed. Bong Joon-Ho's *Memories of Murder* (*Sarin-ui Chueok* 2003) won the Director's Prize at the 2003 San Sebastian International Film Festival and the Cognac International Thriller Film Festival (Cine21 2003). In 2004, Park Chan-Wook's *Oldboy* (2003) won the Grand Prize at the Cannes International Film Festival (Cine21 2004a). Some of these genre films also went on to achieve commercial success in some Western film markets such as in the US, the UK, Italy, and France. For example, the copyright of *A Tale of Two Sisters* (*Janghwa Honglyeon* 2003) was sold to DreamWorks, a major American film company which intends to remake the film for Hollywood, for US$2 million. This was the highest selling price at the time for Asian film copyrights bought by Hollywood (Film2.0 2003). *Oldboy* is another example of a commercially successful Korean genre film in the West: it established a new record as the best-selling Asian film in the UK in December 2004 (H. L. Kim 2004).[10] Besides the international film festival circuit and Western commercial success, the recent Western embrace of the South Korean genre film is also apparent from film review Internet websites, such as Imdb.com, Rottentomatoes.com, BeyondHollywood.com, and Twitch.net. These websites provide detailed information and reviews of the latest South Korean genre films and it is from these websites that Western cult fandom can be observed. In particular, it is evident that *Oldboy* has inspired a new level of online cult fandom of the Korean genre film as an unprecedented number of film website users have praised the extreme violence of *Oldboy*'s main protagonist, Dae-Soo.

The above examples of *Hallyu* and Western cult fandom show the ways in which contemporary South Korean popular culture travels across national and cultural borders. It appears that contemporary South Korean popular culture is hybridized and influenced by various foreign cultures through transcultural flows largely facilitated by advanced media technology and globalization. This hybridity contributes to the aspect of *mugukjeok* (무국적, 無國籍, non-nationality) in globalized South Korean popular culture, which is the principal trait that enables South Korean popular culture to be globally consumed. In his book, *Recentering Globalization*, Koichi Iwabuchi suggests the concept of "*mukokuseki*" (non-nationality or non-Japaneseness), where he emphasizes "culturally odorless" aspects of Japanese consumer products such as the Sony Walkman or computer games. He argues that the trait of being culturally odorless *mukokuseki* in these Japanese consumer products is one of the main reasons behind their global popularity. In this book, I use the term *mugukjeok*, the Korean equivalent for Japanese *mukokuseki*, which shares the same Chinese characters "無國籍" with *mukokuseki*. I use the concept of *mugukjeok* here within the paradigm of transcultural hybridity, to refer to how popular cultural flows enable the mixing of particular cultural elements (national, traditional, and specific) with globally popular cultural elements, which then causes those particular cultural elements to become less culturally specific. Thus, the concept of *mugukjeok* in this book does not mean complete odorlessness or *non*-nationality; rather, *mugukjeok* implies the transcultural hybridity of popular culture, which is not only influenced by odorless global elements, but also by traditional (national) elements.[11]

The quote by JYP at the beginning of this chapter regarding the notion of deleting "*Hal*" (Han, 한, 韓, Korea/nness) from *Hallyu* can be understood within the paradigm of global *mugukjeok*. The *mugukjeok* traits in South Korean popular culture are particularly evident in the newly constructed hybrid Korean masculinities as represented by BYJ of *Winter Sonata*, Rain of *Full House*, and Dae-Soo of *Oldboy*. Many forms of non-Korean global masculinities — such as metrosexual, cute (Japanese かわいい, *kawaii*), and cool masculinities — cross cultural boundaries through disjunctive media cultural flows and hybridize contemporary South Korean masculinity. The consequent hybridity of South Korean masculinity creates *mugukjeok* traits which, in turn, contribute to its global popularity. Nevertheless, JYP's concept of the deletion of Koreanness from *Hallyu* does not fully explain the *mugukjeok* traits of hybrid Korean masculinity because his view ignores South

Korea's local specificity which forms the context surrounding the creation of South Korean popular cultural products. For example, it is a specific type of South Korean traditional masculinity, Confucian *seonbi* (선 비, scholar-official) masculinity, that is the basis for *mugukjeok* South Korean masculinity. Therefore, instead of using JYP's concept of the deletion of Koreanness from *Hallyu*, I argue that the *mugukjeok* traits of South Korean masculinity have to be explained through the notion of the transformation and reconstruction of South Koreanness that are driven by the "transcultural" hybridization processes between Korean traditional masculinities and global masculinities.

This book investigates the hybridity of contemporary South Korean popular culture and the transcultural desire of audiences in the various regional markets using the example of hybrid South Korean masculinity, based on a series of empirical reception studies of audiences in Japan, Singapore, and the West. It is argued that South Korean masculinity is hybridized and transformed due to disjunctive globalizations and transculturations, where South Korean masculinity is multifariously reconstructed and re-identified based on the ambivalent desires of audiences who mobilize mixed cultural practices arising from *mugukjeok* and the local specificities of each region.[12] These local specificities are driven by the particular reciprocal and contextual relationships between South Korea and each region that is evident from postcolonialism (Japan), trans-pop-consumerism (Singapore), and neo-Orientalism (the West). Through examining these three different sets of contextual specificities, this book demonstrates the different ways in which the ambivalent desires of each set of regional viewers embrace hybrid South Korean masculinities, which include soft masculinity, global masculinity, and postmodern masculinity.

To carry out the empirical research for this book, I employed methodologies such as participant observation, data collection through interviews and archival research, and survey research through questionnaires. I conducted both individual and focus group interviews with more than thirty interviewees and collected more than a hundred completed questionnaires in Japan, Singapore, and Australia.[13] To maintain the confidentiality of the participants, I use pseudonyms in this book to indicate each participant. Apart from the pre-arranged interviews, I coordinated additional interviews with owners and managers of DVD/CD shops and with a director of a film distribution company at the actual field research sites. In addition, I interviewed Park Chan-Wook, the director of *Oldboy*; Mika Kuroiwa, an NHK producer in Japan; Lee Gyeong-Hui, the chief editor of the *Hallyu* magazine, *Platinum*; and Christian Were, a brand manager of the film distribution company, Madman, in Australia. Because the sample size is relatively small, they cannot be representative of audiences of each cultural group. However, this research shows the different kinds of newly emerging transcultural consumption practices of global audiences in various popular culture consumer markets. In particular, in order to collect more reliable and up-to-date data on these groups of audiences, I have conducted longitudinal analysis of small sample groups. For example, apart from interviews and questionnaires, I have spent more than two years on follow-up research to further discover and define the characteristics of each audience group. This follow-up research has included close and constant observation of fan club website forums and film review websites, frequent emailing and online chatting with these audience groups and content analysis of newspaper and magazine articles which contain information on these audience groups. As a result of such persistent longitudinal research I was able to collect detailed and in-depth data on the various regional audiences of South Korean popular culture. Such longitudinal empirical research has also enabled me to come to an understanding of the diversity of the consumption practices of these regional audiences in relation to South Korean masculinity.

This chapter contextualizes the trajectories of studies on South Korean popular culture and the hybridization dynamics of transculturation on the one hand, and the conceptual background of the reconstruction of South Korean masculinity on the other. As briefly mentioned above, there are many examples that can demonstrate transculturation and hybridization in the realm of contemporary South Korean popular culture. Due to the limited scope of this chapter, I shall only discuss the most significant example — the Korean blockbuster.

Transculturation and Globalization in South Korean Popular Culture: The Case of the Korean Blockbuster

Hangukhyeong Beulleokbeoseuteo: Globalized and Spectacularized "*Haan*"

In 1999, the Korean blockbuster (한국형 블럭버스터, *Hangukhyeong Beulleokbeoseuteo*) emerged and gained nationwide popularity. The term was first used by South Korean daily newspapers when *Toemarok* was released in mid-1998 (B. C. Kim 2005). In the same year that the production plan for *Shiri* was announced, the South Korean media started to use the term *Hangukhyeong Beulleokbeoseuteo* regularly (G. E. Lee 2001). Its use dramatically increased after the unparalleled success of *Shiri*. By June 11, 1999, 119 days after its release, *Shiri* had sold over 5.8 million tickets nationwide, breaking the record that had been set by *Titanic* in South Korea in 1998 (S. Y. Chang 2000: 408). In *Shiri*, North Korean terrorists obtain CTX, a potent new liquid explosive, by hijacking and threaten to use it against South Korea. Agents from the South Korean secret intelligence service attempt to track down the terrorists. For melodramatic effect, the film's director, Kang Je-Gyu, adds a tragic love story between a South Korean agent and a North Korean female spy who become lovers and who eventually end up putting guns to each other's heart. As the film's slogan, "Korean-style action blockbuster," indicates, the film contains Hollywood action blockbuster genre characteristics such as "edge-of-your-seat action, suspense, blood, sweat, and emotion" (Altman 1999: 46). In terms of production and distribution, *Shiri* also follows the conventional characteristics of Hollywood blockbuster genre films, which are high-budget and wide-release. The total budget of *Shiri* was US$2.5 million, which was the highest production cost of a single film in South Korean film history up to 1999. Also, the film was played on 588 screens, which represented almost one third of the total number of screens (1,856) in South Korea at the time (G. H. Lee 2007a).

Shiri is often praised because of its seamless combination of spectacle — adapted from the Hollywood action blockbusters — and the pervading presence of indigenous South Korean content that stem from the national memory of loss (caused by the traumatic split between North and South Korea) and the national desire for reunification. *Shiri* depicts typical images of action films: car chases, explosions, and gunfights. In terms of spectacle, *Shiri* gained the approval of critics and audiences alike because of these action sequences. The film presents nine spectacular sequences at roughly thirteen-minute intervals in 123 minutes of total running time (G. W. Kim 2002: 49). It starts with a shockingly violent scene of North Korean guerrillas in training. This strategy of using a shocking scene in the beginning of the film follows the "five-minute rule" of successful Hollywood films, which is that a film only has five minutes to grab the audience's attention (G. W. Kim 2002: 48–49). Following this scene in *Shiri*, even bigger spectacles are shown, the biggest of which is a massive scene set in the Olympic stadium which is filled with 50,000 extras. It is these action scenes that exemplify how *Shiri* embodies the characteristics of the Hollywood blockbuster.

Since *Shiri*'s release and its subsequent enormous success, the South Korean media has taken an optimistic view of the future of South Korean cinema, which has shown that it can beat Hollywood giants like *Titanic*. "Some of the media noted that *Shiri*'s total production budget is only about two minutes of *Titanic*'s" and "some argued that while those culturally advanced countries like France and Japan struggle as they are attacked by Hollywood productions, Korea is the only one who is defeating them, in spite of IMF intervention" (G. W. Kim 2002: 19). In this euphoric climate, *Shiri*'s success was quickly followed by bigger blockbusters.[14] Another film featuring the split between North and South Korea, *Joint Security Area* (*Gongdong Gyeongbi Guyeok JSA* 2000), sold over 6.5 million tickets in 2000, and in the following year, the nostalgic gangster noir, *Friend* (*Chingu* 2001), sold over 8 million tickets (Korean Film Council 2001; 2002). On February 18, 2004, another Korean blockbuster, *Silmido* (2004), broke the box-office record again, selling 10 million tickets nationwide. Two months later, the war blockbuster, *Taegukgi* (*Taegeukgi Hwinallimyeo* 2004), broke *Silmido*'s record in only two weeks. In 2005, another film with a Korean War setting, *Welcome to Dongmakgol* (2005), also ranked high in the South Korean box office by selling more than 8 million tickets (Korean Film Council 2006).

The obvious commonality shared by the above films (except *Friend*) is the presentation of indigenous themes, such as the Korean War and the reunification issue, within the globalized cultural form of the Hollywood blockbuster. The success of these films lies in the retelling of the trauma of the Korean War. This trauma has engraved its symbolic meaning of *haan* on South Korea's national identity, which then became a driving force behind the success of the films in the domestic market. The Korean blockbusters have clearly mobilized the notion of *haan* to appeal to the South Korean psyche. The meaning of *haan* is peculiar to Korea; it is intrinsically and intricately connected with the everyday lives of Koreans.[15] Korean *haan* can be compared to African-American *blues* in terms of oppression and emotional expression: "It is the ethos of groups or racial mourning. Many years of social injustice, political oppression, economic exploitation, or foreign invasions create the collective unconscious *haan* or *blues*" (Min et al. 2003: 6–9). For Koreans, *haan* evokes a sense of shared destiny and suffering that is considered vital to the building of a national identity (Allen 1999: 129). *Haan* has been one of the most significant themes of Korean national film over the past decades.

Besides the South Korean domestic market, some of these blockbuster films, like *Shiri* and *Taegukgi*, have also achieved significant success in some overseas markets such as the US, Japan, and Hong Kong (Cine21 2004b; Cine21 2004c).[16] The noticeable global recognition of these films is the result of transcultural media entertainment flows, where the Korean indigenous theme of *haan* has been spectacularized and globalized within the paradigm of the globally popular genre form of the Hollywood action blockbuster. For instance, in *Taegukgi*, the theme of *haan* is portrayed through the characters of two brothers who are separated and find themselves on opposite sides of the border between North and South during the Korean War. This separation of the two brothers is a poignant analogy of the divided nation of North and South Korea. The film's director, Kang Je-Gyu, portrays this national sentiment within the Hollywood action blockbuster form, depicting realistic battle scenes that are reminiscent of the Omaha beach sequence of a Hollywood film, *Saving Private Ryan* (1998). As Ethan Alter writes:

> [*Taegukgi*] bears an unmistakable Hollywood imprint. Kang uses every convention in the book, from the ragtag squad of colorful misfits to the corny framing device that bookends the film. Still, the movie's scope overcomes its generic narrative: The battle scenes are terrifically filmed, often reaching *Private Ryan*'s level of intensity, and despite your better judgment, you do get caught up in the melodrama. (2005)

As the above quote suggests, *Taegukgi* demonstrates the influence that Hollywood films can have on the work of non-Hollywood filmmakers. In this case, *Taegukgi* exemplifies cultural hybridity, where the national sentiment of *haan*, represented in a melodramatic plot, is incorporated into the globalized media aesthetic form of the Hollywood blockbuster. By narrating Korea's historical trauma through the Hollywood blockbuster genre, these culturally hybridized films become both familiar and unfamiliar to non-Korean audiences, and it is such cultural hybridity that is the crucial factor in helping these Korean blockbusters travel across national and cultural boundaries.

Shiri, Uncanny Amalgamation between Ours and Others

Many South Korean scholars link the success of the Korean blockbuster with the context of the economic rise and fall of South Korea after the 1988 Seoul Olympics. South Korea began to be referred to as a "dragon economy," along with Singapore, Taiwan, and Hong Kong. In this economically affluent period, South Koreans were optimistic about a strong economic future. With the prospect of a national average income of US$10,000, this sanguine mood reached its peak when South Korea became the twenty-ninth regular member of the Organization for Economic Co-operation Development (OECD) on December 12, 1996 (G. W. Kim 2002: 16). In 1997, however, the International Monetary Fund (IMF) crisis occurred unexpectedly. The economy collapsed under the accumulated contradictions of overextended *chaebol* (or *jaebeol* — family-controlled conglomerates in South Korea), insolvent banks, and inflexible labor markets, and Korea began an unfamiliar era of economic depression and social dislocation (B. K. Kim 2000: 173). All of a sudden, South Korean society panicked as the number of homeless and jobless people escalated. In response to this, rapid globalization was advocated by the South Korean government, which proposed that business had to be stimulated to produce global commodities in order to overcome this economic depression. As Rob Wilson argues:

> Given the era of rampant globalization and the cybernetic transgression of all media and national borders, President Kim Dae-Joong has advocated opening South Korea ever more dramatically to foreign trade and investment, under the IMF-challenged slogan of "globalization," as some kind of hegemonic neo-liberal solution to the Asian recession and currency crisis. Korea seems to be fast coming undone, as coherent national-film imaginary, in these rampant global/local dialectics. (2001: 310)

The 1997 IMF economic catastrophe changed the whole paradigm of South Korean society rapidly and triggered a new national trauma in South Korean modern history. In this chaotic, and what was perceived as a shameful, moment, *Shiri* arrived at what, in hindsight, looked like the right historical time in South Korean modern history to heal the trauma. Before filming took place,

Shiri's director, Kang Je-Gyu, declared that "he would make a Korean-style action blockbuster which would equally match Hollywood ones" (G. W. Kim 2002: 18). When the film did, in fact, triumph over Hollywood blockbusters at the box office, *Shiri* gave hope to South Koreans that South Korean blockbusters could be as good as those of the Americans (2002: 17–21). As some film critics have observed, the most remarkable factor of *Shiri*'s success was, ironically, the IMF crisis. For example, the film critic, Kang Han-Seop, argues that the success of *Shiri* was due to the exceptional explosion of patriotism in the era of economic crisis rather than the film's quality (2003: 66). Another film critic, Byeon Seong-Chan, argues that "uncanny nationalism did its work [on the success of *Shiri*], which had spread in the whole society in the form of collective unconsciousness after the IMF crisis" (2004: 42). Kim Gyeong-Wook also points out that *Shiri*'s success is a mysterious social phenomenon caused by an irrational and non-critical frenzy and collective enthusiasm for nationalism, and observes that "some people have claimed that *Shiri* won victory in restoring independence to Korean cinema which had been colonized by Hollywood" (2002: 6). She also argues that after the economic currency collapse and the subsequent IMF intervention, a complex social phenomenon emerged in South Korean society. This phenomenon was a mixture of a sense of shame about "ours" and frantic enthusiasm for America as a progressive symbol of globalization (2002: 18–21). Kim Gyeong-Wook's position is that *Shiri* represents a re-emergence of South Korean national identity and also expresses the ambivalence by South Koreans towards globalization. This ambivalence towards globalization can be seen in the way that *Shiri* appeals to the most intimate "national" sentiment of South Koreans — *haan* — by means of the most globalized cinematic form of the Hollywood blockbuster. This ambivalence was, in fact, already evident at the very beginning of South Korean cinema. Joo Chang-Gyu highlights this contradictory nature:

> There are already contradictory powers working within the concept of "Korean cinema" since cinema itself, which is obviously rooted in the West, flowed into this country through its colonial experience by means of the extension of capitalism, and it adapted to the non-Western public as a form of national entertainment. What are the persistent characteristics of Korean cinema history, which is a mixture of colonialism, capitalism, nationalism, and the consciousness of working class people? (2001: 184)

As Joo argues above, South Korean cinema was initially contradictory in its birth because it was based on the Western technology of film, but this Western technology eventually became localized to South Korea's socio-political context, which is a mixture of such historical events as colonialism, capitalism, and nationalism. This, I suggest, describes the cultural hybridization of South

Korean cinema. Joo's notion of Korean cinema as "contradictory" and "a mixture" remains crucial to the discussion of the ambivalent traits of *Shiri*. The history of the film's success shows contemporary South Korean cinema's ambivalent state where the national sentiment of *haan* was encroached upon by globalization, and Hollywood film conventions were absorbed into the South Korean national identity.

In *The Fantasy of Blockbuster: Narcissism of Korean Cinema*, Kim Gyeong-Wook severely criticizes such cultural absorption that characterizes South Korean cinema's uncritical imitation of Hollywood. She states: "under the US-led globalization dynamics [after the IMF crisis], Korea obsessively learned how to completely mimic America[n culture, socio-economic system and lifestyle] and how the whole Korean society could be Americanized" (2002: 17). Kim further argues that *Shiri* is located somewhere where Korea(n cinema) discards "Ours" (Koreanness) and obtains something "Americanized" which is disguised as globalization (2002: 18). She also applies this criticism to post-*Shiri* films such as *Phantom* (*Yuryeong* 1999), *Bichunmoo* (2000), and *The Warrior* (*Musa* 2001). For her, *Phantom* is another Hollywood copy while the other two films are benchmarking products of Hong Kong and Japanese martial arts films that demonstrate South Korean cinema's desire to become global (or non-national/*mugukjeok*) (2002: 20–21). Here, Kim's criticism brings a fundamental question. If, as Joo Chang-Gyu has argued above, the origin of South Korean cinema is "contradictory" and "a mixture," how can South Korean cinema's "Koreanness" be defined? A film critic, Kang Han-Seop, points out that the current mainstream film discourses in South Korea reflect South Korea's inferiority complex and shows its yearning for originality and purity. He states:

> South Korean cinema today has not been forcefully constructed by Hollywood … For the past 100 years, it has been naturally developed through the reciprocal collision, restraint and adaptation between filmmakers, capitalists (cinema owners and investors), and audiences within the fluctuating changes in different levels and aspects of South Korean cinema. (2004: 129–30)

Kang further argues that South Korean cinema can only be identified by the form and content of *today*'s South Korean cinema, which is based on the cultural evolution point of view (2004: 130). Kang's argument clearly demonstrates how South Korean cinema can neither be pure Korean nor completely dominated by Hollywood, and how the question regarding the seeking of "Koreanness" in the South Korean cinema discourse is in contradiction to its hybrid identity. Thus, I suggest that the Korean blockbuster has to be understood within the framework of cultural hybridization rather than within a cultural imperialist paradigm that erects the false dichotomics of Korean/non-Korean, ours/others, subordinate/dominant.

The Korean Blockbuster: An Indigenized Global Form

In *The Location of Culture*, Homi Bhabha argues that colonial presence and its ambivalent identity are revealed when the subordinate culture recognizes dominating discourses "as they articulate the signs of cultural difference and re-implicate them within the deferential relations of colonial power" (1994: 110). This discrimination process between colonial culture and its double, the subordinate culture, is represented through disavowal. It is this that creates colonial hybridity. As Bhabha argues:

> Hybridity is the sign of the productivity of colonial power, its shifting forces and fixities; it is the name for the strategic reversal of the process of domination through disavowal (that is, the production of discriminatory identities that secure the "pure" and original identity of authority). Hybridity is the revaluation of the assumption of colonial identity through the repetition of discriminatory identity effects. (1994: 112)

Bhabha's theory of postcolonial mimicry is emblematized in his phrase, "almost the same, but not quite." This phrase illustrates the fact that when the subordinate culture copies colonial or the dominant culture, local practices of reinterpretation and redeployment always occur and create "difference" between the original and its double. He also argues that between the Western (dominant) sign and its colonial signification, "a map of misreading" has emerged in the subordinate culture which highlights the subordinate's sovereign ability to accept or reject the dominant culture. Supporting this point, Leela Gandhi also argues that colonial mimicry is "an ambivalent mixture of deference and disobedience" (1998: 149). These points tie in with Roland Robertson's "glocalization" theory, which emphasizes the mitigating effects of local conditions on global pressures (1995). These arguments above all acknowledge the indigenous/subordinate culture's ability to discern and reinterpret the authority of the dominant culture.

However, as seen in the earlier section, the cultural imperialist argument in the South Korean cinema discourse only stresses Hollywood/America's dominant influence on South Korean cinema. This argument, which interprets the global omnipresence of the Hollywood film by using the dichotomies of dominant/dominated and center/periphery, creates a homogeneous view of global audiences. Such a paradigm is based on the false assumption that such global audiences blindly absorb Hollywood/American values without reinterpreting them. In this paradigm, globalization is simply the synonym of a blanket Americanization of the world as led by Hollywood. In *Modernity at Large*, however, Arjun Appadurai asserts that "globalization does not necessarily or even frequently imply homogenization or Americanization ..." (1996: 17). He argues that various cultures and ideologies are brought into new societies and they tend to become indigenized in one way or another (1990: 295). Anthony Giddens also suggests that globalization is increasingly becoming "de-centered," that is, that globalization is not under the control of particular nations or large corporations (1999). Rico Lie also argues that "cultural imperialism is no longer seen as an adequate way to denote the process of intercultural contact and changing cultures," and provides Reebee Garofalo's summary of the four weaknesses of the theory of cultural imperialism. First, the theory of cultural imperialism overstates external determinants and undervalues the internal dynamics of localities; second, it conflates economic power with cultural effects; third, it assumes that audiences are passive and renders local creativity less significant; and fourth, it often creates the patronizing view that the authentic and organic native culture of the developing world is under siege by the synthetic and inauthentic culture of the developed West (quoted in Lie 2003: 59).

In contrast to the above critics who emphasize the adaptive power of local cultures, the cultural imperialist view only highlights South Korean cinema's mimetic tendencies and its neo-colonial desire of the dominant culture that is Hollywood while failing to acknowledge local power dynamics such as the ability to discriminate and re-examine the dominant culture. As Koichi Iwabuchi also asserts, the concept of cultural imperialism implies that the recipients of dominant culture consume this culture automatically and without a critical cultural lens (2002a: 39). In the light of this, I suggest that the cultural imperialist perspective is inadequate to explain the current phenomenon of hybridity in South Korean cinema because it overlooks three major points. First, the premise that South Korean cinema "discards Koreanness" is not applicable since South Korean cinema has always been "contradictory" in nature and has been "a mixture" of local and foreign influences. Second, it ignores the ability of South Korean audiences to make critical judgments of Hollywood blockbuster conventions. Third, it ignores the hybridized presence of South Korean cinema through the articulation of difference through postcolonial mimicry.

Finding Its Lack: Similar but Different

In her article, "Disappearing South Korean Women: Unconscious Optics of the Korean Blockbuster," Kim So-Young argues that *Hangukhyeong Beulleokbeoseuteo* is "a local translation of the Hollywood blockbuster" since it contains Korea's geopolitical space and themes (2001: 28). The term *Hangukhyeong Beulleokbeoseuteo* (the Korean blockbuster), demonstrates the polarity between its two chief characteristics: "Korea(n)" indicates an indigenous and national identity while "blockbuster" designates the big-budget foreign entertainment influence of Hollywood. Kim points out that this newly coined term explains "how Korea's geopolitical characteristics are interpreted targeting the local, the Asian region, and the global market in the form of film production" (2001: 27). She argues that the foreign cultural form known as the Hollywood blockbuster has been adapted, modified, and indigenized to the domestic South Korean market. She points out that it is important to consider how subordinate cultures such as the Korean blockbuster can subvert the dominant practices of the Hollywood blockbuster (2001: 27). Kim's point is based on Walter Benjamin's view of translation. In his essay, "The Task of the Translator," Benjamin highlights the importance of the translator's effort in differentiating in the translation from the original based on the specific linguistic and contextual aspects of the local. Employing Benjamin's argument, Kim So-Young suggests that the Korean blockbuster phenomenon has to be discussed within the framework of a local and regional "translation" process, that can also be a "subversive practice," of the Hollywood blockbuster, rather than a concept of the reproduction of "the same thing" repeatedly (2001: 27). In the article, she clearly points out that "it is obvious that the Korean blockbuster is a repetition of the Hollywood blockbuster. However, the practice of repetition does not always bring about sameness. There is a subversive repetition, as well as a subordinated repetition, in terms of reproduction" (2001: 27).

Kim So-Young's point aptly explains how local translation practices complicate and hybridize Korean cinema. In fact, *"hyeong"* from *"Hangukhyeong Beulleokbeoseuteo"* can be interpreted as "style." Thus, the literal meaning of the term could be "South Korean-style blockbuster," as distinct from the Hollywood "style" blockbuster. Alternatively, *Hangukhyeong* can also be interpreted as "South Koreanized," which implies the South Korean indigenization of the Hollywood blockbuster. The best example of this indigenization is, as has been discussed previously, how the national sentiment of *haan* has been spectacularized and globalized through the form of the Hollywood action blockbuster in films such as *Shiri*, *Taegukgi*, and *Joint Security Area*. The term *Hangukhyeong Beulleokbeoseuteo* thus demonstrates the dynamic relationship between the contradictory processes of globalization and localization.

Kim So-Young's argument about the *Hangukhyeong Beulleokbeoseuteo* is important because it introduces the notion that a new style of South Korean film has emerged, one that is an indigenized, localized, and Koreanized version of the Hollywood blockbuster. This view suggests that the recent development in South Korean cinema is a re-adaptation of hegemonic Hollywood culture that has resulted in a new localized form. This can be explained using Roland Robertson's concept of "glocalization," which emphasizes how the globalization of a product is more likely to succeed when the product is adapted specifically to each locality or culture that the product is marketed in. According to Robertson, glocalization is "the creation of products or services intended for the global market, but customized to suit the local cultures" (1995: 28). This can also be described by the Japanese term, *dochakuka*, which means "a global outlook adapted to local conditions" (1995: 28). This term comes from the Chinese characters "土着化" (*tu zhuo hua*) which has also been used in South Korea with a different pronunciation "토착화" (*tochakhwa*). It refers to "how [certain forms of institution, culture, or customs] have become totally indigenized and adapted to the local" (Naver Dictionary 2004). Kim So-Young points out that the Korean blockbusters are "a compromise between foreign forms and local materials," offering "both a voluntary mimicry of, as well as imagined resistance to, large Hollywood productions, playing of various logics of both identity and difference in the global cultural industry" (2003). Her argument, acknowledging South Korea's local awareness, is based on the *tochakhwa* (indigenization) practice in South Korea of the Western blockbuster genre. In an article in the film magazine *Cine21*, "South Korean Cinema Manifesto," Kim So-Young emphasizes the similar (mimicked) and different (indigenized) aspects of hybridity in South Korean cinema in this way:

> While Korean cinema surely has its own exclusivity, it also contains non-simultaneous simultaneity with tradition, genre, conventions, and track of thoughts, which the world cinema history has accumulated and has influenced globally and concurrently. Even though the Korean film's domestic market share reached over 50% that means neither we see "pure" Korean films nor we think in a "Korean" way ... it is because the colonies copy the dominant [ideology and cultural forms] and reproduce it. They imagine the copied production as theirs and their own achievement unless the colonies break into the process of the postcolonial transformation. As a non-Western and non-hegemonic country, the speculation of "Korean" cinema would come to notice when this attachment/tie [to the dominant] is cut off or when it is represented why it cannot be cut off. (2004)

Undeniably, the Korean blockbuster syndrome and the tendency of recent South Korean cinema seem to strengthen the connection to Hollywood's dominant cultural productions. Post-IMF crisis films like *Shiri* and *Taegukgi* tend to present Korean content with a "Hollywood tongue" (S. Y. Kim 2001: 27). Kim So-Young's words aptly support my argument that South Korean cinema is not pure but that it is highly hybrid. Her point here is that this hybridity can be called "Korean" as soon as South Korean cinema reveals its difference from, as well as its similarity to, dominant Western culture. Instead of criticizing South Korean cinema's lack of purity, Kim So-Young suggests that this hybridity can be regarded as constituting "Koreanness" in contemporary South Korean cinema discourse.

Similar to Kim So-Young, Chris Berry also argues for understanding South Korean blockbusters in terms of postcolonial indigenization when he discusses the films of Park Chan-Wook. In an interview, Park Chan-Wook says: "at one time, I tried to catch up with Hollywood movies, but it was useless. So, I decided to produce movies that appeal to Koreans' native sentiments" (quoted in Berry 2003: 217). In his breakthrough blockbuster, *Joint Security Area*, Park depicts the poignant relationship between North and South Korean soldiers at Panmunjeom, the Korean

DMZ (demilitarized zone) peace village. From being enemies, the soldiers become friends, comrades, and brothers; this deepening relationship between the North and South Korean soldiers in the film demonstrates how the "Joint Security Area" becomes less a site of military stalemate and more a place where warm, brotherly interactions establish strong emotional ties. Through portraying such brotherly interaction, the film romantically embodies the desires of both North and South Koreans for reunification. In this film, Park merges the native sentiments of North and South Korea with the blockbuster genre. This creative merging reflects the hybridity of the South Korean blockbuster which clearly demonstrates "different" aspects from the dominant Hollywood form. Hence, regarding Park's comment about making movies that appeal to the native sentiments of Koreans, Berry emphasizes the "difference" of South Korean cinema and argues that "in borrowing the idea and practice of the blockbuster and adapting them to local circumstances, at the very moment of perceiving a local 'lack' Park simultaneously de-Westernizes it" (2003: 217). In other words, as soon as Park realizes local "lack" — an awareness of difference in the South Korean blockbuster from the dominant culture of Hollywood — and supplements this lack by appealing to South Korea's native sentiments, the Hollywood blockbuster is de-Westernized to become the indigenized *Hangukhyeong Beulleokbeoseuteo*. According to the arguments put forward by Kim So-Young and Berry then, the postcolonial awareness of the "lack" in local culture is arguably the main source of power to create not only hybrid, but also indigenized, South Korean cinema. Their arguments well explain the current tendencies towards hybridization in South Korean popular culture within the framework of disjunctive globalizations.

The theoretical frameworks of Kim So-Young and Berry that focus on the postcolonial awareness of the "lack" in South Korean cinema are important in analyzing the transcultural hybridization of South Korean popular culture. On the other hand, South Korean popular cultural products travel very successfully and are consumed transculturally: for example, the two television drama series, *Winter Sonata* and *Full House*, have achieved great regional success in Asia and the Western cult fandom of the Korean genre film, *Oldboy*, is significant. As such, South Korean popular culture is no longer a subordinate culture. A new theoretical paradigm is needed to explain its culturally dominant position in regional and global popular culture. While awareness of its lack is the key to understanding the hybridity of South Korean popular culture, the awareness of its "sufficiency" is the key to explain its global success. I argue that its diversity together with the various aspects of its hybridity are the key factors behind its success in the various global markets. The hybridity of South Korean popular culture and its global consumption demonstrate re/adaptation, re/indigenization, and re/formation of the global cultural hegemony. I argue that South Korean popular culture, rather than being imposed upon by outside forces, confronts and adopts foreign cultural identities, forms, and commodities, and consequently produces a hybrid articulation of South Korean popular culture that enables its movement across cultural boundaries. In other words, the hybridity of South Korean popular culture enables transcultural flow, a flow of culture that is neither uni-directional nor bi-directional, but multi-directional.

Transculturation

Transculturality as Hybridity

Wolfgang Welsch argues that the most appropriate concept to describe today's cultures is "transculturality." He contrasts the concept of transculturality with three other concepts: the classical concept of single cultures, interculturality, and multiculturality (1999: 194). The traditional concept of single cultures was first suggested by Johann Gottfried Herder in *Ideas on the Philosophy of the History of Mankind* (1784–1791). Welsch states that Herder's concept of culture is characterized by three elements: social homogenization, ethnic consolidation, and intercultural delimitation. Regarding the first element, Welsch argues that modern societies are differentiated within themselves to a high degree as evident in the multicultural aspects of everyday lives that have produced differences between classes, genders, and races. The socially homogenous view of the single cultures concept does not capture the multicultural reality of modern-day societies. Secondly, he argues that the idea of ethnic consolidation is only applicable when cultures are envisaged as "closed spheres or autonomous islands" (1999: 195). This view completely ignores the historical evidence of intercultural mingling. Finally, Welsch describes the third element of the concept of single cultures — intercultural delimitation — as cultural separatism. He argues that this third element is a form of cultural racism.

In relation to the more recent concept of interculturality, Welsch argues that this concept focuses on the conflict between different cultures. He suggests that the concept of interculturality is also problematic because it still stems from an idea of cultures as separate or forming closed islands. Finally, Welsh observes that the concept of multiculturality espouses the idea of one society as composed of several different cultures. He argues that this concept still shares the same presupposition as the classical concept of single cultures where cultures are clearly distinguished and homogeneous. The only difference is that the concept of multiculturality implies that these different cultures exist within the one society or community while the concept of single cultures posits each culture as constituting a whole society. Welsch claims that the problem with the concepts of single cultures, interculturality, and multiculturality is that the term "culture" no longer implies homogeneity and separateness.

Because the description of cultures as islands or spheres does not describe accurately the globalized reality of contemporary societies, Welsch proposes the concept of transculturality and posits three reasons to support this concept. First, he argues that transculturality is a consequence of the inner differentiation and complexity of modern cultures. Second, he points out that cultures today can no longer be explained by ideas of separatism or homogenization because they are interconnected and entangled with each other. Third, he suggests that today's cultures are characterized by hybridization which can apply at the levels of population, commodities, and information. Therefore, Welsch argues that there is no longer anything absolutely "foreign" or exclusively "our own." For Welsch, transculturation theory is an alternative to the theory of cultural imperialism which emphasizes homogenization over heterogenization, Westernization over indigenization. In contrast to the cultural imperialism theory, the concept of transculturality prioritizes locality and particularity. This relationship between transculturation and cultural heterogenization has been explained by many scholars. Lull, for example, argues that "cultural influences always interact with diverse local conditions producing a range of heterogeneous dialogues" (1995: 147). Iwabuchi also suggests that "in contrast to the homogenization thesis, this view [heterogenization] is concerned more with sites of local negotiation. It suggests that foreign goods and texts are creatively misused, recontextualized in local sites, differently interpreted according to local cultural meaning" (2002a: 40). Likewise, what Welsch highlights here is that the concept of transculturality can describe both the homogenizing tendencies of globalization and the heterogenizing aspects of local desires and particularities. Transculturality illustrates the complex relationships between and within cultures today: it emphasizes not isolation but intermingling, not separation but disjunctive interactions, not homogenization but heterogenization.

Welsch's theories on transculturality can help explain the hybrid aspects of contemporary South Korean popular culture, and its ability to flow across cultural boundaries and infiltrate foreign markets, in four ways. First, South Korean popular culture is multilayered in itself and reflects the inner complexity of modern Korean society such as diversities in class, gender, and race. Second, South Korean popular culture is decidedly intermingled with the foreign as can be observed from the local indigenization of the Hollywood blockbuster. Third, through the processes of selective adaptation via transculturation, South Korean popular culture becomes a hybrid that is not exclusively and purely "our own/Korean" nor absolutely "foreign/ other." Fourth, the hybridity of South Korean popular culture is heterogeneous in ways that are different from the heterogeneity of other cultures and has diverse aspects due to a continuous transculturation process.

Transculturality as *Mugukjeok*

The Korean word *mugukjeok* (무국적, 無國籍) means "lacking in or having no nationality." It shares the same Chinese characters as the Japanese word *mukokuseki*, introduced by Iwabuchi in his book *Recentering Globalization* (2002a: 29). *Mugukjeok* is an example of transculturality. After *Shiri*'s success, South Korean film productions became more competitive by becoming more globalized, more amalgamated, and more non-nationalistic (*mugukjeok*); these *mugukjeok* films are different from earlier nationalistic South Korean films. Another example of *mugukjeok* can be seen in popular music, where artists such as Rain and Se7en are highly influenced by American R&B and hip-hop singers such as Usher and Justin Timberlake. When Rain performed his debut song, *Bad Guy*, at his concert in Madison Square Garden in February 2006, he replicated some of Usher's dance moves and some media in the US have pointed out that his style virtually clones that of American popular music (Walsh 2006). Undoubtedly, this has been instigated by JYP, Rain's producer, whose very first quote at the beginning of this chapter regarding his desire to achieve *Hallyu* without *Hal* (*Han*, Korea/nness) suggests that Rain has become that very embodiment. Rain and his regional success demonstrate the ways in which *mugukjeok* functions in the globalization and transculturation of South Korean popular music.

South Korean popular culture's *mugukjeok* is similar to Meyrowitz's idea of "no sense of place" (1985). Meyrowitz's definition highlights the influence of media flow that creates communities with "no sense of place" who share culturally neutral presentations. In order to explain the *mukokuseki* of cultural commodities, Iwabuchi suggests the concept of "cultural odorlessness." He argues that culturally odorless products such as Pokemon, Nintendo, and the Sony Walkman tend to be characterized as racially and ethnically softened or as having had their identities erased (2002a). This culturally hybrid odorlessness can also be explained through Appadurai's concept of "mediascapes." Mediascapes refer to the capabilities of the media in producing and disseminating information as well as images through transcultural flows. He argues that the most important aspect of mediascapes is that they provide images and narratives to culturally diverse audiences (1996: 35). Mediascapes enable cultures to flow, mix, metamorphose, and become odorless. These practices create non-nationality or *mugukjeok*. *Mugukjeok* is the inspiration for the creation of "sodalities" between different cultural groups, which eventually stimulate active transcultural consumption. Appadurai further explains:

> Part of what the mass media make possible, because of the conditions of collective reading, criticism, and pleasure, is what I have elsewhere called a "community of sentiment" (Appadurai 1990), a group that begins to imagine and feel things together ... Collective experiences of the mass media, especially film and video, can create sodalities of worship and charisma ... These mass-mediated sodalities have the additional complexity that, in them, diverse local experiences of taste, pleasure, and politics can crisscross with one another, thus creating the possibility of convergences in translocal social action that would otherwise be hard to imagine. (1996: 8)

This point can be summarized as: when one culture flows into another, there must always be interventions and metamorphosis, which emphasize the interaction between two different cultures and create commonalities that are conducive to transcultural consumption. Jan Nederveen Pieterse defines globalization in this way as an ongoing production of a "global mélange" through the hybridization process (2004: 43–44). The transcultural flow is, in short, a repetition of the processes of production, consumption, modification, and reproduction. In other words, cultures are deterritorialized and reterritorialized and contribute to the creation of diverse *mugukjeok* styles. Such a perspective is more productive than a nation-centric view of global cultural power. The theoretical framework of *mugukjeok* is critical to understanding the transcultural consumption of South Korean popular culture because this popular culture is received by diverse audiences located in such different places as Japan, Singapore, and the West.

Transculturality as Audience Reception

The transculturality of South Korean popular culture can also be examined using the theoretical framework of media audience reception studies. Pertti Alasuutari, in the introduction of the edited book, *Rethinking the Media Audience*, suggests that there are three generations of reception studies (1999: 1–21). The first generation of reception studies, characterized as reception research, employs a semiotic approach in analyzing the way that media messages are created and received. Stuart Hall's well-known concepts of "encoding and decoding" (1980) typifies reception research. Hall's semiotic approach sees communication as a process whereby certain messages are sent and then received with certain effects, where these effects depend on how audiences interpret media messages. Hall argues that all messages can be decoded differently by different audiences. This approach involves a shift from examining the effect of the impact of media messages on audiences to a focus on the interpretations of audiences (Alasuutari 1999: 2–4).

The second generation of reception studies refers to empirical reception studies and is characterized as the audience ethnography paradigm. While the first generation puts more emphasis on the interpretation of media texts and messages by particular audiences, the second generation focuses more on analyzing "interpretative communities" — the audiences (1999: 5). Alasuutari further argues that: people representing the second generation of reception studies like to emphasize that they are doing or that one should do proper ethnographic case studies of "interpretive communities." One even talks about an "ethnographic turn" quite comparable to the previous "linguistic turn." Like classic anthropologists such as Malinowski (1961), it has been argued that a proper ethnographic study in audience ethnography entails at least several months' stay in the "field" (Drotner 1992) — a demand which, strangely enough, is presented at a time when anthropologists and qualitative sociologists are increasingly questioning the whole notion of a "field" (Gupta and Ferguson 1997).

The third generation of reception studies, according to Alasuutari, applies discursive or constructionist views to audience research. This generation "brings the media back to media studies, but conceives of the media and media messages in a broader sense than just as an encoded text and then decoded by a particular 'interpretive community'" (1999: 7). The objective of the reception research of the third generation is to illustrate contemporary "media culture" and it mainly focuses on the role of the media in everyday life in the postmodern contemporary world. In particular, Ien Ang emphasizes that investigating media audiences in a postmodern world only becomes significant when such investigation points toward a broader critical understanding of the particularities of contemporary culture (1996: 4).

Ang's point about the importance of focusing on cultural particularities is echoed by Sonia Livingstone, who observes that audience reception studies "focus on the interpretative relation between audience and medium, where this relation is understood within a broadly ethnographic context" (1998: 237). According to Livingstone, audience reception studies analyze the ways in which different ethnographic groups of viewers interpret media products in different ways based on their particular socio-political contexts. Such an approach describes the ways in which media products are interpreted and incorporated differently by various regional audiences because of their diverse local and specific cultural contexts (Robertson 1995; Appadurai 1996; Hannerz 1996). In line with the notion of third-generation reception studies, this book focuses on the differing practices of reception of South Korean popular culture by three different regional audiences — Japan, Singapore, the West — based on the cultural particularities of each region.

This book also emphasizes the fact that these regional audiences are "active" instead of "passive" audiences. As Wang et al. have argued, the image of contemporary audiences has changed "from [being seen as] passive, fragmented individuals manipulated by media to [being seen as] autonomous social groups which select and interpret program content according to their own interest and cultural background" (2000: 12). This notion of audiences as active can be extended with the concept of "participatory culture." This concept emphasizes the significance of the roles of private individuals (the public) as consumers and, importantly, as contributors or producers; this combination of the roles of individuals as both consumers and producers is well-described by the term "prosumer."[17] Henry Jenkins argues that the "circulation of media content — across different media systems, competing media economies, and national borders — depends heavily on consumers' active participation" (2006a: 3). Jenkins further argues that within participatory culture, audiences actively participate in media production, where the boundaries between producer and consumer, sender and receiver, and corporate media and grassroots have now blurred (2006a: 1–24). Such participatory culture can be detected from many online websites such as Rain's Singaporean fan club website, RainSingapore. com; the film review website, Twitch.net; and the video-sharing website, YouTube. com. In these online websites, South Korean popular culture is dynamically circulated, reproduced, and consumed by active global audiences. It is evident that, empowered by new media technologies, audiences have now become transcultural prosumers. Based on the discursive view of third-generation reception studies, this book focuses on two main aspects of the transcultural consumption of South Korean popular culture: the particularity of cultural context of each region, and the active and participatory aspects of audiences.

Transculturality as Consumption

According to Chua Beng Huat, "consumption is to be treated as a process by which artefacts are not simply bought and consumed, but given meaning through their active incorporation in people's lives. The innovative ways of using undistinguished mass-production goods are conceptualized as 'styles' which are expressive of the individualities/identities of the users" (2000: 5). Chua argues that Asia has arisen as a new consuming market during the last couple of decades despite the 1997 economic crisis that temporarily hindered economic growth. He stresses that the tendency of Asian consumer groups is to be attracted to the American lifestyle and to American ideologies such as liberal values and individualism. Chua also points out that Asia is not only the market for American products, but also for Japanese consumer goods such as cars, television sets, and other electronic products. He explains that Japanese technological "superiority" is recognized among Asian countries. In addition to technological and industrial superiority, Iwabuchi's point of view stresses the influential power of Japanese cultural products and the Japanese lifestyle in many Asian countries.

Iwabuchi argues that Asians, especially the young, desire Japanese technology, the Japanese lifestyle, and Japanese popular culture. He observes that Asian consumers have, since the 1980s, fallen in love with Japanese cultural products such as popular music, television dramas, and computer games. He points out that their popularity in the Asian region is due to the "similar but superior" aspects of Japanese products (2001: 204; 2002a: 8). He argues that "young people in Taiwan or Hong Kong actually perceive the sense of cultural similarity or proximity in positive ways in consuming Japanese popular cultural forms" (2001: 205). This sense of cultural proximity is produced in consumers through the cultural odorlessness of these products. According to Iwabuchi, the urban middle-class culture that is widely apparent across Asia, including Japan, is proof of an odorless culture which can be comprehended in the concept of "sharing Asianness." This "emerging 'Asianness' is primarily articulated in the shared pursuit of urban consumption of Americanized (Westernized) popular culture" (2001: 206). The indigenization of modern Western culture and the sharing of cultural proximity have become driving forces of creating Asianness, and the combination of these forces enables cultural products to travel across the various Asian countries. Iwabuchi describes the significant point of transcultural flows in the Asian region:

> With the emergence of Asian capitalist sphere in which Japanese popular culture finds wider audiences, Japan's exploitative articulation of Asian cultural commonality has been reframed to accommodate itself to the disjunctive transnational flows of capital, cultural products and imagination. Transnational popular cultural flows highlight the fact that it has become no longer tenable for Japan to contain its cultural orientation and agendas within clearly demarcated national boundaries. (2001: 202)

Iwabuchi argues that there is a commonality between Asian countries where they share certain historical aspects such as the process of indigenization of Western modern civilization. This commonality has become strengthened through various transcultural flows. Thus, the sharing of a commonality of Asianness allows culture to travel more easily in the Asian region.

Another scholar, Leo Ching, has also detected the sharing of a sense of Asianness in the region. In his article "Globalizing the Regional, Regionalizing the Global," Ching discusses the relationship between Japanese mass culture and Asianism. According to him, despite the extraordinary economic growth in Asia, there is no corresponding extension of Asian culture on a global scale. However, Japanese mass culture such as popular music and television dramas has achieved massive popularity in the Asian region. In order to examine the possible reasons for this, he focuses on the relationship between mass culture and regional identity — here, regional identity relates to an imagined regional community — and examines two examples: the Japanese morning drama, *Oshin*, and the children's animated series, *Doraemon*. Ching states:

> The tremendous popularity in Asia of both programs has been attributed to a certain commonality, a certain structure of feeling that has rearticulated something that is invariably "Japanese" (as far as the site of production and the manifested cultural codes are concerned) into something that one might call an "Asian consciousness" or "Asiatic imaginary." This culturalist regionalism sets itself against the background of a specific regional economic development under late capitalism. (2000: 249)

According to him, the success of Japanese popular culture is explained by two reasons. First, in spite of the uniqueness and heterogeneity of the different countries in Asia, there is an association or identification as Asian that is common to these countries. Second, despite their specific articulations of Asianness, there is a regional recognition of Japan as a forerunner in the region and as a developmental leader of social and economic progress. Hence, in relation to Japan, the other Asian countries are "alike, but not quite." In short, the popularity of Japanese popular culture in the region can be explained by a concept of shared Asianness with the region and the assumed cultural superiority of Japan. Ching points out that "various notions of 'Asianness' have been constructed through this media regionalism," such as MTV (2000: 256). Hence, transcultural media flows generate the sense of shared Asianness and it is this sense of cultural proximity between Asian countries that stimulates the travel of cultures across boundaries.

Another scholar who has examined these transcultural phenomena is Ding-Tzann Lii who, in her article "A Colonized Empire," discusses how Hong Kong films are a dominant cultural form in relation to the film industries of other Asian countries (1998). Lii argues that the "Hong Kong film industry not only resists foreign domination, but also 'invades' other countries, thereby creating a new type of imperialism." She names this "marginal imperialism." Lii explains:

> Hong Kong is a colony situated at the periphery of the world power system. However, the colony is becoming imperialist and is establishing itself as an empire. What are the implications of the new kind of imperialism associated with the colonized empire? To begin with, Hong Kong imperialism is new in the sense that it is different from the old one, which is created by the Western core (including Japan), and is therefore referred to here as "core imperialism." In contrast, the imperialism as exemplified by Hong Kong movies emerges at the margin of the world system, and occurs primarily within third-world countries. This is why I refer to it as "marginal imperialism." (1998: 125)

Lii argues that the form of marginal imperialism articulated by Hong Kong cinema is different from the original imperialism emanating from the Western core. She argues that in this original imperialistic system, subordinated others are transformed or even erased. However, in the system of marginal imperialism, a process of "yielding" has occurred where "the self" enters into and interacts with "the others." This process creates a new synthesized form with a higher order than the original forms. This concept of "yielding" can be elucidated as the process of indigenization in localization theory. What Lii highlights here is that media from the periphery, such as Hong Kong cinema, can operate to regionalize, to localize (Asianize), and finally, to imperialize the region. Lii maintains that "marginal imperialism has created a yielding mode of articulation, which is different from the incorporating mode of articulation associated with core powers" (1998: 136). The regional popularity of Hong Kong cinema can be explained by the process of localization, which has enabled Hong Kong cinema to become a regionally dominant culture.

The above scholarly approaches can be applied to examining the transcultural influence of South Korean popular culture. For example, in relation to Iwabuchi's and Ching's arguments on the regional popularity of Japanese popular culture, the current popularity of South Korean popular culture can be understood as "similar but superior" to other Asian cultures. The characteristic of "similar" can be explained through Iwabuchi's concept of the "Japanization" trend in the world cultural market, where he stresses Japan's dominant influence within the Asian region, including South Korea. It is evident that South Korean popular culture has been influenced by Japanese popular culture through the Japanization process and has become "similar," in other words, *mugukjeok*. This *mugukjeok* South Korean cultural product indeed reinvigorates the sense of sharing Asianness which allows the products to travel more easily in Japan and other Asian countries.

In addition, the "superiority" of South Korean popular culture can be identified through the notion of "sufficiency" which is characterized by the various aspects of its hybridity. Lii's point of "marginal imperialism" also supports the notion of the superiority of hybridized South Korean popular culture, as she argues that one culture interacts with another and this creates a new synthesized form with a higher order than the original ones (1998: 128). A good example of foreign embracing of "similar but superior" (sufficient) Korean popular culture can be found in the reviews of *Taegukgi* by US film critics. Many critics and reviewers mention that the film shares similarities with *Saving Private Ryan* due to its hyper-realistic depiction of explosions, flying limbs, and bodily mutilation in the combat scenes; at the same time, many of them also point out that the film's powerful narrative of the anguish and grief that are experienced by the two separated brothers who have to point their guns at each other enhances the spectacularized tension of the battle sequences to the point where the tension of these sequences surpasses that of the battle sequences in Hollywood blockbusters (Cornelius 2005; Villarreal 2004; Savlov 2004; Slotek 2004; Kehr 2004). This is a good example of the ways in which contemporary South Korean popular culture has the characteristic of being "similar" as it adapts globally well-known popular cultural elements, and at the same time, has the characteristic of being "superior" as it is hybridized and indigenized during which it creates synthesized forms of a higher order (sufficiency). New hybrid South Korean masculinity can be the best example to explain similar but superior South Korean popular culture.

Hybridity of Korean Masculinity

Korean Masculinity Discourses

In Michel Foucault's book, *History of Sexuality*, sexuality is seen as being constituted by a historical apparatus. He writes: "sexuality must not be thought of as a kind of natural given which power tries to hold in check, or as an obscure domain which knowledge gradually tries to uncover. It is the name that can be given to a historical construct" (1979: 152). If sexuality is subject to socio-historical constructions, as Foucault has suggested, then the essentialist notion of masculinity as being biologically determined should also be questioned. Such a questioning of the essentialist notion of gender has been launched by Judith Butler's concept of gender performativity. In her article, "Performative Acts and Gender Constitution," Butler writes:

> Gender is in no way a stable identity or locus of agency from which various acts proceed; rather, it is an identity tenuously constituted in time — an identity instituted through a stylized repetition of acts. Further, gender is instituted through the stylization of the body and, hence, must be understood as the mundane way in which bodily gestures, movements, and enactments of various kinds constitute the illusion of an abiding gendered self. (1988: 519)

Here, Butler argues that sexuality and gender are culturally constructed through the repetition of stylized performances of gender in time. These stylized bodily performances, in their repetition, establish the appearance of an essential and naturally given gender.

Similarly, R. W. Connell suggests the concept of "doing masculinities" in order to explain culturally constructed masculinity. He argues that "different cultures, and different periods of history construct masculinity differently ... masculinities do not exist prior to social behavior, either as bodily states or fixed personalities. Rather, masculinities come into existence as people act. They are accomplished in everyday conduct or organizational life, as patterns of social practice" (2000b). Masculinity is produced and maintained through culturally specific and repetitive everyday practices, where such practices as those of acting, dressing, or speaking are performed in particular gender-specific ways (Connell 1995: 6, 35, 80). Thus, the above conceptualizations of sexuality and masculinity underscore three points: one, that masculinity is constructed and reconstructed regularly; two, that masculinity is fluid and may be constructed differently in different situations and different cultural contexts; three, that multiple masculinities are produced at any given historical moment. Drawing on Connell's concept of masculinity as multiple and heterogeneous, this section discusses the ways in which South Korean masculinities have been deconstructed and hybridized in relation to South Korea's particular socio-political context and transcultural dynamics.

Moon Seung-Sook uses the term "hegemonic masculinity" to refer to the dominant practices of masculinity within the South Korean local context of Confucian tradition, militarization, and compressed industrialization. In her article, "The Production and Subversion of Hegemonic Masculinity," Moon addresses three components that constitute hegemonic masculinity in the particular context of South

Korea. These three components are: the ability to provide for the family, masculine distance from daily reproductive labor, and military service (2002: 79–113). In this section, drawing on Moon's schematic description of hegemonic masculinity, I discuss three major stereotypical images of South Korean masculinities: patriarchal authoritarian, *seonbi* (*wen*), and violent.

Firstly, South Korean hegemonic masculinity embodies patriarchal authoritarianism where men were traditionally considered to be heads of family and the main providers. Historically, the *yangban* (the aristocracy during the Joseon dynasty) households relegated women to interior spaces while men's domains were exterior spaces, such as a scholars' studio (Moon 2002: 84). This spatial division was based on Confucian patriarchal ideology and created a gendered division of labor. Hence, men were expected to work outside the home while women became domestic housewives. As Confucian patriarchy later transformed into modern industrialized patriarchy, the normative gender constructs of the male-as-provider and the female-as-dependent-housewife persisted. In the realm of capitalist industrialization, men's ability to provide for the family becomes the material basis of men's authority as fathers and husbands. Moon explains that the ideas and practices that define men as the principal income-earners of the family validate men's domestic authority and dominance in South Korea so that men's earning power becomes a primary indicator of their manliness (2002: 84–86).

Moon's argument that South Korea's patriarchal authoritarianism was reinforced by capitalist industrialization is supported by Kim Eun-Shil, who addresses the relationship between patriarchal authoritarianism and the economic development model during the modernization era in South Korea in her article, "Cultural Logic and Patriarchy in the Korean Modernization Project" (2000: 105–30). She argues that during the modernization era, South Korea built a new value structure based on gendered binaries such as masculine/feminine, material/spiritual, modern/traditional, and Western/Eastern. Kim observes that South Korea's modernization is often considered as a process of production, rationalization, and control which is often perceived as belonging to the masculine realm. She further states that South Korean modernization is based on "dynamic achievement and development, desires for infinite growth … and the individual male's desire for modernization and male solidarity" (2000: 117). Such dynamic modernization of the Westernized and production-driven industrial structure in South Korea is initiated and controlled by men because of traditional patriarchy (2000: 118). Such industrialization endows South Korean men with authoritarian power while neglecting South Korean women's productive ability and relegating them to the domestic and subordinate realm. In other words, while undergoing modern industrialization, the patriarchal system allows South Korean men to be controlling subjects as masculinity is associated with development and industrial production while South Korean women either become passive tools or men's subordinates. South Korean authoritarian masculinity is constructed and enabled by South Korea's particular socio-economic context, which is a blend of the traditional patriarchal system and production-driven industrialization.

Secondly, Moon Seung-Sook argues that the separation of men from the daily work of reproductive and caring labor is another element of hegemonic masculinity. This separation is demanded by the role of men as family providers. Because men are required by society to leave the domestic space and earn income while women are required to perform various domestic chores such as cleaning, washing, and caring for children, performing any of these domestic activities is considered unmanly or emasculating (2002: 99). In order to explain the link between masculinity and the required distance from reproductive labor, Moon suggests analyzing the model of *seonbi* masculinity during the Joseon dynasty (1392–1910). *Seonbi* is a term that refers to a Confucian scholar-official who studies Confucian texts to obtain "wisdom" (*wen*, 문, 文). During this period of study, the *seonbi* is not supposed to degrade himself by engaging in any form of manual labor or any economic activity (2002: 99). *Seonbi* masculinity thus indicates mental attainment rather than physical performance. Such a notion of *seonbi* masculinity contributes to men's disengagement from the daily domestic labor which is indispensable for the maintenance of society but devalued and mostly performed by women. Despite its sexist aspects, *seonbi* masculinity is still considered to be an ideal model of Korean masculinity by some scholars because it also represents such traditional virtues as politeness, integrity, faithfulness, loyalty, and cultural-scholarly attainment (Geum 2000: 59–92).

Geum's explanation of the cultural-scholarly attainment aspect of *seonbi* masculinity is supported by Kam Louie's theory of "Chinese *wen* masculinity" (2002). Louie argues that the paradigm of the "binary opposition between *wen* (文), the mental or civil, and *wu* (武), the physical or martial" is important in Chinese conceptions of masculinity but not as evident in contemporary Western conceptions of maleness (2002: 10). Although an ideal man would be expected to embody a balance between *wen* and *wu*, historically, *wen* tended to be considered superior to *wu*. Because Confucius is the god of *wen*, in China, which was a strict Confucian country at one time, *wen* — mental attainment — was often considered to be a more elite masculine form than *wu* — physical attainment (2002: 17–18). Elite Chinese *wen* masculinity has influenced Korea's *seonbi* masculinity because Korea has, historically, been culturally influenced by the Chinese Confucian tradition. It could be pointed out that the notion of *seonbi* masculinity — mental and cultural attainment — is in contrast to the hegemonic masculinity of contemporary South Korea where men are involved with physical work and with business activities as family providers. This contradiction can be explained by the fact that South Korean masculinities are multiple and heterogenous. In contemporary times, many South Koreans still value *seonbi* masculinity as constituting one of the noble masculinities: this is evident from the domestic popularity of male stars in recent television dramas and movies such as BYJ in *Winter Sonata* and Han Seok-Gyu in *Christmas in August* (*Palweol-ui Keuriseumaseu* 1998), in which the male characters embody *seonbi* masculinity. Because it emphasizes gentle and cultured mentality, not strong physical achievement, *seonbi* masculinity has contributed to the construction of soft South Korean masculinity.

Thirdly, Moon Seung-Sook also argues that mandatory military service constitutes another element of hegemonic masculinity within the context of the ongoing military confrontation between North and South Korea (2002: 89).[18] Historically, the military has been the exclusive province of men. In Korea, particularly due to the peculiar political condition of a national split between North and South, military service subjects men to extreme physical hardship and discipline within a strict hierarchical system. Several kinds of abuse, including cases that have led to suicide or murder, are reported every year. On June 19, 2005, a twenty-two-year-old army private killed eight soldiers and wounded four in a grenade and shooting rampage along the DMZ. He later said that this was in retaliation against fellow soldiers who had bullied and abused him (Hwang 2005). Cho Seong-Sook explains that the military service induces routinization and the justification of violence because soldiers are allowed to legally practice violence, which is the means by which they learn the logic of conquest (1997: 168–69). Lee Hyo-Je, the president of the Association of Women's Organizations, states that "violence is widespread in South Korea because militarism justifies violence" (2002). Kim Jeong-Soo also points out that militarism evokes "authoritarianism, violence, homogenization, and blind obedience" (2001).

Many South Korean scholars have insisted on the socio-political connections between violent South Korean masculinity and militarism. In *The Republic of Korea of Yours*, Park No-Ja argues that Korean militarism, particularly the military service, drives the society violent and dehumanizes Korean men (2001: 97–119). He further suggests that the military system creates human robots that commit violence without feeling their conscience (2001: 108–9). Another scholar, Kim Kyung-Hyun, also suggests that the military dictatorships of the past were responsible for violent Korean masculinity. In his book, *The Remasculinization of Korean Cinema*, he argues that violent masculinity that has been portrayed in South Korean films is the effect of the political, economic, and cultural implications of the harsh rule of military dictators from the 1960s to the 1980s. He states, "Throughout the early 1980s, the films that featured the transformation of aimless and anxious men undergoing the process of maturity through violent, introspective searches were ubiquitous" (2004: 5). Thus, it is evident that such a political environment and social system have created frustration and anxiety in South Korean men and that their rage against the military dictatorial government can only be explored through violent acts. Violent South Korean masculinity is constructed due to Korea's specific political condition of national division and militarism.

Through discussing the three representative features of South Korean hegemonic masculinity — patriarchal authoritarian masculinity, *seonbi* masculinity, and violent masculinity — I have examined how Korea's specific socio-political contexts have helped to create heterogenous and contradictory masculinities. Since the early 1990s, various socio-political events have deconstructed these hegemonic masculinities. For example, the IMF catastrophe has caused a crisis in terms of the traditional roles of men as primary household income-earners.

An attempt at the deconstruction of South Korean masculinity is evident from Min-Ki, the male protagonist of the melodrama, *Happy End* (1999). Kim Kyung-Hyun suggests that Min-Ki transgresses the normative boundaries of gender by performing various household chores in the kitchen and by watching television dramas with keen interest (2004: 254–58). He argues that the connection between domesticity, as represented by the kitchen and daytime soaps, and masculinity, as represented by the jobless and middle-aged Min-Ki, demonstrates the deconstruction of conventional gender roles. This is a perfect example of the deconstruction of the paradigm of *seonbi* masculinity where men are expected to remain separated from daily domestic labor. However, Min-Ki only demonstrates the incomplete deconstruction of South Korean masculinity. Kim Kyung-Hyun notes that, by having Min-Ki kill his unfaithful wife, Bora, the film ultimately carries the message that "the man must resort to violence in order to recover himself from trauma" (2004: 258). It is evident that Min-Ki reverts back to violent masculinity after the attempt at deconstructing hegemonic masculinity. Despite his attempt to deconstruct hegemonic masculinity through subverting gender roles, Min-Ki, by killing Bora, fails to complete the deconstruction of hegemonic authoritarian South Korean masculinity.

In his article, "The Gaze of the Consuming Subject: Construction of Masculinity," Cho Heup argues that *Happy End* contains the theme of the crisis of patriarchal hegemony. This is because Bora's adultery and her whoring body are "provoking texts which are against the traditional patriarchal system" (2004: 134). He also points out how the film shows that "the only way of recuperating patriarchal ideology is through violence" and that Min-Ki still fits into an image of a traditional patriarchal violent man (2004: 134). However, Cho points to the other male character in the film, Il-Beom — Bora's lover — as exemplifying the deconstruction of South Korean hegemonic masculinity. Cho argues that Il-Beom represents soft masculinity through his caring and gentle image. Referring to further examples like Sang-Woo in *One Fine Spring Day* (*Bomnareun Ganda* 2001) and In-Woo in *Bungee Jumping of Their Own* (*Beonjijeompeureul Hada* 2001), Cho argues that there is a new tendency towards representing soft and neutral masculinity in South Korean films in recent years. These soft male characters are good examples of how South Korean masculinity has been transformed. This transformation demonstrates that South Korean men are now "doing" different masculine acts in terms of the different socio-cultural contexts of recent South Korea. The central process enabling the doing, or performance, of different masculinities is, I argue, transculturation.

The Soft Masculinity of Bae Yong-Joon: *Mugukjeok* and Postcolonialism

In chapter 2, I focus on Japanese fandom of Bae Yong-Joon (BYJ) and examine the ways in which South Korean masculinity is reconstructed through the ambivalent desires of middle-aged Japanese female fans. These desires are evident in the mixed cultural practice of postcolonial *mugukjeok*; via this practice, the fans create new South Korean soft masculinity. First, *mugukjeok* is an example of the cultural proximity that is created through transcultural flows between South Korea and Japan.[19] In terms of masculinity, *mugukjeok* is evident from the ways in which the two countries commonly produce and consume pretty boy (*kkonminam*) images which possibly originate from the *bishōnen* of Japanese *shōjo manga*. This *bishōnen* image has repeatedly appeared in pastiches and been commodified by various regional pop-stars, in the course of which this image has evolved to eventually create the "shared imagination" of pan-East Asian soft masculinity.

Second, BYJ's *wen* masculine image, in relation to the nostalgic "shared imagination" of Confucian tradition, also embodies *mugukjeok* soft masculinity. Here, postcolonialism is evident from the "retrospective" and "nostalgic" ways in which Japanese fans embrace the *wen* masculine image of BYJ. This can be related back to the colonial experience between Korea and Japan. In brief, the Japanese embrace of BYJ, particularly his *wen* masculinity, can be explained as a kind of consumption of the simulacrum of Japan's past; in other words, the Japanese embrace of BYJ is the result of the commodification of memory. Thus, the chapter demonstrates how the soft masculinity of BYJ is constructed based on the disjunctive cultural practice of "counter-coevality" (caused by temporal lag) and "cultural proximity" (due to spatial adjacency).

Chapter 2 is based on audience reception research conducted in Japan in August and September 2005. I interviewed a total of eighteen of BYJ's female fans from Tokyo and Okinawa, and divided them into four focus groups that had five, four, seven, and two participants respectively. Seven of the participants were in their thirties, three were in their forties, six were in their fifties, and two were in their sixties. I also collected fifty-six questionnaires at the *Saitama Super Arena*, where the promotional event for BYJ's film, *April Snow*, was held on August 31, 2005.

The Global Masculinity of Rain: *Mugukjeok* and Regional Pop-Consumerism

Chapter 3 focuses on the ways in which South Korean masculinity is reconstructed through the global desires of Rain's Singaporean female fans. This reconstruction is evident in the mixed cultural practices between *mugukjeok* and pop-consumerism in Asia, during which new South Korean global masculinity is created and transculturally consumed. First, *mugukjeok* is evident from the pragmatic ways in which Rain is globalized where his masculinity becomes non-nationalized due to the hybridization of Confucian traditional masculinity with a type of global masculinity that is mainly exemplified by the figure of the "cute" (Japanese *kawaii*) boy and by such American stars as Justin Timberlake and Usher. Rain's hybridized global masculinity demonstrates how South Korea's popular cultural products relentlessly adapt global popular cultural elements in pragmatic ways and combine them with traditional masculine images to appeal to the complex desires of transcultural viewers.

Second, regional pop-consumerism is another driving force behind the reconstruction of Rain's hybrid global masculinity. This regional pop-consumerism can be connected to the consumerist lifestyle of the "new rich" in Asia. The new rich in Asia can be characterized as a new middle-class in some Asian countries, based on their economic power as a new consumer group. Chua Beng Huat explains that, with the expanding desires of the new rich, a new lifestyle of consumerism has emerged in Asia (2000: 3). In Singapore, this new consumerist lifestyle is complicated because the Westernized values and commodities that come with this new lifestyle clash with the different traditional ways of life that co-exist in Singapore's multicultural society (2003: 20). Rain's Singaporean fans, who constitute a good example of the new rich in Asia, perform complex consumption practices that characterize their global lifestyles. It is these consumption practices that constitute the trans-pop-consumerism of Singaporean fans in relation to Rain's hybrid global masculinity.[20]

Chapter 3 is based on focus group interviews, survey questionnaires, and participant observation of an official fan club website, RainSingapore.com. In December 2005, and July and August of 2006, I interviewed five members of Rain's Singaporean fan club. One is in her twenties, three are in their thirties, and one is over fifty. Four of them are Singaporean-born working women of Chinese (Mandarin-speaking) ethnic backgrounds and the other is a Malaysian-born Chinese who has been living in Singapore for more than fifteen years. One is married and four are single.

The Postmodern Masculinity in *Oldboy*: *Mugukjeok* and Neo-Orientalism

Chapter 4 focuses on Western cult fandom of the Korean genre film, *Oldboy*, and discusses how postmodern South Korean masculinity is reconstructed through the ambivalent desires of Western spectators based on the mixed practice of *mugukjeok* and neo-Orientalism. This chapter examines how the Western desire for the Other is expressed, transformed, and redefined by consuming hybrid South Korean masculinity, as exemplified by the "savage but cool" Dae-Soo, and how this transformed desire, "with a distinctly postmodern slant," is different from earlier Orientalist desires towards the primitive Other. This Western desire is ambivalent because it seeks the strangeness of Otherness and, at the same time, the familiarity of modern "coolness." Hence, Western audiences of *Oldboy* experience the hybrid "time between dog and wolf," which refers to the time when they cannot identify whether Dae-Soo is a "cool" friend or a savage stranger.[21] This "time between dog and wolf" epitomizes the current ever-fluctuating postmodern era, an era characterized by "the demise of the tradition of Aristotelian logic, through which Western society has long defined itself via a series of polar oppositions, the central of which were Good versus Evil, and Us versus Them" (Booker 2007: xv); this is the time when Western audiences ambivalently embrace postmodern South Korean masculinity that is fragmented and constantly transforming.

Chapter 4 is based on the empirical research on the online cult fandom of *Oldboy* in various film review websites. In order to discuss the online fandom of this film, I examine reviews and comments on forums and discussion boards of film review websites such as IMDb.com, RottenTomatoes.com, AintItCool.com, BeyondHollywood.com, and TwitchFilm.net. In addition to online participant observation, I conducted one focus group interview with three male fans of *Oldboy* in their twenties and two individual interviews with two male fans of *Oldboy*; both of whom are in their thirties. These interviews were conducted between November 2004 and September 2007 in Melbourne. From participant observation on the film review websites and through the interviews, I discovered that the majority of the fans of *Oldboy* were males in their twenties and thirties. Hence, the gender dynamics between the audience and South Korean masculinity in this chapter appear to be different from those dynamics between the female fans and the male South Korean stars that are analyzed in chapter 2 and 3. Thus, in chapter 4, I focus on the West's ambivalent reception of *Oldboy*, where this reception fluctuates between Western male identification with South Korean cool masculinity and Western desire for the primitiveness of South Korean masculinity.

I use "Euro-American" interchangeably with the term "Western" in this chapter, because the West is conventionally defined as Europe and its direct colonial offshoots such as the US and Australia, while the East, in many instances, simply denotes "Asia." As Guillermo Gómez-Peña clearly points out in his article "The New Global Culture," binary models of understanding the world are no longer functional due to digital technology and global communication (2001: 7). However, in discussing the neo-Orientalist Western reception of South Korean genre films, I want to examine how Orientalism still persists and functions even in this ever-fluctuating postmodern global era, where advanced technology blurs the boundaries between such binary oppositions as local and global, Us and Them, East and West. I chose the term "the West" to refer to the websites and their users after spending considerable time participating in and observing these websites.[22] The term embraces the origins and backgrounds of websites where most users are English-speaking Euro-Americans.

Bae Yong-Joon, Soft Masculinity, and Japanese Fans:
Our Past Is in Your Present Body

> Bae Yong-Joon is gentle, humble, sincere, and loyal. He is a man like a real man (おとこらしい おとこ).
>
> — Gan, questionnaire respondent

> [I like his] gentleness and politeness. He has something we Japanese have already lost.
>
> — Pan, 54, questionnaire respondent[1]

On April 4, 2004, a new word, "*Yonsama*," appeared in the headlines of many entertainment and sports newspapers in Japan and South Korea: "Welcome *Yonsama*! 5,000 fans at Haneda Airport," "*Yonsama* has arrived! Over 5,000 go crazy," "*Yonsama* paralyzes Haneda Airport," "Japan's middle-aged women's infatuation with *Yonsama*," "*Yonsama* beats Beckham!" (Herald Kyungje 2004; J. W. Cho 2004a; Nikkan Sports cited in J. W. Cho 2004b; D. M. Park 2004; D. J. Lee 2004; Sankei Sports 2004). Many of these newspapers devoted their front pages to describing the welcome given to the South Korean actor, Bae Yong-Joon (BYJ), by the 5,000 "fanatic" Japanese fans that greeted him at the Haneda International Airport. The articles pointed out that most of the fans were middle-aged women.[2] Many of these fans had arrived at the airport the night before BYJ's arrival and had stayed up all night in order to find the best location from which to see him. Many of them had also brought gifts and flowers for him. Thousands of fans took photographs of him with their digital and mobile phone cameras. The evening television news programs reported the "intensity" with which these middle-aged female fans greeted BYJ and how many of them had eyes filled with tears while holding their welcome placards. Some of the media pointed out that the number of fans who welcomed BYJ was much bigger than the number of fans who welcomed David Beckham.[3]

Bae Yong-Joon has gained remarkable recognition in Japan after the South Korean television drama *Winter Sonata* was first screened on NHK in April 2003.[4] In the next two years, the complete series of *Winter Sonata* was rebroadcast four times on NHK due to the overwhelming number of requests for reruns by viewers who mostly belonged to the middle-aged and older brackets (Heo and Ham 2005: 13). The third run was retelevised on NHK's terrestrial television channel at 11:10 p.m. every Saturday.[5] Even though this scheduled time was not the prime time, the average audience share for the series was 14.4%, which was double the shares for other programs showing in the same time slot. Its shares peaked at 22.2%, which was the highest share achieved by a drama series aired in Japan at that time (Chae 2005: 10).[6] The enormous success of *Winter Sonata* in Japan has created what is known as "the *Yonsama* syndrome." This refers to the popularity of *Winter Sonata*'s main actor, Bae Yong-Joon, among fans. *Yonsama* is an appellation that is a combination of BYJ's name, Yong, and the Japanese word, *sama*. Normally, in the Japanese context, *sama* is used to address royalty and aristocrats and connoted respect for members of these classes. In this regard, *Yonsama* can be translated as "Prince Yong" or "My Dear Lord Yong" and indicates the immense respect that Japanese fans have for BYJ. Japan's prime minister, Junichiro Koizumi, even once commented on BYJ's popularity among voters: "I would like to emulate *Yonsama* to become a *Junsama*" (C. D. Lee 2004). In relation to the phenomenon of the celebrity, Francesco Guardini has suggested that a "new form of monarchy has emerged in our time." He has argued that sports stars, singers, film actors, and supermodels are like new kings and queens and that they operate like a new aristocracy (quoted in Ndalianis 2002: vii). In 2004, *Yonsama* became a new king of popular culture in South Korea and Japan.

The *Yonsama* syndrome has opened up a new era of the Korean Wave (*Hallyu*) in Japan, drawing attention not only to South Korean popular culture but also to South Korean traditions, food, and language. The popularity of BYJ created a new attitude to South Korea in Japan and many Japanese became interested in learning about South Korea and its culture. This new attitude is different from the established attitudes held by Japanese towards South Korea. These conventional attitudes were largely created by the media which had presented certain images of South Korea. For example, during the 1980s and early 1990s, a narrow picture of South Korea was presented in the Japanese media through images of anti-government protests and political demonstrations that were occurring in South Korea then. However, the arrival of *Hallyu* has transformed conventional Japanese attitudes: in the *Kyodo News* article, "[South] Korean boom is changing Japanese people's perceptions," one Japanese fan confessed that "it was a kind of awakening" (Suk 2005). The article suggests that the *Yonsama* syndrome has helped to reduce the political tensions between Japan and South Korea that were created due to various historical conflicts between the two countries. A report in the *Australian Financial Review* also suggests that Japan's views of South Korea have changed because of South Korean television dramas and stars. According to the article, "Historical Enmities Melt as Japan Finds 'Asian Cool'," the Japanese had previously looked towards the West but have started to "consume" the East:

> *Yonsama* seems to have got under the skin of this most sophisticated of cities. He has almost single-handedly sparked a fascination in Japan with *Hallyu* (South Korean style). In 2004, South Korean products topped the list for the

most popular of the year in Japan, as ranked by Nikkei Marketing Journal. The top TV commercial for the year in the annual Commercial Grand Prix featured *Yonsama*. Shopping trips to Seoul are now all the rage for young Japanese women. South Korean beauty treatments, South Korean films, South Korean language studies are all enjoying record popularity. This love affair with all things South Korean sits oddly in the context of the tetchy history between the two countries. But it is part of a phenomenon that is now sweeping East Asia: the allure of ethnic Asian. Rising middle classes across the region are becoming fascinated with each other and with the intangible of "Asian cool." (Ryan 2005)

As the article has described above, BYJ has become an icon of transnational cultural flows between South Korea and Japan, despite their history of conflict. Examples of these conflicts include Japan's colonial occupation of Korea (1910–1945); the use of Korean women as "comfort women" by Japanese soldiers during the occupation; South Korea's criticism of Japan's new history books which excluded or minimized the extent of Japan's wartime atrocities; and the ongoing territorial dispute between the two countries over the island of Dok-do/Dakeshima. Although there are still unresolved political problems between the two countries, it has been suggested that BYJ has changed many Japanese people's perceptions of South Korea and its culture (G. M. Shin 2006: 245). South Korea is now seen as something "fashionable" and "cool." A Korean-Japanese (*Zainichi Kankokujin*, 在日韓國人) woman I interviewed in Japan in August 2005 confessed that "Japanese people used to treat us as if we were not human beings, but after *Yonsama*, their attitudes have been changed completely." Through the popularity of *Winter Sonata*, South Korean values and culture have become a topic of debate and interest in Japan. BYJ, in particular, has become an object of desire for Japanese female audiences, particularly for middle-aged female fans.

Middle-aged Japanese female fans demonstrate their desire for BYJ through a series of everyday practices that constitute what I refer to as "transcultural consumption practices." These practices primarily consist of watching *Winter Sonata* on television and many of these fans have seen it more than once. Apart from watching *Winter Sonata*, these viewers also hire DVDs of other dramas of BYJ from the local DVD shops. Most of the major DVD rental shops have a separate South Korean television drama section and some shops even have a separate BYJ section where customers can find comprehensive collections of television dramas that star BYJ as the leading actor. From bookstores in *Shin-Okubo* (also known as "Korea town"), they also purchase South Korean popular culture magazines and BYJ's photo album (Figure 2.1). From a neighborhood variety shop, fans buy gifts such as mugs, key chains, and mobile phone accessories that come with BYJ photos (Figure 2.2). Fans also visit Korean restaurants to have BYJ's favorite dish or a Korean barbeque accompanied by some energy drinks advertised by BYJ. The peak of the consumption of BYJ, however, occurs in tourism. Fans travel to South Korea to meet *Yonsama* or to visit the locations where his dramas have been filmed. There have been more than one million visitors to the house in Chuncheon that was chosen to be the home of Joon-Sang (BYJ's character in *Winter Sonata*) and approximately 600,000 of these visitors were Japanese tourists. The success of *Winter Sonata* and the *Yonsama* syndrome have seen Japanese tourism to South Korea surge by 40% in the first ten months of 2004 (Onishi 2004). More recently, Japanese fans have been busy booking trips to Jeju island to see BYJ on the set of his new television series, *Legend* (*Taewangsashingi* 2007) (Bae and Staines 2006). The many ways by which BYJ is consumed shows that he has become an object of transcultural consumption by middle-aged Japanese women. These consumption practices have been the stimulus behind an estimated US$2.8 billion increase in economic activity between South Korea and Japan, according to the Dai-ichi Life Research Institute (Onishi 2004).

Figure 2.1 Japanese magazines with cover stories of BYJ at a bookstore in Tokyo

Figure. 2.2 A variety shop in Shin-Okubo with BYJ posters

The reason behind this phenomenal popularity of BYJ is the type of masculinity that he embodies, which I refer to here as "soft" masculinity. This soft masculinity is a hybrid product constructed through the transcultural amalgamation of South Korea's traditional *seonbi* masculinity (which is heavily influenced by Chinese Confucian *wen* masculinity), Japan's *bishōnen* (pretty boy) masculinity, and global metrosexual masculinity. This transculturation creates *mugukjeok* (non-nationality) which helps BYJ's soft masculinity to freely travel across national boundaries. *Mugukjeok*, a concept used to describe a cultural practice that has no particular national trait, is an example of "cultural proximity." I also argue that the construction of BYJ's soft masculinity is reinforced by the postcolonial desires of Japanese female fans that engender "retrospective" and "nostalgic" sentiment. According to Chris Rojek, the view of the past that retrospective films convey is "out of time." He states that to create this "past," "pastiche and stereotypes are applied to present the simulacrum of historical reality" (1995: 119). The Japanese consumption of BYJ's soft masculinity can be partly explained as a consumption of a simulacrum of Japan's past. Thus, in this chapter, I focus on the BYJ phenomenon within the framework of the Japanese embrace of South Korean masculinity and discuss how this Japanese embrace is underpinned by "counter-coevality" (a colonial gaze that sees temporal lag) and "cultural proximity" (due to spatial adjacency), based on the disjunctive spatio-temporal contexts of South Korea and Japan.

The *Yonsama* Syndrome

Reading the *Yonsama* Syndrome through *Hallyu* Discourses

In *The Secret (DNA) of Hallyu*, Yoo Sang-Cheol and his co-authors attempt to explain the *Yonsama* syndrome through a cultural imperialist and cultural nationalist perspective. They argue that South Korea's "uniqueness" (unique DNA) is the reason for the regional success of South Korean popular culture (Yoo et al. 2005). They argue that *Hallyu* embodies South Korea's unique aura and "sentiment" and that these are the main aspects of South Korean popular culture that contribute to its regional popularity.[7] The former minister of culture, Lee Eo-Ryeong, states that the most significant driving force of the *Yonsama* syndrome is BYJ's special characteristic of being "gentle" and "sensitive." According to Yoo et al., this persona supposedly represents "the aura of South Korea," which has enabled South Korean popular culture to penetrate the rest of Asia. Their perspective is both a cultural nationalist and cultural imperialist one as they subscribe to the notion that a group of behavioral characteristics such as gentleness and sensitivity can be described as South Korean and assume a mono-directional cultural flow from the dominant to the dominated. Their argument, however, only focuses on the South Korean aspects of South Korean popular culture and neglects to consider the fact that South Korean popular culture is a transcultural product. Furthermore, Cho Han Hye-Jeong has argued that the cultural imperialist perspective on cultural flows is not applicable to contemporary cultural markets as it does not take into account multi-directional cultural flows (2005: 21). Yoo et al.'s argument ignores the multi-directional transcultural flows that contribute to the hybridized characteristics of South Korean popular culture. Despite this, Yoo et al.'s argument is useful in one respect: they analyze BYJ's popularity within the framework of what they call "*sopeuteu paweo*" (soft power) (2005: 57–58). In his book, *Soft Power: The Means to Success in World Politics*, Joseph S. Nye states: "Soft power is a staple of daily democratic politics. The ability to establish preferences tends to be associated with intangible assets such as an attractive personality, culture, political values, and institutions, and policies that are seen as legitimate or having moral authority ... It is also the ability to attract, and attraction often leads to acquiescence. Simply put, in behavioral terms soft power is attractive power" (2004: 6). This concept is useful in understanding the popular trend of pan-Asian contemporary cultural products that share the power of "soft" content, such as images, design, and characters. The idea of "softness" is useful in describing today's popular cultural products as they are always changing and evolving through transculturation.

In regards to the transcultural circulation of South Korean popular culture, Kim Hyeon-Mi presents a postcolonial view in opposition to the cultural imperialist and cultural nationalist argument. In *Cultural Translation in the Era of Globalization*, she stresses that the success of South Korean dramas in the region is mainly due to the "simultaneity of desires" among women from the different countries in Asia who constitute a new Asian middle-class (2005: 242):

> The class position of "[this] new middle class" allows these women to consume the images and products. Through consumption and interpretation, these women experience the new modernity. During this process, the foundation of Asian familism such as a dichotomy of personal/public spaces and stereotypes of female/male roles has been questioned or strengthened and women have introspected themselves and have become subjects who yearn for a new identity ... Rather than being a product of South Korean popular culture's uniqueness or superior quality, the Korean Wave may be a result of the "ability" of a most secular capitalistic materialist desire to appease the newly emerging desires and diverse anxieties in the Asian region. (2005: 243)

In Kim's account, BYJ's popularity in Asia is not based on his superior ability as an actor or his unique "aura" of South Koreanness, but based on his images and characteristics which satisfy the diverse and hybridized desires of Asian fans. I, however, question this point of the "simultaneity of desires" among all Asian consumers, including the Japanese viewers. I believe that the desires of Japanese fans for South Korean popular culture must be distinguished from the desires of other Asian consumers because, unlike other Asian countries, Japan has a colonial and postcolonial relationship with South Korea. Also, Japan has, to some extent, shown a tendency to assert cultural superiority over the rest of Asia and Asian cultures (Heo and Ham 2005: 60; Iwabuchi 2002a: 8).

In *Japan, Consuming Korea: Hallyu, Women, Drama*, Hirata Yukie proposes the notion of "everydayness" and coevality to explain the ways that middle-aged Japanese female fans consume South Korean popular culture. Quoting Kuroda Fukumi's book *Seoul My Heart* (ソウル マイ ハ-ト 1988), Hirata explains that this book indicates the new view held by the Japanese towards South Korea, which began arising around the time of the 1988 Seoul Olympic games. Hirata argues that Kuroda shows a sense of "coevality" towards South Korea; for example, when Kuroda visits South Korea for travel, it is evident that she desires to know more about "Seoul (South Korea) Now" rather than about South Korea's politics, economy, and history (2005: 43–45).[8] Hirata emphasizes that *Seoul My Heart* indicates the new Japanese consciousness towards South Korea. In this book, according to Hirata, a Japanese woman (Kuroda), in viewing South Korea through a coeval gaze, sees the ordinary everyday life of the neighboring country (2005: 44). Further explaining the more recent phenomenon of Japanese female fans consuming South Korean popular culture, Hirata states that in "passing over the imperialistic and male-centered socio-historical context, their [the Japanese women's] gaze is a new trend among women which is created as a result of the 1990s' global consumerism" (2005: 131). Hirata's point well explains Japan's recently changed views towards South Korea, where she mainly emphasizes the notion of sharing the sense of coevality between two countries. It is an irrefutable fact that Japan's view towards South Korea has been radically changed during the past couple of decades due to the various socio-cultural experiences such as the 1988 Seoul Olympics, the 2002 Korea/Japan World Cup, and *Hallyu*. However, I still believe that it is more likely Japan's counter-coeval gaze that is the main driving force behind the Japanese embrace of *Winter Sonata* and BYJ.[9] In this chapter, I thus focus on the retrospective desire of Japanese female fans towards South Korea and South Korean culture that is evident from their nostalgic gaze towards BYJ.

Regarding the *Hallyu* phenomenon, particularly the *Yonsama* syndrome, some South Korean newspapers and magazines have focused on its "industrial benefits" and "cultural dominance," and have emphasized the regional popularity of *Hallyu* within a capitalist framework. Notably, these media articulate imperialist attitudes while describing the successes of *Hallyu* and frequently use such phrases as "conquering China/Japan," "cultural invasion," and "subjugating Asian countries" (D. H. Lee 2004a; S. G. Kim 2004; H. J. Lee 2004; J. H. Tak 2006; H. S. Lee 2005). Baek Won-Dam criticizes such explicit expressions of imperialism and argues that these attitudes resemble the vulgar nature of an "overnight millionaire" and a "prostitute" (2005: 106). As the title of her book — *The Choice of East-Asia, Hallyu* — suggests, *Hallyu* has to be understood in terms of sovereign local reception and cultural choice. Using the examples of China and Vietnam, Baek argues that the local audiences in these countries "chose" *Hallyu* as an "alternative culture" while they were undergoing the process of socio-ideological changes during the 1990s (2005: 33, 163). According to Baek, following the deconstruction of the socialist structure, China could not find its own cultural identity as it entered the capitalist era and, therefore, chose *Hallyu* as a temporary measure to fill the cultural void: "Because there was a cultural vacuum, the marketing strategies of South Korean enterprises [such as casting a South Korean television drama star Ahn Jae-Wook as a commercial model] unexpectedly constructed *Hallyu*" (2005: 33). She argues that Vietnam also chose "*Hallyu* as a transitional substitute" for its new cultural identity as it transitioned from the premodern cultural system to the modern capitalist system and that the reason for this choice was partly due to the similarities between South Korean and Vietnamese cultural traditions (2005: 67, 163). Baek's argument on the sovereign local choices of *Hallyu* in both China and Vietnam is based on the notion of "glocalization."[10] Glocalization is an important concept for explaining the consumption of South Korean popular culture in Asia. In particular, the advantage of Baek's postcolonial approach is that it recognizes multi-directional transcultural flows and the differences in local reception based on local socio-historical contexts. Based on her postcolonial argument, I examine why Japanese audiences chose BYJ and how his soft masculinity is constructed through the paradigm of Japan's retrospective choice.

BYJ, from *Woojungsa* to *Yonsama*

BYJ began his acting career in the film *Ppilgu* in 1994. He later went on to star in television drama series such as *Love Greeting* (*Sarang-ui Insa* 1994), *A Sunny Place of the Young* (*Jeolmeuni-ui Yangji* 1995), and *First Love* (*Cheotsarang* 1997). He started to become more well known after acting as an ambitious film director in *A Sunny Place of the Young*. But it was not until he starred as Kang Jae-Ho in *Have We Really Loved?* (*Uriga Jeongmal Saranghaesseulkka* 1999) that he gained widespread support from a fan club that had members nation-wide. In *Have We Really Loved?*, Jae-Ho is an aspirational young man who had been abandoned by his parents and had had a lonely childhood. Due to his difficult childhood, Jae-Ho holds a grudge against the world. His only aim in life is to become rich and successful. Motivated by this ambition to be rich, he befriends his rich classmate, Hyeon-Soo (Yoon Son-Ha). However, he unexpectedly falls in love with his lecturer, Shin-Hyeong (Kim Hye-Soo), who is like a sister to Hyeon-Soo. These three characters enter into a complicated love triangle that is resolved and Jae-Ho and Shin-Hyeong end up being together. However, Jae-Ho then finds out that he has a terminal brain tumor and he decides to leave Shin-Hyeong. However, because of Shin-Hyeong's wish to continue the relationship, they meet again and are married. In the end, Jae-Ho dies peacefully in Shin-Hyeong's arms because of his illness. In the series, BYJ acts as Jae-Ho, who has selfish desires but is, at the same time, a tragic figure who is devoted to his romantic partner. Many critics have commented that BYJ played the character of Jae-Ho, who has both "evil and pure" desires, to perfection (Woojungsa.com 1999). Despite its relatively low audience share, the drama received enthusiastic responses from netizens (internet citizens), who formed the *Woojungsa* (an abbreviation of the drama's Korean title) fan club on April 30, 1999. The website of this fan club, Woojungsa.com, opened a new era of television drama fan-community culture in South Korean cyberspace. The fan club has various social welfare activities, one of which involved helping orphans named Jae-Ho as a way of commemorating BYJ's character of Jae-Ho in *Have We Really Loved?*.

After a two-year absence from the television screen, BYJ ventured into acting and played a complicated villain in *Hotelier* (*Hotellieo* 2001). However, it was not until 2002 that BYJ managed to expand his acting career beyond South Korea with *Winter Sonata*. This newly found popularity gave both BYJ and his co-star, Choi Ji-Woo, the chance to expand their acting profiles throughout Asia, especially Japan. Following the regional success of *Winter Sonata*, BYJ's historical film, *Untold Scandal* (*Seukaendeul: Joseon Namnyeo Sanglyeoljisa* 2003), was released in 2004 in several Asian countries including Japan, Hong Kong, and Singapore.

Untold Scandal is based on the French novel *Les Liaisons Dangereuses* (*Dangerous Liaisons* 1782). In the film, BYJ plays the role of Jo Won, a notorious playboy from the Joseon Dynasty (eighteenth-century Korea). Jo Won appears elegant and courtly, but he is a sexually voracious young lord who indulges in numerous sexual conquests. He is challenged by his cousin, Lady Cho (Lee Mi-Sook), to seduce the sexually aloof Lady Sook (Jeon Do-Yeon), who is known as "the gate of chastity." This beautiful and conservative widow initially rejects Jo Won's attempts to seduce her but eventually falls in love with him when he tells her that he had room for only one person in his heart, and that person was Lady Sook. However, once Jo Won achieved his goal and won the challenge, he leaves Lady Sook who then takes her own life in despair.

The film achieved great success in South Korea because of its glossy evocation of the decadence and hypocrisy of the Joseon Dynasty. It had visually outstanding costumes and art direction, lush landscapes, and beautifully framed and well-lit sequences. However, its box-office record outside South Korea did not match its success within South Korea, and this was particularly so in Japan. Critics have argued that BYJ's character of Jo Won did not meet the expectations of Japanese audiences, who preferred him as the sweet, innocent, and well-mannered Joon-Sang in *Winter Sonata*. This suggests that the *Yonsama* syndrome does not automatically guarantee the success of "any" BYJ film in Japan (G. J. Shin 2004). It is arguable that *Untold*

Scandal did not resonate well with middle-aged female fans in Japan and in other Asian countries because of BYJ's nudity, the strong sex scenes, and Jo Won's slyness in the movie. The poor reception of *Untold Scandal* in Japan suggests that BYJ's fans desire a Joon-Sang who is tender and soft rather than a Jo Won who is dangerous and dominant (Figures 2.3 and 2.4).

Figure 2.3 A scene from *Winter Sonata*

Figure 2.4 A scene from *Untold Scandal*

BYJ, Joon-Sang, and Soft Korean Masculinity

BYJ's character, Kang Joon-Sang, in *Winter Sonata* has changed many Japanese people's perceptions of South Korean men. South Korean scholar, Kim Eun-Shil, who analyzes the effects of the *Yonsama* syndrome on the postcolonial relations between Japan and South Korea, states: "To the Japanese, South Korea used to be associated with images of the 'dark, noisy, and smelly,' but now *Yonsama's* middle-aged fans associate South Korea with 'beautiful things' and see *Yonsama* as an idealized man" (quoted in Onishi 2004). In particular, it is evident from the responses to my research questionnaires that Japanese women's perceptions have changed from viewing South Korean men as overly macho and uncivilized to viewing them as possessing highly idealized attributes. For example, in response to the question, "Is BYJ's character/ image different from those pre-existing images of South Korean men which you have seen from other movies, dramas or in your real lives?," forty-six out of fifty-six participants answered "Yes." Out of these forty-six, thirty-eight participants used such negative expressions as "dark, scary, sly, aggressive, and violent" to describe how they saw South Korean men previously. In particular, many of them use the word "scary" (こわい):

> Before, they had scary images. After I knew BYJ, the images of South Korean men have become better and I feel friendly towards them. (Dan, 52, questionnaire respondent)

> Previously [South Korean men's images were] violent and scary. But BYJ is tender, gentle and he takes his life seriously. (Nan, 50, questionnaire respondent)

As these responses above suggest, after watching BYJ in *Winter Sonata*, the perception of these Japanese fans of South Korean men has changed dramatically from viewing them as scary and macho to viewing them as tender and gentlemanly. One of the participants, Kan (49), explains that the perception of South Korean men as scary was mostly the result of the media representations of "protesting [South Korean] students against the dictatorship during the 1980s." One of the interviewees, Ba (42), also points out that "some South Korean middle-aged men I see in [television] dramas are quite bossy and they don't treat women fairly." As Kan and Ba have described, the preconceived idea of South Korean men as scary was created through images that were presented in the media. These negative images were created during the socio-political crisis in the 1980s in South Korea that can be traced back to historical national traumas such as the Japanese occupation era.

During the thirty-five years of Japanese occupation, Koreans were exploited and Korean traditions, industries, and culture were completely suppressed. Following the Liberation in August 1945, another traumatic historical event, the Korean War (1950–1953), further devastated North and South Korea. Due to these historical events, South Koreans have been portrayed in the past as a poor and filthy people living in an undeveloped country: a good example of this is the US television drama series, *M*A*S*H* (1972–1983). In particular, as a neighboring country and a former colonial power, Japan treated South Korea as an inferior country with a second-rate culture in the past. An article in the *Wall Street Journal* describes this Japanese attitude towards South Korea:

(But) in Japan the South Korea craze is particularly surprising, because it has gripped a generation that has never shown much interest in Japan's nearest neighbor. Japan's colonial rule in South Korea, from 1910 to 1945, left some now-older Japanese conflicted about the country or dismissive of it. For decades, many Japanese looked down on South Koreans as inferior both racially and economically. (Fuyuno 2004)

This article points out that the older generation, born during the period of Japanese occupation, has changed its point of view about South Korea after the advent of BYJ in Japan. Many of these fans express their surprise at seeing a new South Korean male image in the form of the tender and soft BYJ. From the above analysis, it is arguable why *Untold Scandal* was not successful in Japan: this was because the character of Jo Won resurrected the old images of South Korean men as strong, scary, and dominant. The popularity of *Winter Sonata* in Japan indicates that Japanese female fans now embrace the newly constructed soft South Korean masculinity as exemplified by the character of Joon-Sang in *Winter Sonata*.

In chapter 1, employing Judith Butler's concept of gender performativity, I have discussed the ways in which masculinity is culturally constructed through the repetition of stylized bodily performances such as acting, dressing, and speaking. In the next three subsections, through examining the characteristics of Joon-Sang in *Winter Sonata*, I discuss three key aspects of BYJ's bodily performance that reinforce his soft masculinity. They are "tender charisma," purity, and politeness.

Tender Charisma

The main plot of *Winter Sonata* is about the experience of first love, memory loss, and unknown family ties. The drama begins with the innocent and humorous encounter between Joon-Sang (BYJ) and Yoo-Jin (Choi Ji-Woo), both of whom eventually fall in love with each other and become high school sweethearts. Because of an accident, Joon-Sang loses his memory and he becomes separated from Yoo-Jin for ten years before they meet again. On the day of Yoo-Jin's engagement ceremony with her high school friend, Sang-Hyeok, she runs into Joon-Sang on the street. However, he cannot remember Yoo-Jin because he now lives his life as Min-Hyeong, a Korean-American architect. Even though Yoo-Jin thinks that Min-Hyeong is not Joon-Sang, her first love, she cannot help being reminded of Joon-Sang when she sees Min-Hyeong. She is torn between Min-Hyeong and Sang-Hyeok. Later, Joon-Sang recovers his memory; however, the situation becomes even more complicated as secret family ties between Joon-Sang and Yoo-Jin are revealed.

In *Winter Sonata*, BYJ, who plays the role of Joon-Sang/Min-Hyeong, embodies a well-mannered gentleman who puts his lover, Yoo-Jin, first. Throughout the series, Joon-Sang's gentle and selfless consideration for Yoo-Jin is signified through his devoted demeanor and his tender smiles. Some Japanese scholars declare that the key aspect underlying BYJ's popularity is his "soft smile" (Endo and Matsumoto 2004). In addition, Joon-Sang is able to selflessly sacrifice his own welfare for Yoo-Jin's sake. For example, when Sang-Hyeok is hospitalized as he pines for Yoo-Jin, who had separated from him to be with Joon-Sang, Joon-Sang takes Yoo-Jin to the hospital and encourages her to see Sang-Hyeok:

Joon-Sang: You can go in now.
Yoo-Jin: (without looking at his face) You shouldn't do this.
Joon-Sang: Yes, I should ... You are worried about him. Aren't you?
Yoo-Jin: (tears in her eyes) Joon-Sang ...
Joon-Sang: I'm fine. You can go ...
Yoo-Jin: (without looking at him, with trembling voice) What if I can't come back?
Joon-Sang: (frightened expression) !!!
Yoo-Jin: If I see Sang-Hyeok, I might not be able to come back. Then ... what should we do?
Joon-Sang: (sorrowfully) That's ... ok. That's better than watching you suffer in pain.

The above scene describes how Joon-Sang endures emotional hardship for Yoo-Jin's sake and it appears as if he would bear any pain for Yoo-Jin. Joon-Sang is an idealized embodiment of a man who is able to express outward emotion (through the act of crying) for Yoo-Jin while maintaining a strong will inside. According to Kim Ho-Seok, the character of Joon-Sang has both feminine and masculine aspects which can be characterized as "tender charisma" (cited in Yoo et al. 2005: 81). Fans often view the real-life BYJ through this idealized screen image of Joon-Sang.

Many of the Japanese fans I have interviewed have often described BYJ as an ideal and perfect man who has both "manly charisma" and "feminine tenderness." In other words, the masculine attribute of tender charisma symbolizes the ideal man for these fans:

He is different from any other actor or any other guy. He is tender but not weak. His dialogues are so sweet, poetic, and intelligent but at the same time he has such a charismatic manner. (Ga, 54, focus group interviewee)

In his photo album, he looks so manly and tough! But he is still my prince. Always! Look at his smile ... how sweet! (Na, 52, focus group interviewee)

In the above responses, Ga described BYJ as an ideal man who is both "tender" and "charismatic" while Na's remark about BYJ's "toughness" and "sweetness" suggest that for her, the combination of these qualities in one body is desirable. Kuroiwa, a producer at NHK, also emphasizes BYJ's "tender charisma" as constructed by what she refers to as his neutralized images:

> Bae Yong-Joon is very neutral. Not very sexual[ly appealing], not very manly but not too feminine either. When the woman wants to be led by somebody, he does that. He is gentle, charming, and polite but at the same time, when he has to say something he says something. He is the man when the woman wants him to be a man. He fulfills all the needs of middle-aged Japanese women. (personal interview)

Kuroiwa's point highlights the fact that BYJ's sexually neutral "tender charisma" is one of the most significant aspects contributing to the middle-aged Japanese female fandom of BYJ in Japan.[11] In BYJ's star images, masculinity and femininity are hybridized and unified in an ideal manner for his fans: in the words of one of my interviewees, Sa (38), BYJ is "gentle and feminine, yet sometimes very manly." BYJ's neutral masculinity stays in the third space; though it contains a feminine aspect, it is "not feminized." This "tenderly charismatic" neutral masculinity of the third space can be explained through the traditional Confucian ideology of the ideal man who possesses "a tender exterior and a strong inner will" (외유내강, 外柔內剛, *oeyunaegang*).[12] This feature, *oeyunaegang*, is one of the key characteristics of *seonbi* masculinity during the Joseon Dynasty and is still considered to be one of the principal qualities of a cultured man in South Korea. It is evident that BYJ performs soft masculinity through mobilizing sexually neutral images characterized by *oeyunaegang*. The earlier mentioned responses from the fans demonstrate that such soft masculine images of BYJ's "tender charisma" resonate well with many Japanese fans.

Purity

The way that Joon-Sang represents "purity" also constitutes the soft masculine image of BYJ. This purity is mainly signified by the portrayal of "first love" between Joon-Sang and Yoo-Jin. Many Japanese viewers mention that Joon-Sang and Yoo-Jin's pure first love reminds them of simpler times during their younger days (Onishi 2004). Since *Winter Sonata* was broadcast in Japan on NHK, NHK has received phone calls, e-mails, and more than 20,000 letters from viewers who want to describe their own experiences of love and loss (Tabata 2003; Wiseman 2004). Some of the fans I interviewed point out that the main characters in *Winter Sonata* are portrayed in a more innocent manner than other characters in recent Japanese television dramas:

> Today's Japanese dramas contain too much representation of sex. But in *Winter Sonata* we don't see those embarrassing sex scenes. They [the characters] love purely. (Ga, 54, focus group interviewee)

These viewers, who do not like the explicit representation of sex in Japanese dramas, prefer the idealistic depiction of "pure" and innocent love in *Winter Sonata*. For these viewers, watching the innocent relationship between BYJ and Choi Ji-Woo unfold in *Winter Sonata* allows them to remember their younger selves: for example, some of these viewers state that BYJ is an "old-fashioned gentleman who reminds me of my first love" and that "the high school setting takes us [Japanese women] back to the days before marriage" (quoted in Wiseman 2004). In relation to this, Baek Seung-Gook argues that the major attraction of *Winter Sonata* is the fact that its story stimulates in Japanese viewers the nostalgic memory of their first love (2005: 174). Baek states that "the sender of *Winter Sonata* encodes 'pure love' in the message [drama content] and the Japanese viewers decode them" (2005: 175). According to him, the drama employs "pure love" as a cultural code and it uses various audiovisual methods to deliver this coded message to the receivers (2005: 175–78). In other words, there are dramatic signifiers in *Winter Sonata* that imply first love, for example, when Joon-Sang plays a piece entitled "The First Time" on the piano for Yoo-Jin. This piano music is an example of a signifier of first love (Y. S. Kim 2005). The notion of encoding certain cultural codes can also be applied in relation to conceptualizing the construction of BYJ's soft masculinity in *Winter Sonata*. As Joon-Sang plays the piano for Yoo-Jin, the image of soft masculinity is encoded into his piano-playing body. In other words, BYJ's soft masculinity is constructed as he performs certain actions such as the gentle playing of a piano piece which signifies a first love that is pure.

Another example of the construction of soft masculinity through the portrayal of purity is the kiss scene between Joon-Sang and Yoo-Jin. In episode two, while Joon-Sang and Yoo-Jin are playing with snowmen, Yoo-Jin steals a kiss from Joon-Sang by kissing him on the cheek when he least expected it. The white snow of the landscape in the scene signifies purity. In addition, Joon-Sang's innocent and surprised look after Yoo-Jin's unexpected kiss reinforces a sense of purity. This innocent look, as performed by BYJ, encodes the message of the innocent "purity" of a teenage boy's first kiss and reinforces the soft masculinity of BYJ. This encoded message of soft masculinity is first established in the bicycle-riding scene in episode one. In this scene, Joon-Sang rides a bicycle along a path by the river while Yoo-Jin sits behind him holding his waist. Romantic background music is played as they ride along the path surrounded by a glowing sunset, the sparkling river, and golden-brown shrub. Dressed in their high-school uniforms, which signify youth, the smiling and happy lovers look pure and innocent. To explain the representation of first love in this scene, Kim Gi-Gook uses Jean Baudrillard's concept of "simulacra and simulation" (2005: 95). According to Kim, this bicycle scene is a perfect model of first love for many Japanese fans. He argues that *Winter Sonata*'s "romantic images are Baudrillard's simulacra" and that the viewers indulge in an imaginary reality of romantic first love that, in fact, never actually existed.

One of my interviewees, Na (52), said: "I watched *Winter Sonata* more than 20 times ... especially I watched the bicycle scene again and again. It reminds me of my first love from high-school." It is evident that Joon-Sang's bicycle-riding bodily performance helps to create the soft masculine image of a teenage boy who reminds Na of her first love. For this fan, Joon-Sang's image in a high-school uniform is a simulacrum of a pure and golden past and is, therefore, a retrospective site of nostalgia. Here, Joon-Sang's high-school uniform and bicycle signify the purity of a teenage boy, and this sense of purity enhances the construction of BYJ's soft masculinity. Thus, it is evident that BYJ's soft masculinity is constructed through certain bodily performances such as acting (playing a piano and riding a bicycle), facial expressions (the look of innocent surprise as being kissed), and dressing (wearing a high-school uniform). It is also evident that this reconstructed soft masculinity of BYJ satisfies the nostalgic desires of Japanese fans for their golden past.

Politeness

Another aspect of BYJ's soft masculinity is his politeness. In *Winter Sonata*, BYJ is portrayed as well-mannered and thoughtful. He speaks to Yoo-Jin in a respectful manner and is always considerate of her needs. As one of my interviewees, Ba, said:

> I was so surprised [when I saw his polite image from the drama] because I thought South Korean men were very rude and authoritative. (Ba, 42, focus group interviewee)

As Ba has remarked above, BYJ's polite image surprises her because it is different from pre-existing images in Japan of Korean men as rude and authoritative. In *Winter Sonata*, his politeness is demonstrated through the ways in which he cares for Yoo-Jin. For example, when Joon-Sang finds out that he and Yoo-Jin share a common father, he decides to keep this a secret as he wants to protect her from any traumatic experience. In episode 18, they travel to a small beachside town. Yoo-Jin is excited because it is their first trip together; unbeknown to her, Joon-Sang is unhappy because it is a farewell trip for him.

Yoo-Jin: Let's make lots of memories. I want to remember every single thing!
Joon-Sang: (voice only) I don't want to leave anything behind, Yoo-Jin ... anything that would remind you of me.

From the above scene, it is clear that Joon-Sang attempts to protect Yoo-Jin from being hurt by making sure that nothing would be left behind for Yoo-Jin that would remind her of him. Even after he finds out that they are not actually blood relations, he leaves Yoo-Jin as he believes that Yoo-Jin would be happier with Sang-Hyeok. Apart from the polite image of Joon-Sang, many fans also view the real-life BYJ as a polite young man. Most of the interviewees and the questionnaire participants I met in Japan mentioned BYJ's politeness and considerateness:

> He is so polite and considerate. [Look at] how he treats his fans. So considerate! ... We love his politeness and modesty. (Na, 52, focus group interviewee)

> He is humble and polite ... I like the way of he greets others. (Chan, 42, questionnaire respondent)

For these fans, BYJ's politeness is singled out as the most significant factor in their desire for him. In particular, these fans make an emotional connection with the way he treats his fans as a family. This is seen in the way that BYJ calls his fans "my family" and always shows his respect and consideration for them. For example, on his second visit to Japan in 2004, over a thousand fans gathered outside his hotel. As BYJ tried to leave the hotel, hundreds of fans converged on his car. During the chaos that ensued, about ten fans were injured and hospitalized. The Japanese media criticized BYJ, suggesting that it was his changing of his schedule that had led to the incident. However, before negative public opinion spread too far, BYJ held a press conference and politely apologized for the incident and said, "I was too naïve. I believed that such an accident would never happen. I'm so sorry about what has happened to my valued family" (Choi 2004). The deep regret for his action was enhanced by his tears. The Japanese media soon turned their focus from the incident to his polite apologies and the fact that he had cried. Later, each fan who was injured in the incident received a personally autographed letter from BYJ, who addressed each fan as being part of his family. Here, his sincere apology and crying gesture are signifiers of his polite manner. Such an encoded polite image reinforces BYJ's soft masculinity. Some interviewees have also noted the polite way that BYJ greets his fans:

> Of course he has the prettiest face and sweetest smile and that is why I love him. But I love him also because of his polite and considerate attitudes ... He bows to his fans with his two hands together. We don't see that [polite manner] any more here. (Ra, 48, focus group interviewee)

> Even the way he waves his hands is so noble. (Ga, 54, focus group interviewee)

As Ra explains above, BYJ's greeting gesture of "bowing to his fans with his two hands together" signifies his politeness and consideration. Ga even suggests that the way BYJ gently waves his hands is "so noble." It is evident that such polite and gentle bodily performance helps to construct BYJ's soft masculine image which is different from the images of young Japanese men and also different from the pre-existing images of Korean masculinity in Japan. Such refined bodily performance makes him unique and special; as Ran said, "I've never seen this kind of man in my whole life. From him [his body], we can feel such an aura of nobility." It is thus his polite body that many Japanese fans specifically desire and resonate with.

The desire of Japanese fans for BYJ's soft masculine and polite body is also evident from their appreciation of the fake *Yonsama* (Figure 2.5) who appeared at the *Saitama Super Arena*, where the promotional event for BYJ's film, *April Snow*, was held. At this event, over thirty thousand Japanese (mostly female) fans gathered to see BYJ and it was during this event that a Japanese man appeared dressed up as BYJ. Some of the fans took photos of this fake *Yonsama* even though he did not look like BYJ. However, through the mobilization of certain bodily performances of BYJ, such as smiling and politely putting his hands on the chest, the fake *Yonsama* was able to successfully signify BYJ through the use of these bodily signifiers. Because of his polite bodily gesture, the Japanese fans were able to identify this anonymous Japanese man with *Yonsama*. As a bodily signifier, the fake *Yonsama*'s polite gesture encodes BYJ's soft masculinity and because this coded message is familiar to the receivers (the fans), they were able to decode the bodily signifiers as signifying BYJ's polite body. The Japanese fans' appreciation of the fake *Yonsama* clearly demonstrates the ways in which BYJ is identified with his soft masculine body of politeness.

Figure 2.5 The picture of a fake *Yonsama*

Cultural Proximity and *Mugukjeok* Soft Masculinity

As observed, BYJ's masculine image can be characterized as having the three aspects of tender charisma, purity, and politeness. I have shown how these three key aspects form the foundation of his soft masculinity and how they are embraced by Japanese fans. Now, I want to discuss the ways in which the transcultural flows between Japan and South Korea operate in constructing South Korean soft masculinity as represented by BYJ. These transcultural flows create *mugukjeok* soft masculine images that circulate in Asia and which drives the Japanese fandom of BYJ. This *mugukjeok* soft masculinity can be conceptualized by analyzing the disjunctive socio-political contexts of Japan and South Korea. These contexts include the shared traditions of East Asian Confucian ideology, the Japanese colonization of Korea, and the extensive influence of contemporary Japanese popular culture in the Asian region ("Japanization").[13]

Confucian *Seonbi* Masculinity

According to Chua Beng Huat, the popularity of South Korean dramas in Asia is partly due to the fact that these dramas espouse values that are common with the values of other Confucian countries such as China, Hong Kong, Japan, Taiwan, and Singapore (Chua 2004: 216). Numerous South Korean scholars also point out that cultural proximity, driven by sharing traditional values of Confucianism, is one of the significant reasons for the popularity of South Korean popular culture in the Asian region. Kang Jin-Seok suggests that there are two major reasons for why *Hallyu* has become a leading popular culture in Asia: the first is the close cultural proximity of Confucian countries in the region as enabled by the similarity of sentiment (정, 情) shared by these countries; the second is the effective use of visual images (Kang 2004: 74–76). The close cultural proximity of these countries is mainly due to the sharing of Confucian ideas such as the importance of maintaining family values and the importance of filial piety. A Chinese studies scholar, Lee Min-Ja, also claims that the popularity of some South Korean dramas such as *What Is Love?* (*Sarangi Mwogille* 1991) in China is due to the sentimental empathy of sharing Confucian values and familism (2006: 91).[14] According to the suggestions of these scholars, there are some common values and sentiments that are central to the dominant social ideologies in these Confucian countries. In particular, considering the widespread Confucianism among East Asian countries, the sharing of common values can be explained using the concept of pan-East-Asianism. Pan-East-Asianism is constructed through the transcultural flows between different cultural groups that subsequently create *mugukjeok* values and ideas among East Asian countries including Japan and South Korea.

Sharing common *mugukjeok* values is clearly demonstrated from the notion of "East Asian Confucian masculinity." It appears that East Asian countries share certain beliefs of the ideal man that is based on Confucian ideology. Kam Louie explains the ideal model of Confucian masculinity as a combination of *wen* (文), the mental, and *wu* (武), the physical (2002: 10). According to traditional Confucian ideology, an ideal man (君子, *junzi*) embodies a balance of both *wen* and *wu* (Louie 2002: 11).[15] Historically, however, *wen* was considered to be superior to *wu*. Because Confucius is the god of *wen*, in China, which was a strict Confucian country at one time, *wen* — mental attainment — was often considered to be a more elite masculine form than *wu* — physical attainment (2002: 17–18). Due to the transcultural flows of Confucianism, this model of Chinese *wen* masculinity influences the formations of masculinity in East Asian cultures. In Korea, *wen* masculinity was widely practiced by the Confucian scholar class, *seonbi*, throughout the Joseon Dynasty.

Many aspects of BYJ's soft masculinity are related to traditional Confucian *seonbi* masculinity. As observed earlier, his image of "tender charisma" embodies the model of an ideal Confucian man who possesses *oeyunaegang* ("tender exterior and strong inner will"). This model *oeyunaegang* masculinity is based on the basic teaching of Confucianism that is relevant to the key virtues of *seonbi* (J. G. Lee 1999: 307). "Politeness" is also one of the basic virtues that is required from *seonbi*.[16] Through practicing Confucian moral virtues such as *oeyunaegang* and politeness, *seonbi* from the Joseon era tried to achieve the goal of becoming the Confucian ideal man, *junzi* (군자, 君子). Such Confucian moral ethics as practiced by the *seonbi* are historically influenced by China. Because of Chinese cultural influence, Japan and Korea have traditionally shared the various ideologies and practices of East Asian Confucian culture. Because BYJ exemplifies the characteristics of "tender charisma" and "politeness," which are the basic virtues required by *seonbi* masculinity, BYJ embodies the traditional virtues of pan–East Asian Confucian culture. These traditional values as embodied by BYJ also transmit well to Japan due to the close cultural proximity between Japan and South Korea. In other words, BYJ's soft masculinity can be conceptualized within the framework of the shared *mugukjeok* Confucian values between Japan and South Korea.

Korean Popular Culture, Post/Colonial Mimicry[17]

Apart from Confucianism, the unique historical and political relationship, mainly characterized by the Japanese colonization of Korea, between the two countries has been reinforced to create *mugukjeok* values that South Korea and Japan have shared. Throughout the Japanese colonization period, all cultural sectors in Korea were suppressed by the Japanese colonial government, *Joseon chongdokbu* (조선 총독부). In 1938, Japan enforced strong policies to weaken Korean culture in order to demoralize Koreans as colonial subjects and to obliterate Korean culture. The Japanese government implemented various cultural control policies "such as a prohibition against speaking Korean, requirements that Korean nationals become Japanese and that Korean names be changed to Japanese-style names, the enforcement of a conscription system for Korean people, and restriction of freedom of speech by closing Korean newspapers, including *Donga Ilbo* and *Chosun Ilbo*" (Min et al. 2003: 31).[18] These cultural controls can be related to the *kominka* (황민화, 皇民化) policy, which is the Japanese assimilation policy that was implemented from 1937 to Japan's defeat in World War II (Peattie 1984: 121). *Kominka* can be translated as "Japanization" or "the imperialization of subject peoples," which articulates Japan's transnational political and cultural power and was a policy that attempted to assimilate colonized peoples such as the Ainu, the Okinawans, the Taiwanese, and the Koreans into Japanese society (Iwabuchi 2002a: 9).[19]

Indeed, it was not only under the strict *kominka* policy, but also during the entire Japanese occupation of Korea between 1910 and 1945 that all Korean cultural sectors were deprived of their freedom of creativity and expression. Above all, Koreans were forced to think and behave according to the colonizer's norms and institutions and they also had to express themselves in the language of the colonizers. After having experienced such absolute suppression under Japanese colonial rule, Koreans held paradoxical attitudes towards Japan. For example, a Korean nationalist director, Na Un-Gyu, produced an anti-occupation film, *Arirang* (1926), in protest against what he saw as cultural genocide. On the other hand, other directors produced pro-Japanese occupation movies, such as Lee Byeong-Il's *Spring of the Peninsula* (*Bando-ui Bom* 1941) and Park Gi-Chae's *Korean Strait* (*Daehan Haehyeop* 1943) (S. L. Kang 2006). In particular, Lee Byeong-Il, who had studied film in Japan, vigorously adapted advanced film techniques from Japan such as the technique of utilizing the camera's depth of field and the tracking shot on the street (S. Y. Kim 2006). It is evident that Lee and Park's admiration of Japan is contradictory to Na Un-Gyu's resistant attitude. These paradoxical attitudes of the oppressed towards the oppressor can be explained by Albert Memmi's analysis on the "colonized mentality." Memmi argues that the colonial condition creates an ambivalent colonized mentality, where the colonized hate and desire the colonizer at the same time. He writes: "how could the colonized deny himself so cruelly ... how could he hate the colonizers and yet admire them so passionately?" (quoted in Gandhi 1998: 11). As a colony of Japan, Korea had an aversion to Japan while experiencing longings for what Japan had to offer. Likewise, the Korean cultural sector not only resisted Japan in relation to the freedom of expression and its own sovereignty, but also learned from and mimicked Japanese culture and its products.

The cultural shadow of Japanization continues to exist after Korea gained independence from Japan and exerts a continuing influence on current South Korean society. This occurs especially in the realms of popular culture and South Korean popular culture often struggles to avoid copying Japanese popular culture. During the 1990s, Japanese popular cultural products were avidly consumed in the Asian region. According to Iwabuchi:

> The rise of Japanese cultural export[s] can, I suggest, be read as a symptom of the shifting nature of transnational cultural power in a context in which intensified global cultural flows have decentered the power structure *and* vitalized local practices of appropriation and consumption of foreign cultural products and meanings. (2002a: 35)

As Iwabuchi claims, apart from the ongoing popularity of American popular culture within the Asian region, Japanese popular culture gained a new cultural status in Asia. The Asian regional consumption of contemporary Japanese popular culture can be understood as a new form of "Japanization." Due to the development of advanced technologies such as the Internet and cable television, the Japanization of Asian countries has become faster and more efficient. In the case of South Korea, the phenomenon of Japanization is detected not only from the consumption of Japanese popular culture but also from the way that South Korean popular culture mimics Japanese popular culture. For example, even though there was a strict ban on importing Japanese popular culture until October 1998, some South Korean television dramas successfully merged and copied the plots, characters, and settings of Japanese television dramas (D. H. Lee 2005: 125–26). South Korean popular culture celebrities are also often suspected of imitating Japanese stars and some have actually admitted to being "influenced" by Japanese pop-stars in terms of fashion, image, and dancing and singing styles.

One of the recent examples related with the issue of South Korean popular culture imitating Japanese popular culture is found from the plagiarism debate over the songs of South Korean idol boy band, Big Bang. When Big Bang released their second mini album, *Hot Issue* in November 2007, one of the songs *Fool* (*Babo*) was suspected of being plagiarized because of the similarity of the melody with *P.I.A.N.O*, the popular *Shibuya-kei* genre music composed by a Japanese artist Daishi Dance — *Shibuya-kei* is a sub-genre of Japanese popular music which is best described as a mix between jazz, pop, and electro-pop. Later, Daishi Dance declared that Big Bang did not plagiarize *P.I.A.N.O*, and the debate was over. Regarding this issue, G-Dragon, the composer of *Fool* and band leader, explained that he has been a fan of Daishi Dance and has been highly influenced by the *Shibuya-kei* genre. In August 2008, G-Dragon collaborated with Daishi Dance to compose the title song, *Day by Day* (*Haru Haru*), of *Stand Up*, the third mini album of Big Bang (A. W. Nam 2008; J. A. Lee 2008; W. G. Kim 2008).

Some Asian studies scholars, including Chua Beng Huat, claim that the popularity of South Korean dramas in Asia is partly due to the similarity of these dramas with Japanese dramas. Chua suggests that because South Korean dramas resemble Japanese dramas and because Asian viewers are already used to watching Japanese dramas, these Asian viewers readily consume South Korean dramas (Chua 2004: 217). As observed earlier, South Korean popular culture has been highly influenced by Japanese popular culture ever since the Japanese occupation. This Japanization of South Korean popular culture has created a hybridized *mugukjeok* South Korean popular culture. In her article, "The Cultural Construction of South Korean Trendy Drama," Lee Dong-Hoo also claims that any local cultural products tend to be produced through the process of cultural hybridization. She states: "One of the major mechanisms of the construction of South Korean popular culture is hybridization through the re-adaptation of Japanese popular culture which is an adaptation of Western media culture or global consumer culture" (2005: 127). In other words, South Korean popular culture can be understood through the notion of a product of hybridization, Japanization, and *mugukjeok*.

It appears that BYJ's soft masculine image exemplifies a hybridized, Japanized, and *mugukjeok* South Korean popular cultural product, and that the characteristics possessed by such a product enable BYJ's soft masculine image to freely travel across cultural boundaries between Japan and South Korea. The best example of the Japanization of BYJ's soft masculinity is evident from the transcultural flows of Japanese *bishōnen* masculinity.

Kkonminam BYJ, Japanization of the Pan-East Asian Pretty Boy

BYJ's soft masculine image is often exemplified through his feminine appearance. In *Winter Sonata*, BYJ's Joon-Sang is a bespectacled architect with dyed-brown hair who wears a scarf tied in a different way in each scene. Soon after the success of *Winter Sonata*, imitations of Joon-Sang's glasses, scarf — and even his hair — became popular items among BYJ's middle-aged Japanese fans (Yamaguchi 2004). These items were bundled into what was referred to as a "*Yonsama* triple set" where the wig cost ¥13,440 (US$120), the scarf ¥5,145 (US$46), and the glasses ¥26,250 (US$233). Despite the high price of these items, they were very popular among Japanese female fans, who purchased these items to commemorate BYJ or to personalize his character of Joon-Sang in *Winter Sonata*. Some husbands of these fans even wore these items to please their *Yonsama*-crazy wives (D. H. Lee 2004b). The advertising photos promote how ordinary Japanese men can become as sweet and gentle as BYJ after wearing the *Yonsama* triple set. These ads show before and after pictures of "*Yonsamaized*" Japanese men who undergo the transformation to become more tender- and feminine-looking. This transformation provides evidence that the above representation of BYJ contributes to the construction of his soft masculinity.

Along with his "noble" smile and "feminine" presentation, BYJ's "pretty face" seems to appeal to middle-aged Japanese female viewers the most (H. T. Hwang 2004). Many South Korean plastic surgeons suggest that BYJ is able to project a tender and mellow image because of his slim feminine face and small nose (Yoo et al. 2005: 80–81). These plastic surgeons also suggest that his face shows the perfect mixture of both feminine and masculine sides, which is commonly detected in Japanese pretty boy (*bishōnen*) stars (Yoo et al. 2005: 80–81). It is arguable that the similarity between BYJ and Japanese *bishōnen* stars is one of the reasons why Japanese fans are able to embrace BYJ's soft masculine image easily.

Pretty boy *bishōnen* images appeared in the South Korean entertainment industry in the late 1990s. There have been many beautiful men and pretty boys in the history of global entertainment. Some of the most obvious examples are Alain Delon, James Dean, Marlon Brando, and Brad Pitt. Although these foreign celebrities have been popular in South Korea, it was only after the late 1990s that such a tendency to idolize pretty boys has become a cultural phenomenon that has created a significant impact on many levels of South Korean society. Television commercials, dramas, and billboards have glorified pretty boys. This socio-cultural phenomenon is referred to as the *kkonminam* syndrome, where pretty feminine males in entertainment media become hugely popular. Such images of pretty boys have replaced the previous images of tough and macho South Korean men as characterized by Choi Min-Soo, Jeong Woo-Seong, and Park Sang-Min. Choi Min-Soo, an enduring icon of "the South Korean tough guy," consolidated his tough guy image playing a tragic gangster character in a television drama series called *Sandglass* (*Morae Shigye* 1995). Park Sang-Min became popular as an unbeatable street fighter in a series of three films by the well-known South Korean auteur director, Im Kwon-Taek. In the trilogy, *Son of the General 1, 2*, and *3* (*Janggun-ui Adeul* 1990, 1991, 1992), Park plays a legendary gangster, "Kim Doo-Hwan." Jeong Woo-Seong plays a rebellious young man in his 1997 film, *Beat* (*Biteu* 1997), and became a new symbol of the tough guy. Since the late 1990s, however, these macho characters have gradually disappeared from the screen and *kkonminam* characters have flourished instead.[20]

The Korean term, *kkonminam* (꽃미남), is a coined word that is a combination of 꽃 (flower) and 미남 (a beautiful man). The origin of the word is uncertain. The most widely agreed-upon opinion is that this word originated from the pretty boy characters from girls' comics. When the pretty boys appear in the comic book, the background is almost always filled with flowery patterns, and that is the reason that people began calling pretty boys *kkonminam*. Generally, *kkonminam* refers to men who are pretty looking and who have smooth fair skin, silky hair, and a feminine manner. Kim Yong-Hui explains that "the *kkonminam* syndrome is developed from a consequence of the deconstruction and the hybridization of female/male sexual identities rather than males merely becoming feminized" (2003: 104). According to Kim, *kkonminam* are able to satisfy complex human (especially female) desires because the *kkonminam* possesses both feminine and masculine attributes. The rise of the *kkonminam* phenomenon suggests that the new era of soft masculinity has arrived.

The pretty boy images of South Korean male stars are influenced by the *bishōnen* (미소년, 美少年, beautiful boy) images of Japanese *shōjo manga* (少女漫画) characters. *Shōjo* means a girl (or girls) and *shōjo manga* refers to a genre of *manga* (comics) especially written for girls and which normally describes the lives of teenage girls at school and their romantic relationships with their *bishōnen* boyfriends.[21] A similar genre of comic book, called *sunjeong manhwa* (순정만화), also exists in South Korea. This Korean term, *sunjeong manhwa*, is often used to describe a pretty boy, as in the conventional expression, "as pretty as a male lead of *sunjeong manhwa*." In both *shōjo manga* and *sunjeong manhwa*, the main female character is often an ordinary girl while the main male character is an extraordinarily good-looking boy. The pretty boy characters from *shōjo manga* and *sunjeong manhwa* share similar features — the male characters are tall with long legs, and they have slim feminine faces, long and/or wavy hair, and sweet smiles. This is because the *kkonminam* from *sunjeong manhwa* is deeply influenced by the *bishōnen* from *shōjo manga*. During this process of transculturation, *mugukjeok* pretty boy images, such as the images of the *kkonminam* from *sunjeong manhwa*, are created. *Manga* and *manhwa* have been imaginative sites that produce *bishōnen* and *kkonminam* images for female fans who actively desire *mugukjeok* soft masculinity.

In the case of the popular cultural sector, *mugukjeok* pretty boys are highly visible among boy bands in various East Asian countries. These include Japanese popular music *bishōnen* bands such as SMAP, Arashi, and KAT-TUN; South Korean popular music boy groups such as HOT, Shinhwa, SS501, TVXQ, and SHINee; and Taiwanese boy bands such as F4. Among these boy bands, SMAP is the original model representation of East Asian soft masculinity. Considering SMAP as the "perfect female fantasy," Fabienne Darling-Wolf argues that their unique characteristic of "extreme androgyny" reinforces their popularity:

> The extreme androgyny of several of the members is often surprising to the western observer. The five men's bodies are hairless and lean and their costumes in concert often cross gender boundaries — they wear form-fitting shorts, hot pink suits, or long animal-print coats with huge flowers pinned on their collars. (2004: 360)

Apart from these highly feminized appearances, according to Darling-Wolf, SMAP also performs the ideal of the "new man," and highlights the caring and sensitive aspects of masculinity. This phenomenon developed in the media during the 1980s. For instance, SMAP members would show their awareness of significant changes in gender roles by publishing cookbooks and taking care of children in television shows (Darling-Wolf 2004: 361). SMAP's managing agency is known as a *bidanshi fakutorii*, or "pretty man factory," suggesting that the feminized masculinity of SMAP members has become a commodity under production (Cogan 2006: 83). This commoditized soft masculinity has been reproduced in many other East Asian countries as is evident from the abovementioned East Asian male pop-stars where they share the soft masculine images of feminine prettiness. Due to the fact that the feminized masculine images of these pretty boys possess very similar characteristics, it is almost impossible to recognize their nationalities by their appearance. This is because of the *mugukjeok* aspect which has been created as a result of the transcultural flows of *bishōnen* masculinity; this *mugukjeok* aspect, in turn, enables these East Asian male pop-stars to cross cultural borders easily. BYJ is the best example of how the *mugukjeok* image of a pan-East-Asian pretty boy circulates in the region.

Pan-East-Asian pretty boy pop-stars can be described as Japanized, hybridized, and *mugukjeok*. The South Korean term, *mugukjeok*, means "no nationality" which implies no particular national taste or odor, that is "culturally odorless," as suggested by Iwabuchi (2002a: 27). BYJ's soft masculine image is actively embraced in many Asian countries including Japan because his image reflects the "odorless" aspect of a *mugukjeok* pretty boy. This aspect has been mentioned by some of the fans that I interviewed:

> I think it's because of those comics ... when we were girls we read lots of girl's comics ... he reminds me of those handsome boys in the comic books. (Ba, 42, focus group interviewee)

> [I like him because of] definitely his smile. Well ... it's a typical *bishōnen* smile. Pure and sweet. (Sa, 38, focus group interviewee)

Both Ba and Sa mention that BYJ's image is similar to Japanese *bishōnen* images and that they like (embrace) him because of this similarity. In other words, the culturally odorless image of *bishōnen* in BYJ's star text reinforces the Japanese embrace of BYJ. This cultural odorlessness can also be explained by Appadurai's term, "mediascapes," which refers to the capabilities of mass media in producing and disseminating information and images through transcultural flows (1996: 35). BYJ's culturally odorless *bishōnen* image can also be explained using another of Appadurai's concepts, the concept of "shared imagination" (1996: 8). What Appadurai argues, in relation to this concept, is that collective experiences through the mass media can create "sodalities" of worship and taste, and can eventually enable communities or cultural groups to participate in "shared imagination." Likewise, transcultural media influences between various Asian countries create odorless — culturally acceptable — images of pretty boys. The consequences of mediascapes, popular cultural flows, cultural mixing, and metamorphosis all combine to create the odorless and *mugukjeok* images of the pan–East Asian pretty boy. BYJ is popular among Japanese audiences partly due to his *mugukjeok* pretty boy image. This image is culturally acceptable in Japan because it shares similarities with *shōjo manga*'s pretty teen boys or *bishōnen* bands. BYJ's soft masculinity is a localized form of Japan's *bishōnen* masculinity. Therefore, Japanese audiences readily embrace BYJ's soft masculinity as they are already used to viewing pretty boy images.

Counter-Coevality and Postcolonial Soft Masculinity

As examined earlier, the construction of BYJ's soft masculinity is based on the cultural proximity of Japan and South Korea. In this section, I discuss another aspect of the construction of BYJ's soft masculinity: this is the counter-coevality between the two countries. This counter-coevality is produced by the post/colonial context of Japan's colonization of Korea, and this counter-coevality constructs the notion of a temporal lag between the two countries. Such counter-coevality is evident from two different ways in which Japanese fans desire their "past" from BYJ's "present" body. First, they demonstrate nostalgic desire for BYJ's polite body and second, they apply traditional ideologies in interpreting his postmodern hard body.

Desiring the Past: Our Memory Is in Your Present Body

In the earlier sections, I observed the ways in which Japanese fans reminisce about their "olden days" when they embrace BYJ's images of purity and politeness. Shin Gyeong-Mi argues that the *Yonsama* syndrome reflects Japanese people's yearning for the "good days" of the Sho-Wa (昭和) era (2006: 241). The Sho-Wa era lasted from 1926 to 1988, the year when the former Japanese emperor, Hirohito, died. During this era, Japan experienced rapid economic growth. Shin states that "*Sho-Wa* nostalgia is a phenomenon which reflects the yearning for the era of the fast economic growth of 1950–1970 by the Japanese who are tired of today's economic depression" (2006: 241). She then adds that the main themes of *Winter Sonata* (pure love, devotion, and politeness) resonate deeply with Japanese viewers in their thirties, forties, and fifties who had grown up during the *Sho-Wa* era. This suggests that for these middle-aged Japanese viewers, *Winter Sonata* enabled them to engage in *Sho-Wa* nostalgia which highlights their collective desire for the "good" old days. In particular, as observed from the quotes of the fans in the earlier sections, this collective desire for the good old days can be detected from their longing for traditional Japanese virtues such as politeness.

This idea of collective desire can be further explained through the notion of "the flow of the public's consciousness of time," which is suggested by Ma Jeong-Mi. She argues that "the star image is a signifier which can exemplify 'the flow of the consciousness' of time" (2005: 324). Ma further explains that "an actor becomes a star when the image of the actor reflects the collective psyche of the public of a particular time" (2005: 324). In the case of the Japanese fandom of BYJ, his polite image exemplifies "the flow of the consciousness" of the Japanese viewers. It is in his politeness that they find traditional Japanese virtues, virtues that they believe Japan once had but that now have been lost:

> I think he is a real man. [He is] Intelligent, humble, polite, takes care of others, elegant, and has a strong will. We used to have that kind of man in Japan. But now it's hard to find that kind of character [virtue] from young Japanese men. (Tan, 64, questionnaire respondent)

> Today's Japanese male actors? Oh no! They are rude, too shallow, and vulgar. We can't even compare them with him [BYJ]. (Ma, 64, focus group interviewee)

According to Tan, such values as humility, compassion, elegance, and politeness can rarely be found in contemporary Japan. Ma also remarks that Japanese young men are rude and cannot be compared with the polite BYJ. These fans see the lost virtues of Japan's past in BYJ's polite image. In this sense, BYJ's body is a retrospective site. Likewise, BYJ's soft masculine image as signified by his polite body became an object of Japanese female fans' retrospective desire. As is evident in the above remarks by Tan and Ma, BYJ's soft masculinity becomes the site of Japan's imagined past; however, this soft masculinity is not conceived as "an equal interlocutor but marked by a frozen, immutable temporal lag" (Iwabuchi 2002b: 552). NHK producer Kuroiwa explained this as follows:

> Only one month after (the drama *Winter Sonata* has been aired) we received many long letters from the audience. "Oh … I had the same experience when I was young …" they recall the memories of their first love and really wanted to express themselves … When Bae Yong-Joon visited Japan, he acted so gentlemanly and politely. We used to have such men in Japan but not any more. They [the middle-aged Japanese female fans] really hate the way the Japanese young generations behave. (personal interview)

Both Tan and Kuroiwa point out that Japan "used to" have such values, and their remarks imply that there is a temporal lag between South Korea and Japan. To Japanese audiences, South Korea is still "the past." The above quotes show — through desiring BYJ's polite body — how Japanese middle-aged female fans articulate Japan's counter-coeval gaze at South Korea. BYJ's body has become the repository for the nostalgic desires and memories of these middle-aged Japanese viewers.

In relation to nostalgia and the commodification of memory in the modern world, John Frow argues that "many accounts of postmodernity mourn a loss of history and of memory" (1997: 7). In Frow's view, memory is not historical memory, but rather a memory that is made up of an immense accumulation of "spectacles." Citing Guy Debord's *The Society of the Spectacle*, Frow states:

> In Debord's analysis the "present age" is defined in more precise terms as a set of social relations of production, and the "sign," "copy" and so on reappear as the category of the "spectacle": the fetishized form of the commodity in a

system of representation which is in part to be understood as the system of the mass media, including advertising and design; in part more specifically as the social force of television (which can often be directly substituted for the word "spectacle"); but at times more generally as the visual, or the forms taken by the gaze within a consumer-capitalist society. (1997: 5)

Therefore, in the case of the Japanese viewers of *Winter Sonata*, their retrospective gaze at BYJ's body reinforces their desire for the "spectacle," which is only a signification and a simulacrum of the real world and real history. In the case of BYJ, the retrospective gaze of Japanese fans magnifies their desire towards the coded and imagined world, as exemplified by BYJ's politeness in his soft body. Through the nostalgic gaze of Japanese fans, his soft body becomes a spectacle of Japan's glorious past. This nostalgic gaze is produced through the denial of coevalness. Frow argues:

> The concept of coevalness or contemporality is intended to specify the conditions under which the interests of both "observed" and "observer" societies can be put into relation. Coevalness is assumed to be grounded in the shared intersubjective time that precedes all more culturally specific experiences of time, and it is this that opens the way for "truly dialectical confrontation." The word coevalness is equivalent to the German *Gleichzeitigkeit*, and is meant to include the senses both of co-occurrence in physical time (synchronicity) and of co-occurrence in typological or epochal time (contemporaneity) ... Its counter-concept, *Ungleichzeitigkeit* (non-synchronicity, the uneven layering of times within any historical formation) seems to me in fact to provide a more adequate way of understanding the *unequal* relations that hold within a synchronic framework characterized by uneven development and a global division of labour. Not everyone occupies the same NOW ... (1997: 9)

As Frow suggests above, different cultural groups have different structures for the experience of time. Frow's concept of "unequal time" can be explained through my term "counter-coevality." Counter-coevality emphasizes the view of "not" sharing the synchronic time structure between the observer/consumer and the observed/commodity while Frow's idea of "non-synchronicity" emphasizes the aspect of multiple histories and relativization of cultures. In the case of the Japanese fandom of BYJ, the commoditized memory of Japan's past reinforces the desire of Japanese fans for BYJ's politeness and for his soft masculinity. Such desire is driven by their counter-coeval gaze at South Korea.

Japan's counter-coeval gaze at South Korea is due mainly to the temporal lag created by the disjunctive procedures and phases of modernization that took place in both countries. Unlike Japan's voluntary active modernization since the mid-1800s, known as *Meiji Ishin* (明治維新, *Meiji* Restoration), Korea went through a forced and compressed modernization phase in the early to mid-1900s that was initiated by Japan and led by America. During the colonial era (1910–1945), Japan was able to quickly establish modern infrastructure in the social and cultural spheres through the exploitation of the colonized Asian countries, including Korea. Matsuzawa Tessei explains that under Japan's imperialistic aggression and colonization, there was an influx of Korean and Taiwanese immigrants into Japan, who were then exploited by the Japanese government "in construction, transport, gravel yards, factory services etc." (1988: 154). Even after the occupation, while Japan experienced rapid economic growth from the 1950s to 1970s (*Sho-Wa* era), South Korea experienced the devastating Korean War and the post-War reconstruction. After the division of the Korean peninsula, along with America's political intervention, South Korea experienced a dark era of dictatorships from 1962 to 1988. During this era, under the catchphrase of "turbo modernization," South Korea underwent rapid and compressed economic development but, at the same time, experienced socio-political conflicts such as the Kwangju Massacre and the retrogression of democracy (Min et al. 2003: 25-58; Standish 1994: 70).[22] While Japan experienced a flourishing modernization period, South Korea's modernization phase was interrupted by a dark era of turbulence. Hence, the difference in the progression of the phases of modernization in South Korea and Japan created a significant temporal lag. The two countries occupy a "different *now* and *then*." This asynchronous temporal experience is the main reason for the counter-coeval gaze of Japanese fans at BYJ's soft masculinity.

The experience of the temporal lag between Japan and South Korea is described by Koichi Iwabuchi. Iwabuchi states that it is "the [idealized backward] 'Asia' where Japanese consumers find their lost purity, energy, and dreams" (2002b: 550). As explained by Iwabuchi, Japanese audiences find their lost virtues from BYJ's soft masculine body. Iwabuchi argues that "the politics of the transnational evocation of nostalgia is highlighted when it is employed to confirm a frozen temporal lag between two cultures, when 'our' past and memory are found in 'their' present" (2002b: 549). In the case of BYJ's polite image, Japanese fans find their "past" and "memory" in BYJ's "present" body. BYJ's polite body exemplifies the nostalgia of the fans where counter-coevality is evident.

Postmodern Body, *Momjjang*

The counter-coeval desire of Japanese fans is also evident from the ways in which they embrace the images of BYJ's muscular hard body in his photo album *The Image: Volume One*. His muscular body reflects the "*momjjang*" syndrome, a socio-cultural trend that began in South Korea in the early 2000s. The literal meaning of *momjjang* (몸짱) is "body-master." The word *mom* (몸) means "body" and *jjang* (짱) is the vernacular for "the great" or "the best." *Momjjang* is a neologism that refers to the socio-cultural phenomenon of having a good-looking body in South Korea. The term was first used in 2003 (Yoo et al. 2005). For women, *momjjang* normally refers to a skinny and toned body while for men, the word refers to a toned muscular body. This phenomenon began when a forty-year-old woman published images of her *momjjang* body on an Internet website run by her. Beginning with a couple of photos of this *momjjang ajumma* (a middle-aged woman), the *momjjang* syndrome began to take hold in South Korea.

South Koreans began focusing on shaping their bodies to make themselves look good and sexually attractive. The *momjjang* syndrome has also led to significant changes in lifestyles where South Koreans spend more time and money on their body by taking up activities such as yoga and exercise and buying healthy food. Gradually, the *momjjang* fever led to the "well-being" phenomenon. Lee Mi-Rim explains this phenomenon:

> In the post-modern era, along with the growing interest in the human body, creating a great body became a phenomenon ... The well-being lifestyle — rather spending time and money for sports dance, yoga, meditation, exercise, and low fat, organic foods — became a barometer of modernization. The general concept of well-being refers to a lifestyle or culture which pursues a beautiful happy life through the harmony between physical and spiritual health. This well-being life specifies living well; living a healthy, easy, and balanced life. It emphasizes the spiritual aspect more than the material aspect ... (M. R. Lee 2005)

Lee points out that the well-being phenomenon indicates that the focus of South Koreans has changed from pursuing the "material" to pursuing the "spiritual." According to her, the former is a "modern" pursuit which is often characterized by the focus on financial stability and economic growth and the latter is a "postmodern" pursuit which is characterized by the focus on well-being, body, and health. Indeed, the *momjjang* syndrome is neither new nor exclusive to South Korea; it is a global phenomenon. It is a local adaptation of the global well-being phenomenon that has been circulated through new media and communications technologies such as the Internet and satellite television and usually in the form of advertising.

Since the early stages of the global consumer market, the human body has become an object of visual media marketing strategies. In *The Body in Late Capitalist USA*, Donald M. Lowe argues that "post-war advertising utilizes the technologies of the look in relaying juxtaposed images and signs." Later, he adds, "advertising, using images of the new sexuality, captures, mobilizes, and directs the fantasy of the addressee" (1995: 133). According to Lowe, the new sexuality of the post-war era in the US is distinctive because of its promise of new kinds of sexual pleasure as well as its aspect of consumption that contradicts the form of repressive, disciplinary sexuality that restricts sexual expression to the mere fulfillment of the function of human reproduction (1995: 131). In the late capitalist era, as the human body becomes an object of indulgence, the consumption of the body (and body-related products such as fashion, beauty, and food) has become a crucial part of the late capitalist lifestyle. Lowe argues that the late capitalist lifestyle is "very much a sexual lifestyle" that is "based upon the consumption of sexualized commodities." Lowe suggests that the "gay lifestyle" is an ideal example:

> By the 1970s, gay culture has emerged as an alternative lifestyle. On the basis of lifestyle consumption, an urban male homosexual minority with sufficient income transforms itself into the gay lifestyle (although this was less true for lesbians). Gays display themselves as consumers of clothing, holidays, theatre and cinema, restaurant meals, cosmetics, and household goods ... As Dennis Altman has suggested, the interesting point is that, increasingly, gay lifestyle has become avant-garde fashion in popular culture, as "the adoption of styles and fashions associated with an increasingly visible and assertive gay minority" has become an obvious trend. (1995: 135)

According to Lowe, the gay lifestyle has become an "icon" of late capitalist lifestyles, as gay fashions and styles have become leading trends in consumer markets. The widespread influence of gay fashions, for example, is evident in the globally recognized lifestyle of "metrosexuality," whose prime exemplar is David Beckham, a soccer player from the UK. According to British journalist Mark Simpson, "the typical metrosexual is a young man with money to spend, living in or within easy reach of a metropolis — because that's where all the best shops, clubs, gyms and hairdressers are" (Simpson 2002). As Simpson explains, a metrosexual refers to a man who makes an effort to cultivate an aesthetic style and good taste on fashion, beauty, art, and culture. While a metrosexual may embrace lifestyle habits that are commonly identified as typically belonging to fashionable, urban homosexual men, the term usually refers to heterosexual men who are seen to be more in touch with their feminine side.

BYJ is often referred to as being a symbol of metrosexuality. According to the article, "The Rampant Republic of Mr. Beauty, the Era of Male Consumption" in *Film2.0*, fashionable and body-conscious men have become an object of consumer marketing in contemporary South Korea. At the center of this trend, there are many metrosexual stars including BYJ (S. H. Han et al. 2006). For example, in the LG credit card television commercial, BYJ is portrayed in a series of juxtaposed images as a young professional living a busy urban life while enjoying modern leisure activities such as travel, dining, fashion, music, and the arts. In this commercial, his image is similar to Joon-Sang from *Winter Sonata* (J. M. Ma 2005: 332–33). He is an idealized embodiment of the urban young professional who engages in a:

typical metrosexual lifestyle such as swimming, shooting, travelling in a convertible sports car, walking into the luxurious restaurant while holding a bunch of flowers, and playing a trumpet at a Jazz bar in a fashionable brand suit. (J. M. Ma 2005: 332–33)

BYJ is a commercial barometer for the popularity of metrosexuality. Regarding the global trend of metrosexuality, Kang Yoo-Jeong argues that there are two major elements behind the rise of metrosexuality: one element is the manifestation of the contemporary male desire to become more physically attractive; the second element is the support of a global consumerist industry catered towards promoting the metrosexual lifestyle (Y. J. Kang 2006). These two elements are well-illustrated through the juxtaposed images of BYJ in the LG-card commercial, where the contemporary male desire to be physically attractive and industrial capital are entwined within metrosexual lifestyles that emphasize the consumption of fashion and aesthetic styles.

Apart from the active consumption of updated fashions and aesthetic styles, this metrosexual lifestyle is also exemplified through various fitness activities such as exercise, yoga, and diet to transform male bodies into a more desirable form. As observed from BYJ's LG card commercial, the building of an ideal body through fitness activities is crucial for a metrosexual lifestyle. First initiated by gay lifestyles, physical fitness soon became a vital element of a global trendy lifestyle. Barry Glassner explains that the concern with personal physical fitness has become more widespread over the past couple of decades, especially among middle and upper class Americans (1989: 180). He argues that the contemporary concern with personal physical fitness is a postmodern pursuit because it restores human faith in the human body, faith that was lost during the modern era of the ascendancy of machines, science, and technology (1989: 181). Hence, building and maintaining an idealized physical body has become an essential part of the postmodern lifestyle. The *momjjang* syndrome is a "localized" form of this global trend towards the pursuit of the ideal physical body. The *momjjang* phenomenon shows that South Korea shares some postmodern values with the rest of the world, especially the developed Western world. Some scholars criticize the *momjjang* syndrome for promoting highly unrealistic ideals about the human physique and for contributing to the commercialization of sex (Hong et al. 2004). However, the *momjjang* syndrome also shows that, after the materialistic modern era, South Korea has entered the "well-being" postmodern era.

The rise of the *momjjang* syndrome has led to a boom of well-being/*momjjang* marketing in almost every industrial sector. The South Korean entertainment industry is not an exception. Star management companies adopt *momjjang* marketing to produce their "star" images. South Korean fe/male stars are transformed into *momjjang* through strict training regimes, exercises, yoga, and controlled diets.

In particular, South Korean male *Hallyu* stars aggressively employ their *momjjang* images to target foreign (mostly Asian) audiences. An excellent example is found in BYJ's photo album and photo exhibition where he displays his *momjjang* body. In November 2004, BYJ released his first photo album, *The Image: Volume One*, to commemorate the tenth year of his acting career. This was followed by photo exhibitions in major cities in Japan and South Korea (G. E. Yoon 2005). The photo exhibition was held in Seoul, Busan, Tokyo, Osaka, Nagoya, Fukuoka, and Sapporo. These exhibitions were attended by more than 300,000 fans and the total earnings were donated to various charitable organizations in both countries (G. E. Yoon 2005). In Japan, despite the high price of the photo album (¥14,700/US$130), all 50,000 of the limited editions of the album were sold out in five days. A second reprint of more than 200,000 copies of the photo albums were also sold out in Japan (G. U. Kim 2008).

Consuming BYJ's Hard Body as Soft Masculinity

When BYJ's photo album, *The Image: Volume One*, was released, it created a big impact on Asian fans because BYJ showed a dramatically different side of his image by displaying his muscular and semi-nude body. In the photo album, BYJ is depicted as a darkly tanned and muscular fighter with bloody clothes which is in stark contrast to his soft and tender image. For this photo album, BYJ spent an entire three months just training with a personal trainer in California to create his new *momjjang* body. In relation to BYJ's new body, there were three general responses from the eighteen Japanese fans I interviewed: four fans rejected these images (some even denied having looked at those images); two fans approved of and accepted these images; and twelve fans were ambivalent about the images. Na (52) and Cha (35) are two interviewees who rejected BYJ's *momjjang* body. Na said: "I don't like those (muscular and half naked) images. I think they are too sexy." Cha said: "I didn't have a look at them yet because I'm afraid that my BYJ fantasy might be destroyed." Cha denied BYJ's new sexy look because she desired that her imagined memory of Joon-Sang in *Winter Sonata* remained intact. Only two of the interviewees found BYJ's new body physically attractive in the photo album:

> I actually became a fan after I saw the photo exhibition. Before this I thought he was just a boring man. Only for those old bored *ajumma* [a middle-aged woman], but from those photos I found him very sexy. Then I started watching his dramas. (Ba, 42, focus group interviewee)[23]

Ba was a single woman in her early forties. She ran a private English-language school and studied in the US for five years when she was younger. Her overseas experience in the US may have given her a different view on BYJ's muscular body from those of the other middle-aged Japanese fans that I interviewed. However, the majority of my interviewees showed an ambivalent and reluctant acceptance of BYJ's *momjjang* body:

> I was so shocked and disappointed when I first saw his nude [and sex scenes] from the movie *Untold Scandal*. I was even crying ... When I saw his photo album, finally I decided to take it as one of his challenges and I respect his efforts. (Ga, 54, focus group interviewee)

> He wasn't just trying to sell his body through selling photo books. That was a kind of fan service. Also he donates the entire profits to the poor in Asian countries. I respect his works and his will power. (Sa, 38, focus group interviewee)[24]

As observed from these comments, unlike Ba's open and approving attitude towards BYJ's new sexy images, the majority of his Japanese fans are unable to accept BYJ's *momjjang* body without adding justifications and explanations for why BYJ chose to display his body in the photo album. As Ga and Sa explained above, it is not his sexy and muscular body that they desire but his will power or challenging spirit. Some of these interviewees who were ambivalent about BYJ's *momjjang* images suggest other reasons for accepting his new images:

> I saw his dark and mean side from those photos. I like to discover his other sides because they show his efforts. (Ra, 48, focus group interviewee)

In relation to the reception of his sexy muscular images, Ra emphasized that she enjoyed discovering the different sides to BYJ. As observed from the above three comments from the interviewees who felt ambivalent about BYJ's *momjjang* body, it is evident that they felt compelled to provide explanations for BYJ's choice in making the photo album by mentioning his effort, will power, and hard work. Instead of embracing his *momjjang* body unreservedly, BYJ's middle-aged Japanese female fans prefer and desire his refined qualities.

The desire for his refined qualities by these fans is further evident in their responses to the question, "please explain the most significant aspect of BYJ which attracts you the most," in the questionnaire that they completed. Among 56 participants, more than half of them (32) responded that they were attracted to BYJ because of his personality and "the way that he lives and thinks." Some of BYJ's personality traits listed as attractive by these participants included his sincerity, his seriousness, his humility, his willpower, and his industriousness:

> He is such a faithful and sincere person ... He donated such a large amount of money [to the poor and the sick people in Asia]. He always says that he'll return

the blessing [from his fans] to the fans. I like such loyalty. (Ka, 33, focus group interviewee)[25]

[His] appearance is very good. But I'm attracted to what he has inside. Sincerity, humbleness, he always takes his life seriously. He always tries to progress and to become better with aspiration [向上心] like building up his body for a photo book. He has the most important male value inside of him. (Han, 52, questionnaire respondent)

Ka and Han insist that his moral maturity is the most important factor that makes him an ideal male figure. In particular, for Han, his muscular body only reinforces his mature mentality. From their explanations in relation to BYJ's *momjjang* body, it is clear that these Japanese fans desire BYJ not through his muscular body but through the mental strength and maturity that has enabled him to build his body. In other words, these fans embrace his *momjjang* body within the framework of *wen* masculinity where cultural attainments, such as mentality and moral maturity, are predominantly required to become an ideal man. Here, the counter-coeval gaze of the Japanese fans is evident in the way that they view BYJ's postmodern *momjjang* body through the lens of premodern *wen* masculinity. The persistence of this counter-coeval gaze is clear as these fans transform his postmodern muscular images into a form of premodern masculinity. Thus, the nostalgic desire of the fans for *wen* masculinity is demonstrated here.

The nostalgic desires of Japanese fans for BYJ's *wen* masculinity can also be explained from the notion of *gaman* (が-まん), which refers to "the ideals of tolerance, endurance, perseverance, and control of personal desire" that are "all highly valued personal qualities in Japanese culture" (Light 2003: 114–15). The fans desire traditional Japanese virtues by reading BYJ's cultured manner as displaying *gaman*. The nostalgic desire of the middle-aged Japanese female fans for BYJ's muscular body is also shown through the way that they interpret the cultivation of BYJ's muscular body as being the result of his *gaman*. Finally, the nostalgic desire of the fans is also evident from their description of BYJ as "おとこらしい おとこ" (*otokorashii otoko*). Regarding the question of "the most significant aspect of BYJ which attracts you the most," Jan said:

He has masculine appeal (男性的魅力) ... [such as] sensitiveness, softness, nobility, and dignity. (Jan, 64, questionnaire respondent)

BYJ is gentle, humble, sincere, and loyal. He is a man like a real man (おとこら しい おとこ). (Gan, questionnaire respondent)

Both Jan and Gan described BYJ as having "masculine appeal" (男性的魅力) and "a man like a real man" (おとこらしい おとこ, *otokorashii otoko*) respectively, mentioning his soft masculine — refined — characteristics. In other words, they consider him as an ideal manly man based on the traditional ideology of *wen* masculinity. Jan and Gan display a similar preference for *wen* masculinity as the fans who preferred to view BYJ's postmodern *momjjang* body through the paradigm of *wen* masculinity. Such a perspective demonstrates the nostalgic desire of the fans that fixes BYJ's masculinity in the past. Thus, it is evident that BYJ's soft masculinity is constructed by the counter-coeval desire of Japanese fans in the reception of his *momjjang* body and that this counter-coeval desire is underpinned by the temporal lag between Japan and South Korea due to their post/colonial relationship.

Conclusion

The middle-aged Japanese female fandom of BYJ can be conceptualized through the disjunctive "pre-post-modern" paradigm of time and space between the two countries. This is a reflection of what Appadurai has argued: "space and time are themselves socialized and localized through complex and deliberate practices of performance, representation and action" (1996: 180). This disjunctive spatio-temporal paradigm is evident in the hybridized model of BYJ's soft masculinity as a transcultural product, which circulates based on the cultural and geographical proximity between Japan and South Korea and on the counter-coeval gaze of Japanese fans.

As observed, because of "cultural proximity," BYJ's soft masculinity is constructed as a result of the inter-Asian transcultural flows of various masculine forms such as Confucian *wen* masculinity and *bishōnen* masculinity. This transcultural hybridization creates a shared imagination of *mugukjeok* pan–East Asian soft masculinity as represented by BYJ. Through examining the responses of the fans, it is evident that this *mugukjeok* aspect enables BYJ's soft masculinity to freely travel across the cultural boundaries between Japan and South Korea.

It is also "counter-coevality" that reinforces the construction of BYJ's soft masculinity within the Japanese fandom. As examined, counter-coevality is shown from the nostalgic longing of the fans for Japan's traditional virtues which are identified by them as existing in BYJ's polite body. Counter-coevality is also detected from the way the fans embrace BYJ's postmodern *momjjang* body through the premodern ideology of Confucian *wen* masculinity. Thus, it is evident that South Korean soft masculinity is reinforced by the counter-coeval desire of Japanese middle-aged female fans. This counter-coevality demonstrates the temporal lag between Japan and South Korea which is due to the post/colonial relationship.

Thus, it is my conclusion that South Korean soft masculinity, as represented by BYJ, is constructed by the transcultural flows that create *mugukjeok* and by the counter-coeval desire of the fans that is derived from the postcolonial socio-cultural contexts of Japan and South Korea.

3

Rain, Global Masculinity, and Singaporean Fans:
Fly Anywhere, Click Anytime

> Cloud-Japan has started registration for a tour package to this [Lotte] concert. Good seats have been set aside for Cloud Japan members. Unfortunately, this is only for Japanese fans. (I hate to say this but Japanese fans are not the only ones who can afford to pay) ... I am willing to pay for a tour package to get an R ticket to this Lotte concert but unfortunately, there seems to be nothing available for me as I am not Japanese!
>
> — a letter of complaint to Rain's agency, J.Tune Entertainment, written by Ni, 32, a Singaporean fan[1]

South Korean singer and actor, Rain, was selected as one of "the world's most influential 100 people" by *Time* magazine (Walsh 2006).[2] The article, by Brian Walsh, calls him "The Magic Feet from Korea" and describes him as a performer with "[an] angelic face, killer bod, and Justin Timberlake–like dance moves" and one who "has ridden the crest of *Hallyu*, or the Korean wave, the Asia-wide obsession for that country's pop culture." Walsh writes:

> Yet even if Rain, whose style virtually clones American pop, fails to make it in the US, the trend he represents is here to stay. Rain is the face — and well-muscled torso — of pop globalism. Before he visited the U.S., Rain already had a fan base, thanks to Internet music sites, satellite TV, and DVDs of his soap operas. Those are the same media that make it easier than ever for growing numbers of Americans to get their fix of Japanese anime, Bollywood films, and Korean music — and vice versa. Pop culture no longer moves simply in a single direction, from the West to the rest of the world. Instead, it's a global swirl, no more constrained by borders than the weather. Rain, after all, falls on everyone. (2006)

The article describes three levels of transculturation in relation to Rain as the face of "pop globalism." First, it shows how Rain, a popular South Korean cultural product, is highly influenced by Western (American) popular culture. Rain localizes elements of Western popular culture even as he adopts them. This process, "glocalization," is the first level of transculturation. Second, the article illustrates how popular cultural flows, thanks to the advent of new technology, have aided the emergence of Rain as a regional star in Asia. "Regionalization," through cultural flow via technology, is the second level of transculturation. Third, the article describes how Rain, a popular culture star from the "rest" (the non-West), enters the center (the West). This is the third level of transculturation which is the "globalization" of popular culture. The above transculturations have enabled Rain to become culturally hybridized, to move freely across cultural borders and to become a popular regional icon throughout Asia.

Rain's stardom began with the Asian regional popularity of the South Korean television drama series, *Full House*, in which he plays the male protagonist, Young-Jae. When *Full House* was aired in the Asian region in 2004, the drama achieved about 50% of high audience share in countries such as Indonesia, Thailand, the Philippines, and Hong Kong (JYPE 2006; E. J. Lee 2006). However, it was not until Rain held his Asia concert tour entitled "Rainy Day" in 2005 and 2006 that his regional stardom became highly visible. This concert tour was held in various Asian cities such as Seoul, Busan, Tokyo, Osaka, Hong Kong, Taipei, Beijing, and Bangkok, and more than 172,000 tickets to the concert were sold out. One of the most significant aspects of this Asia concert tour is that in each city those who attended were not just the local fans but also fans from other Asian countries. This particular aspect of the multinational constituency of the fans attending his concerts can also be observed in his 2007 world tour concert, "Rain's Coming." For instance, when the premiere showcase of "Rain's Coming" was held at Jamshil Olympic Main Stadium in Seoul in October 2006, almost a quarter of the forty thousand fans who attended were from overseas (Garcia 2006). In the Bangkok leg of the same showcase in June 2007, more than fifty Singaporean fans — members of Rain's official Singaporean fan club, RainSingapore.com — flew to Bangkok to attend.[3] Many regional fans also traveled to more than one city to catch a repeat performance of the same concerts when Rain embarked on his "Rainy Day" Asia tour and "Rain's Coming" world tour.

Some of these Asian fans flew to the US to attend Rain's concerts held in New York in February 2006 and in Las Vegas in December 2006. While these fans responded positively to these concerts, the US media responded sceptically because they saw Rain as a singer who mimicked US pop-idols. Many described Rain as "Justin Timberlake-like" and "Usher-like" (Pareles 2006; Louie 2006; Sontag 2006). Some criticized Rain for imitating the styles of "old-fashioned" American popular music. Jon Pareles, in the *New York Times*, writes:

> On the three albums he has released since 2002, Rain and his songwriter, producer, promoter, and mastermind, Jin-Young Park [JYP] have imported and digested pop-R&B from the English-speaking world, emulating it with South Korean lyrics. Since Rain's voice is lower and huskier than Mr. [Michael] Jackson's, he dabbles in other pop-R&B approaches: the acoustic-guitar ballads of Babyface, the light funk-pop of Justin Timberlake, the crooning of George Michael and the importunings of Usher. Seeing him onstage was like watching old MTV videos dubbed into Korean. (Pareles 2006)

In opposition to such criticism of Rain as blatantly Americanized, Rain's producer, Park Jin-Young (JYP), claims that Rain is hybridized. He explains that "Rain expresses Korea's sentiment and Asia's delicacy which are elements that African-American music does not have" (quoted in W. G. Kim 2006). He compares Rain's hybrid style to that of Ang Lee's movie, *Crouching Tiger Hidden Dragon* (2000) and suggests that the two share similarities. Like *Crouching Tiger Hidden Dragon*, which expresses aspects of Chinese culture and tradition in the aesthetic form of the Hollywood blockbuster, JYP says that Rain's music expresses aspects of South Korean culture and tradition in the musical form of American popular music. JYP's explanation, however, does not clarify how Rain's music and performance style is hybridized through the processes of glocalization and regionalization. Also, the US media's criticism of Rain's music as merely imitating American popular music does not explain the regional popularity of Rain: why is Rain, and not Usher, popular in the Asian region? To answer this question and to show how Rain's hybridity is engendered by glocalization and regionalization, this chapter analyzes how Rain's masculinity has been constructed through the hybridization of various regional masculinities, and how the resulting hybridized masculinity of Rain resonates with the desire of regional Asian fans.

In this chapter, I focus on the ways in which the driving force behind Rain's regional popularity is the newly constructed South Korean masculinity that he embodies, which I refer to here as global masculinity. Using the example of the Singaporean fandom of Rain, I argue that the construction of this South Korean global masculinity is reinforced by the mixed cultural practices of *mugukjeok* and the "pop-consumerism" of the "new rich" in Asia. According to Richard Robinson and David S. G. Goodman, the term "the new rich" encompasses "those new wealthy social groups that have emerged from industrial change in Asia" in recent decades (1996: 5). They explain that "the common basis of their social power and position is increasingly capital, credentials, and expertise rather than rent or position in the state apparatus or feudal hierarchy" (1996: 5). Based on the economic power of the new rich as a new consumer group, the new rich in Asia can be characterized as a new middle-class. Chua Beng Huat explains that, with the expanding desires of the new rich, a new lifestyle of consumerism has emerged in Asia (2000: 3). Chua states that the new rich in Malaysia typically have three distinct objects of consumption: housing, cars, and children's education (2000: 3). Chua's research suggests that the consumption of material goods and social services can be identified as a new lifestyle for the new Asian middle class.

Expanding on Chua's research, I argue that the regional popularity of Rain can be understood as driven by the new consumer lifestyles of the new rich that become the basis for an emerging "cultural Asia." As Asia's economic power and technological infrastructure develop, there are complex social implications that result from the new cultural practices of the new rich. One of these implications is evident in the increasing visibility of a group of consumers that I call "trans-pop-consumers." This term describes the group's key characteristic of engaging in the transnational consumption of Asian popular culture through the mobilization of capitalist power to obtain leisure and entertainment in addition to material goods and social services. This notion of the emerging new rich in Asia as trans-pop-consumers is clearly demonstrated in Ni's letter of complaint quoted at the beginning of this chapter. In this letter, she strongly protests that "Japanese fans are not the only ones who can afford to pay" and states that she is "willing to" purchase a costly tour package to attend Rain's concert. It is thus evident that newly emerging trans-pop-consumers from Asian countries other than Japan now have the buying power to obtain leisure and entertainment goods.

Trans-pop-consumers demonstrate three main characteristics: they are culturally hybrid; they pursue a global consumerist lifestyle orientated towards the procurement of leisure and entertainment; and they are technologically savvy. Hence, Rain's Singaporean fans, who constitute a good example of these trans-pop-consumers, embrace the cultural hybridity of Rain's global masculinity, employ advanced media technology to produce and consume *mugukjeok* images of Rain, and frequently cross national and cultural borders in pursuit of the leisure and the entertainment that are provided by their consumption of Rain's overseas concerts. It is through trans-pop-consumerist Singaporean fandom that Rain's *mugukjeok* global masculinity is constructed and reinforced.

Rain: A Globalized and *Mugukjeok* South Korean Popular Culture Product

As briefly mentioned earlier, Rain becomes a globalized and *mugukjeok* popular culture product through three levels of transculturation: glocalization, regionalization, and globalization. These transculturations occur within the framework of South Korea's "turbo capitalism." The term "turbo capitalism" was coined by an American economist, Edward Luttwak. According to Luttwak, "it is precisely speed ... that is 'the new feature of market economics in present-day capitalism'" (cited in Martin and Schumann 1996: 181–82). This turbo capitalism refers to the tremendous speed of structural change of consumer societies based on globalization. Cho Han Hye-Jeong suggests that the regional popularity of *Hallyu* is a result of "turbo capitalism" and that *Hallyu* is a "pastiche of American popular culture" (2005: 34–35). She argues that *Hallyu* is a victory of commercial capitalism which creates products that satisfy the taste of the masses. She claims:

> South Korean popular cultural products are nothing but a South Korean version of American popular culture, and the *Hallyu* phenomenon is nothing but a result of how South Korea's export-oriented industrial system of the manufacturing sector has extended into the popular cultural sector. (2005: 34–35)

Drawing upon her analysis, I further argue that the cultural phenomenon of Rain demonstrates how South Korea's global popular cultural product is an effect of turbo capitalism and the transcultural practice of Americanization in the South Korean popular cultural sector. The cultural phenomenon of Rain is also closely related to "South Korea's crippled modernization" with its tendency to cling to American culture, lifestyle, and ideology. This interpretation is further supported by Kang Joon-Man's concept of the "*ssolim* (쏠림) phenomenon" which describes one of the typical socio-cultural characteristics of South Korean society (2006: 154–71). *Ssolim* means "to dynamically incline to one direction"; when applied to the case of Rain, *ssolim* refers to Americanization. The context of turbo capitalism and *ssolim* are considered by some South Korean cultural studies scholars to be two of the main driving forces of South Korea's remarkable economic growth during the past few decades. Despite the remarkable economic growth of South Korea because of "turbo capitalism" and *ssolim*, there have been some notable criticisms of negative side effects resulting from turbo capitalism and *ssolim*, such as political corruption, dictatorship, centralization, and homogenization. Some scholars use the term "crippled modernization" to address such unbalanced socio-politico-economic development of South Korea (Cho Han 2005: 34, Kang 2006: 158–59).

Thus, in the next three subsections, I discuss how Rain has become globalized through examining the transculturation processes of Rain-making that are driven by turbo-capitalism and *ssolim*: glocalization, regionalization, and globalization. This is evident from the Americanized aspects of Rain. The glocalization of Rain occurs during the production of his first album, *n001* (2002), and his second album, *Running Away from the Sun* (2003). The regionalization of Rain occurs during the period covering the release of his third album, *It's Raining* (2004), the successful run of his first "Asia" tour concert, "Rainy Day," in 2005, and above all else, the successful airing of the television drama series, *Full House*, in 2005. Finally, the globalization of Rain begins with the release of his fourth album, *Rain's World* (2006), and is expanded by the "world" tour concert, "Rain's Coming," as well as his role as Taejo Togokhan in the Hollywood action blockbuster, *Speed Racer* (2008). Rain's management company was changed from JYPE to J.Tune Entertainment in November 2006 after he established his own company. In this chapter, however, I still refer to JYPE because most of the events described here took place before Rain's change of management companies.

Glocalized Rain

The glocalization of Rain epitomizes the Americanized popular cultural sector of South Korea. In other words, the South Korean popular cultural sector plans for and strategically produces Americanized popular cultural products and Rain is one of the best examples. JYPE (JYP Entertainment), a management company of Rain, found and trained him as a multi-entertainment idol from the beginning. This cultivation of Rain reflects the birth and growth of "star planning, development, and management companies" during the mid-1990s:

> In 1995 and 1996, SM Entertainment and YG Entertainment were established retrospectively. In 1997, JYP Entertainment followed them. Their arrivals can be described as beginning an "industrial revolution" of the South Korean popular music sector. This indicates that the era of manufacturing stars was begun. Ten years after, these three major entertainment planning companies, which formulated the system of star planning, scouting, and managing, became the most influential market makers of the South Korean popular music industry. In addition, they have now expanded their influences beyond South Korea. (S. M. Kim 2006)

The abovementioned entertainment planning companies — SM, YG, and JYP — can be identified by two of their significant globalization approaches. First, their artists are immensely influenced by the globally and regionally well-known popular cultures of the US and Japan. After adopting and importing globally popular cultural elements into the South Korean popular cultural sector, they repackage and manufacture culturally hybridized and *mugukjeok* products. Second, these companies resell and export these repackaged and glocalized South Korean popular cultural products to foreign — sometimes back to the originating — markets.[4] In order to appeal to foreign audiences better, it is now essential for these artists to learn at least one second language — English, Chinese, or Japanese — as soon as they begin training. Some of the artists, such as Rain, BoA, and Se7en, are now trained to sing in Japanese to appeal more to Japanese fans (Siriyuvasak and Shin 2007: 117). Some, including Rain, have also released single albums in Japanese and Chinese. On March 17, 2009, BoA released her first full-length album in the US. The eponymous BoA contains eleven songs in English, mostly hip-hop dance music tracks. Indeed, several South Korean entertainment planning companies recently produce multinational idol bands that have Chinese, Japanese, or Thai members in order to approach wider audiences within the region. For instance, there is a Chinese member, Han Kyung, in SM's boy group, Super Junior; a Thai American member, Nichkhun, is in JYPE's boy group, 2PM; also, a Chinese member, Victoria, and a Chinese American member, Amber, are in SM's girl group, f(x).

Observing these two globalizing strategies of South Korean entertainment companies, it is clear that the former strategy describes the operation of glocalization while the latter strategy describes the operation of regionalization and globalization. These characteristics also demonstrate the implication of turbo capitalism in the South Korean popular cultural industry. They are evidence of how the industry rapidly adopts global popular cultural elements and styles to appeal to wider audiences, through which the industry can most efficiently harness regional, and eventually global, "capital." These strategies drive the *Hallyu* phenomenon in Asia, which now is the biggest source of economic profit for the South Korean popular cultural sector. The entertainment companies — SM, YG, and JYPE — played leading roles in the *Hallyu* phenomenon and many regionally popular artists such as HOT, BoA, Shinhwa, TVXQ, Se7en, and Rain belong to [or used to belong to] them (S. M. Kim 2006). All of these stars experience similar star-manufacturing processes, training for a couple of years to become glocalized and regionally acceptable popular cultural products. Among them, Rain is one of the best-selling products.

Before he became a famous singer and actor, Rain was a backstage dancer for Park Jin-Young (JYP), a singer and CEO of JYPE. After spending three years as a backstage dancer and trainee singer, Rain made his singing debut in May 2002 with his first album, *n001*. As soon as *n001* was released, the title song, *Bad Guy*, became a big hit and reached the top spots of various South Korean popular music charts.[5] In the following year, his second album, *Running Away from the Sun*, was released and he won many of the most influential musical awards in South Korea, including "Artist of the Year" from KBS and the "Top Ten Artist Award" from MBC (JYPE 2006). Some South Korean popular music critics and media, however, criticized Rain as an entertainer who is recognized for his dance and fashion, but not for his singing (Cho 2004). Pointing out the inadequacy of manufactured entertainers, popular music critic Im Jin-Mo claims that the major entertainment planning companies, in rushing to satisfy the masses, produce entertainers but not musical artists (quoted in S. M. Kim 2006). Some media critics also point out that Rain is influenced by American idols both in the audio and visual aspects of his performances. Rain has even confessed that he was an "Usher wannabe" and that he was often inspired by the styles of Usher and Justin Timberlake (G. S. Lee 2004). This aspect of Rain as American-pop-idol-like can be partly explained as a characteristic of manufactured entertainers in South Korea. Jeong Chang-Hwan, from SM Entertainment, states that:

> We [entertainment planning companies] study foreign popular music styles and make data out of them. Then, we analyze what kind of generational market we aim for and what kind of group [musician] we want to create. (quoted in S. M. Kim 2006)

As Jeong explains, the American-pop-idol-like Rain can be described as a product resulting from the globalization strategy of entertainment planning companies. This strategy shows the ways in which these companies import and adopt foreign popular cultural elements to manufacture globally familiar products that appeal to wider audiences.

The Americanization of Rain as a popular cultural product is also the result of the musical background and business ambitions of Rain's manager and producer,

JYP. JYP's musical background demonstrates the process of glocalization while his business ambitions articulate the perspective of globalization. The glocalization of JYP is evident, as he has eagerly adopted African-American popular culture into his musical style. Since his debut album, *Blue City*, JYP has devoted his musical career — as a singer, writer, and producer — to African-American music styles such as hip-hop, soul, and R&B. Popular music critic, Kang Heon, acknowledged that JYP has successfully combined African-American sentiment with the South Korean popular music genre to produce such extraordinary successes in South Korea as g.o.d and Rain (Kang 2005). In addition, JYP has also adopted African-American popular culture in relation to fashion and hairstyle. For example, for his third album, *Summer Jingle Bell* (1996), which featured 1970s American disco music, he wore an "afro-perm" hairstyle and shiny stretch disco pants (G. H. Shin 1996). The globalization of JYP can be seen in his ambitious global approach when he crossed cultural borders and exported a glocalized product — South Korean hip-hop — to the US. In 2004, he made his American debut as a producer and songwriter, and his song, *The Love You Need*, was included in the new album of hip-hop artist, Mase, *Welcome Back* (W. G. Kim 2006). In the following year, JYP participated in Will Smith's 2005 album, *Lost and Found*, as a songwriter and producer with a hip-hop song that he composed, *I Wish I Made That* (ibid.).

As a songwriter, producer, and manager of Rain, JYP's inclination towards African-American music and his ambition for the globalization of his own music critically influenced Rain's musical career so that Rain has become Americanized, hybridized, and *mugukjeok*. When Rain performed his debut song, *Bad Guy*, he perfectly recreated Usher's sexy dance moves in global R&B dance music (S. A. Park 2004). The music video of *Bad Guy* also demonstrates this ambition of JYP towards globalization. Filmed in Melbourne (Australia), *Bad Guy*'s music video presents an exotic yet global atmosphere, featuring Australian outback scenes and Melbourne's cosmopolitan streets complete with its signature trams. In addition, the music video has a long prison sequence featuring prisoners and guards of different ethnicities and which resembles the images of Hollywood action films. Rain's first album in South Korea is the most successful, among the albums produced by manufactured entertainers, at bringing together the global popular music genre and local mass audiences. This glocalization process of Rain has continued with his second album. Most of the songs in his second album, including *Running Away from the Sun* and *Are You Happy Coz I Became Popular?*, are highly influenced by African-American music styles such as urban soul, R&B, and hip-hop (S. A. Park 2004; S. Y. Do 2004). The glocalization of Rain is mainly due to the "turbo capitalism" of South Korea's economy and *ssolim* and this process demonstrates the way JYPE employs globally familiar African-American popular culture to target wider audiences and to maximize economic profit. It appears that Rain crosses cultural borders within Asia easily, due to the *mugukjeok* aspects of Americanized performance styles.

Regionalized Rain

Indeed, his regional stardom began from his acting career which eventually led to the success of his singing career. In September 2003, Rain made his acting debut through his breakthrough role as Sang-Doo in the KBS television drama series, *Sang-Doo Let's Go to School* (*Sangduya Hakgyogaja* 2003). In the drama, he plays Sang-Doo, a young single father who has resorted to the life of a gigolo to pay his daughter's hospital bills. The plot summary of this drama series is as follows: One day, Sang-Doo meets his long-lost first love, Eun-Hwan, who is now a high school maths teacher. Even though circumstances (Sang-Doo had been jailed for fighting with a man who tried to pick on her) had separated them ten years ago, Sang-Doo has never stopped loving her. Now Eun-Hwan is engaged to a prominent man, Min-Seok, and Sang-Doo wants to win back her love. In order to approach her, he returns as a student to finish high school and gets placed in Eun-Hwan's class. Playing Sang-Doo, a complex and multi-layered character who is a loving father, a cheeky gigolo, and a lovesick young man, Rain demonstrated, in this drama series, that he is able to act in addition to being able to sing and dance. Rain has also become a fashion icon as well as a popular cultural icon: his fashion and styles, for example, the training-wear look that he wore in *Sang-Doo Let's Go to School* and the Boeing aviation sunglasses that he wore in the *Running Away from the Sun* music video have initiated popular trends. Rain has consolidated his star image as a multi-talented entertainer.[6]

Rain's acting career achieved its peak in 2004 when a television drama, *Full House*, was aired on KBS. This drama enabled Rain to expand his star profile beyond South Korea. Even though Rain started his career as a singer in South Korea, he has become popular in many Asian countries as an actor, primarily because of the regional success of *Full House*. The drama recorded the highest audience shares in several Asian countries, including Indonesia, Thailand, the Philippines, Hong Kong, Vietnam, Taiwan, and Singapore (JYPE 2006). According to regional viewers and media reviews, the most significant selling point of the drama is Rain's "obnoxious," yet "cute and innocent" character, Young-Jae. This image of Rain as "obnoxious, but cute and innocent" is also the main point of attraction for all of the Singaporean fans I interviewed. The popularity of *Full House* has expanded the *Hallyu* phenomenon, which used to be restricted to East Asian countries, into Southeast Asia, where Rain has become an icon of *Hallyu*.

Soon after *Full House* became a hit, Rain's musical career also began to develop in the region. Through music video DVDs, Internet movie clips, and numerous popular music programs on satellite television, images of him singing and dancing spread quickly into Asian countries. His third album, *It's Raining*, sold almost one million copies in the region (E. J. Lee 2006). With an assertive catchphrase of "the most popular stage performer of Asia," Rain's first Asia tour concert, "Rainy Day," commenced in Seoul in January 2005. After Seoul, the tour went to Busan (South Korea), Tokyo, Osaka, Budokan (Japan), Hong Kong, Beijing (China), Taipei (Taiwan), and Bangkok (Thailand, February 2006). All 172,000 tickets were sold out (JYPE 2006). More than 20,000 tickets were also sold out in 30 seconds for the Rainy Day Budokan concert held in September 2005 while 20,000 tickets were sold out in 10 minutes after the online sales was started for the Hong Kong concert in October (H. S. Gil 2006). Due to the phenomenal success of his singing and dancing career in Asia, he was awarded the most significant regional music awards by MTV and Channel V (W. G. Kim: 2005).[7]

Besides setting records in terms of number of awards won, Rain's musical popularity is evident on the streets of many Asian cities. For example, in Bangkok in December 2005, it was common to see posters of Rain's music videos and dramas on the front door of most CD/DVD shops in Chinatown and in the major shopping centers such as MBK (Mah Boon Krong) (Figure 3.1). When I visited Hong Kong in October 2005, the numerous musical and entertainment magazines were filled with photographs of Rain that were taken from his "Rainy Day Hong Kong" concert held on October 8 and 9 at the Hong Kong Convention Center. In December 2005, in Singapore, Rain's music albums and music video DVDs were in HMV, the biggest music shop in Singapore, which is located in the Heeren shopping center; the albums were on the shelf reserved for the best-selling albums and the music videos were repeatedly shown on mounted television screens in the store.

Figure 3.1 DVD/CD shop in the MBK shopping center, Bangkok

In 2006, JYPE and Rain began expanding Rain's regional Asian popularity to wider markets, mainly targeting the US market, and in doing so, began to operate the third phase of transculturation: globalization. For an interview with a daily newspaper, *Chosun Ilbo*, JYP was asked: "Rain is already very popular in Asia. Why on earth are you obsessed with the US market?" JYP answered:

Although it sounds paradoxical, that is because we want to maintain the Asian market. I'm sure China's Rain will appear some time next year. Even though he may only be half as talented as Rain, Chinese fans [including the Chinese Diaspora] would favour him over Rain. A while ago, New Kids on the Block was very popular in South Korea. However, after [a South Korean boy band] HOT's arrival, didn't people almost lose interest in British/American boy-bands like 'N Sync and Backstreet Boys? That's why we can't stop moving forward. Only after achieving success in the best [biggest] stage, that is, the American market, can Rain consolidate his position as Asia's number one. It is essential to enter into the American market to conquer the Asian market with its huge population. (quoted in S. H. Choi 2006)

The above comment indicates how JYP sees success in the global market, and especially the US market, as paramount to Rain's continued regional Asian popularity and how JYP acknowledges the significance of this regional support. Asia is the undoubted backbone of Rain's transcultural popularity. This is evident when JYP uses the term "Asia's star" to describe Rain. In using such a term, JYP erases the specific nationality of Rain and emphasizes his *mugukjeok* aspects. As mentioned in chapter 1, JYP suggests that the next step of *Hallyu* lies in the emphasis of its *mugukjeok* aspects and insists on the notion of deleting *hal* (*han*, Korea/nness) from the notion of *Hallyu*. Many South Korean media, possibly directly employing public relations resources from JYPE, also often refer to Rain as "Asia's star." The television documentary program, *Rain, Beyond Asia* (KBS 2005), also begins with the narrator's reference to him as "the treasure of Asia and the pride of Asia." In an interview in the documentary, JYP again insists that "Asia's star" can now become a global star, stating: "I believe that now is the time for Asia's star to enter into the US [global] market and that it is my job to make it possible." Stressing a *mugukjeok* image of Rain as "Asia's" star rather than a South Korean star, it is obvious that JYPE strategically uses regional Asian fandom to enter the global market.

Globalized Rain

The globalization phase of Rain began with the release of his fourth album, *Rain's World* (2006). There are three clear instances of this globalization phase. First, along with the album's release, JYPE announced Rain's world concert tour, "Rain's Coming," which would go to twelve countries, holding over thirty-five concerts (S. H. Kim 2006). Later, Australia (Sydney) was included, thus the tour actually went to thirteen countries. Second, the global fan club, "the Cloud," was launched which integrated the twelve official fan clubs in various countries. Thirdly, Rain made his Hollywood screen debut in the action blockbuster, *Speed Racer*, directed by the Wachowski brothers who are internationally known for directing *The Matrix* trilogy (1999, 2003, 2003).

Beginning from the premiere showcase, which was held on October 13, 2006 in Seoul, Rain took his world concert tour, "Rain's Coming," to Australia, China, Hong Kong, Indonesia, Japan, South Korea, Malaysia, the Philippines, Singapore, Taiwan, Thailand, the US, and Vietnam during the period of December 2006 to May 2007 (Garcia 2006). This world concert tour is the best example of the globalization strategy of JYPE, where Rain takes the opportunity to enter the global market under the rubric of a "world tour," even if there are only two non-Asian countries, Australia and the US, included. Rain's globalization attempt is also evident in the main theme of the album and the concert tour, which consists of five antithetical concepts: war, peace, pain, hope, and love (G. R. Lee 2006a). These polarized concepts are expressed in the photograph on the album cover, where an angel-like Rain, in a military uniform, spreads his wings. Regarding this contradictory image, JYPE explained:

> This visual image contains the hope that Rain can cleanse the world of dirtiness just as rain can wash dirt away ... Through these five contradictory words, Rain shows how corrupted the world is and suggests how it can be healed [by love, peace, and hope]. (quoted in G. R. Lee 2006a)

At the premiere showcase, Rain performed *Friends*, a song which is about the desire for world peace and love, with dozens of children (G. R. Lee 2006b). In the same concert, Rain's military look and his shout of "Attention!" evoke images of the US army, which now represents a destructive agent rather than a peacemaker in many war zones, including Iraq. This authoritarian military look runs counter to the idea of world peace and love. On the one hand, Rain adopts the globally familiar theme of "world peace" to appeal to global audiences and it appears as if he simply follows the steps of many American singers who perform at charity concerts and create charity works such as the US single, *We Are the World*, that was produced in 1985.[8] On the other hand, Rain employs another globally popular image, that of the US military, which is contradictory to the theme of world peace. This contradiction in the imagery used by Rain's concert and album reveals one of the negative aspects of South Korean planned popular cultural production, which is that elements from global popular culture are selected almost at random and combined in a crude manner, without a consideration of wider political and social contexts, to maximize economic profits.

The second instance of the globalization of Rain is the launching of the integrated global fan club, "the Cloud," in September 2006. "The Cloud" brought together selected local fan clubs from twelve different countries: China, Hong Kong, Indonesia, Japan, South Korea, Malaysia, the Philippines, Singapore, Taiwan, Thailand, the US, and Vietnam (J. D. Park 2006; JYPE 2006). RainSingapore.com is the representative for the Rain fans of Singapore. Using Rain's regional Asian fandom to enter the global market is one of the most significant examples of the globalization strategy of JYPE. The main page of the

Cloud, Rain.JYPE.com, shows this strategy, displaying an ambitious catchphrase, "The No. 1 Superstar in Asia, Expanding into the World" (JYPE 2006). Again, the site emphasizes the fact that Rain is "Asia's star." This unified global fan club is expected to be the main axis of the world concert tour. Over 10,000 global fans attended the showcase of his fourth album, *Rain's Coming*, in Seoul in October 2006 (G. R. Lee 2006b); this was the first event organized by "the Cloud." Many Singaporean fans, including four of my interviewees, from RainSingapore.com also attended the showcase.

The last instance of the globalization of Rain is his Hollywood debut in the blockbuster action film, *Speed Racer*. In the film, he plays Taejo Togokhan, an Asian racer. In this film, one of the significant factors is that the nationality and ethnicity of Taejo are ambiguous because the name, Taejo Togokhan, cannot be identified as belonging to any particular country of origin. Rather, Taejo is portrayed as a generic "Asian" which strengthens Rain's *mugukjeok* identity. There were debates over the name of Rain's character, Taejo Togokhan, on many South Korean websites. For example, thousands of replies are attached to the online article, "Is Rain playing a Japanese? Fans get angry": some netizens such as "nomodem," "vnrwiyg2," and "nepetc" insist that Taejo is named after the first king of the Joseon Dynasty, "Taejo"; some netizens like "bananrep," "irisvocal," and "lhotse97" argue that the name is Japanese since Togo is a popular Japanese name; and other netizens like "red99sim" suggest that Khan is the title for Mongolian kings (Netizens' replies attached to J. Y. Kim 2007). The casting of Rain to play the ethnically ambiguous character of Taejo suggests that Hollywood recognizes the *mugukjeok* aspects of Rain's stardom and uses this strategy to target Asian audiences. Park I-Beom, from the entertainment planning company, IHQ, says: "[when looking for Asian stars for their movies,] the most significant factor Hollywood pays attention to is her/his marketability in Asia" (J. Y. Chae 2006).

It can be argued that his character, Taejo Togokhan, is regressive in terms of the portrayal of an Asian character with an ambiguous national identity that ignores cultural specificity in Western (mostly Hollywood) films. Here, however, I emphasize its *mugukjeok* Asian masculinity that has been constructed through transcultural media flows, rather than Hollywood's exploitation of culturally ambiguous Asian characters. I argue that this new way of employing *mugukjeok* Asian masculinity, as represented by Rain, has to be understood within a different conceptual paradigm from the pre-existing critical paradigm of Hollywood's Orientalist attitudes towards culturally ambiguous Asian characters and Asian cultures. First, this is because the representation of *mugukjeok* Taejo Togokhan clearly reflects the sovereign will of Rain and his management company. For example, in Money Today Star News, a journalist writes: "Rain's character was initially Japanese, but Rain asked the producer to change the character to a culturally ambiguous *mugukjeok* Asian American character" (Y. S. Yoon 2007). Rain's request seems to reflect his intention of not upsetting South Korean (and non-Japanese Asian) fans. And it is interesting to note that Rain's intention coincides with the marketing strategies of Hollywood producers who want to target Asian markets. Second, such a *mugukjeok* character has to be understood through an economic paradigm, as being the blunt result of marketing strategies. Based on the motivations of global capitalism, in recent years, Hollywood eagerly employs *mugukjeok* Asian characters in order to target Asian markets. Such an employment of *mugukjeok* Asian characters, which is based on economic motivation, has to be distinguished from Hollywood's pre-existing exploitation of culturally ambiguous Asian characters, which was, in contrast, based on Orientalism. In November 2009, Rain's second Hollywood movie, *Ninja Assassin*, was globally released, in which he played a leading role, Raijo, a deadly assassin from the "Far East." In an interview on "Good Day New York," a morning show aired on a Fox channel, he introduced himself: "Good Morning New York … This is Rain. I'm an artist from Asia" (myfoxny.com 2009).

The *mugukjeok* Asian identities of Taejo Togokhan and Raijo coincide with the basic marketing strategy of JYPE where Rain is promoted as "Asia's star" rather than as a South Korean star. Such reference of Rain as *mugukjeok* is also evident from the website of the "Rain's Coming" concert (RainWorldTour.com), where Rain's entry into the world market is proclaimed by concert organizer, StarM:

> Rain's Coming brings you the message of passion, challenge, hope, and love. Rain['s] World Tour is the first world tour of the Asian singer. As [the world] of culture and art [is] paying attention to Asia, Rain is the hero of the new Asia. (RainWorldTour.com 2006)

StarM repeatedly refers to Rain as "Asia's star" and "Asia's hero," not South Korea's, which is a strategy that was used by JYPE to emphasize the *mugukjeok* aspects of Rain. The statement also indicates that the world is paying attention to "the new Asia." This concept of "new Asia" fits in with the idea of the emerging "new rich" in Asia, who possess new buying power, particularly in the popular cultural industry. Due to the pragmatic marketing strategies based on turbo-capitalism, Rain is culturally hybridized through the adoption of foreign popular cultural elements in order to appeal to wider audiences. This cultural hybridity constitutes the *mugukjeok* aspects of Rain's stardom. It appears that this hybridized, globalized, and *mugukjeok* aspect of Rain resonates well with the trans-pop-consumerist lifestyles of the new rich in Asia.

Trans-Pop-Consumers, Singaporean Fans

Singaporean fans, it appears, practice trans-pop-consumerism in Asia which is facilitated by three main characteristics of the socio-cultural context of Singaporean society. These three characteristics are: cultural hybridity resulting from the fusion of East and West based on the social context of pragmatism; the pursuit of a newly emerging leisure- and entertainment-oriented consumerist lifestyle; and high technology literacy.

Singapore, the Culturally Fluid City

Singapore is often described as a multicultural society; it is a place where people of different ethnicities, languages, and cultures coexist. Chong Li Choy explains:

> Since its founding in 1819, Singapore[an] society has been open to a wide variety of cultural influences. This is due to the country's historical beginnings both as an immigrant society and as a trading society involving European and Asian traders under a British Administration. As immigrants, the peoples of early Singapore had to adapt to the new social setting and live under a British Administration. (1987: 133–34)

Choy argues that Singapore's historical context, where people from different cultural origins had to find ways to coexist side by side, led to the evolution of a Singaporean society which is culturally fluid (1987: 134). According to Choy, cultural fluidity is the "vagueness in cultural norms and values," which can potentially cause conflicts and contradictions. Contradictions, he says, can be considered acceptable so long as they achieve socially desirable results. In a culturally fluid society, different people adopt different cultural norms and values to the existing social environment to survive and prosper. Cultural fluidity, he comments, enables Singaporean society to absorb the values and practices of new foreign cultures and "pragmatically" integrate them into the existing culture and society (1987: 134).

This ideology of pragmatism is underpinned by the unique historical context of Singapore. Factors such as immigration, colonialism, and rapid social development have helped to shape a pragmatic society. Pragmatism in Singapore is often practiced by the government in the name of national interest and development. Chua Beng Huat argues that pragmatism has been rationalized by the leaders as "the natural," "the necessary," and "the realistic" solution to the problems of nation-building (1995: 59). At the center of this logic, there is "the single-minded pursuit of continuous economic growth as the key to national survival and progress" (Lazar 2001: 61). Another Singaporean scholar, Lily Kong, also argues that the ideology of pragmatism has helped Singapore to become an economically strong city-state in only a few decades (2000: 412). According to the arguments above, it appears that Singapore is a contradictory and globalized society where multicultural elements are pragmatically mingled in order to serve the government's pursuit of economic growth for the nation-state.

As observed, due to Singapore's cultural fluidity, the nation-state tends to be strongly influenced by the West, especially America. In keeping with the logic of global capitalism, Western brands are easily detected everywhere in Singapore. Singapore can be imagined as a space "thoroughly penetrated and dominated by the West" (Chua 2003: 7). At the same time, "Asianization" of Singapore has obviously been buoyed by the rise of capital in Asia since the 1960s (Chua 2003: 24). Starting with the "Speak Mandarin Campaign" in 1979, the Asianization movement was officially inaugurated by the government to strengthen and restore the different cultural heritages of Singaporeans so that they can be confident "in both the traditional worlds of their own respective communities as well as the Western world of science and technology and international trade" (Vasil 1995: 64–65). This Asianization movement is related to certain ideological and moral discourses in Singapore that pitched "reinvented good and wholesome 'Asian' cultures and values against a homogenized, bad, and decadent 'Western' culture" (Chua 2003: 6).

In particular, according to Chua, the Singaporean government has been the source of much ideological discourse that is anti-West generally and anti-American specifically (2003: 22). This discourse is essentially against the cultural contents of the consumer products of America that contain the "moral laxity of individualism." Such moral laxity, according to this discourse, may cause such consequences as high divorce rates, sexual promiscuity, and a drug culture, aspects of which are often reflected in American dramas and films (2003: 23). Throughout the 1960s and 1970s, the Singaporean government censored and banned popular cultural products from the West. These products "constituted 'unhealthy' 'yellow' culture which 'destroy[ed] [young people's] sense of value, and corrode[d] their willingness to pay attention to serious thought'" (Kong 2000: 412). Kong continues:

> The values and lifestyles that were associated with the decadent West ... were purveyed through cultural products such as rock music, foreign films, and television programmes. Night spots such as night clubs with live bands and discos were closed down and bans and censorship were introduced and tightened in a bid to control the insidious danger. (2000: 412)

Singapore's cultural policies throughout the 1960s and 1970s were mainly focused on avoiding negative cultural influences from the "decadent West." As a part of this attempted resistance, the authoritarian government enacted a "strict media censorship" against the Westernization of Singapore (Tan 2003: 413). Based on the social movement of "Asianizing Singapore," the government used media censorship to protect Asian values from the unwanted Western influences of sex and violence. For example, on cable television, "*Sex and the City* was entirely banned because of nudity and the positive depiction of promiscuous lifestyles" (Tan 2003: 413). Later, in 2004, the government allowed the censored version of the series to be broadcast (Rodan 2005). The Asianization movement is a measure of the Singaporean state's fear of the "Westoxication of the Singaporeans" (Chua 2003: 6). Chua explains:

> Ostensibly, official fear is that liberal individualism will make inroads into the cultural sphere of the local population, supposedly leading them away from local "traditional" values and undermining local social cohesion. (2003: 23)

As Chua explains, however, it is "the Western modernity of liberalism that is rejected, not the modernity of capitalism" (2003: 24). Because of these contradictory aspects, "'America' is simultaneously both an object of repulsion and of attraction" (2003: 25). This ambivalent attitude of simultaneously desiring and rejecting America(n products) is evidence of Singapore's pragmatic playing off of East and West against each other to fulfill the complex desires of Singaporeans.

Singapore, the City of Global Consumers

In addition to its pragmatic desires for globalized East/West characteristics, Singapore is also a city of global consumer capitalism. Unlike most other Asian countries, Singapore was a modern capitalist city from its founding. Because of "the absence of any pre-colonial traditional or tribal culture," Singapore was never "culturally and economically isolated on the periphery of capitalism, rather, its very own historical trajectory has been inextricably tied to global capitalism" (Chua 2003: 19). Chua explains:

> Singapore is without doubt a space penetrated by the global marketing strategies of producers of consumer goods. This penetration is, of course, facilitated by a highly-developed telecommunications and information technology infrastructure, and transport facilities that are central to economic development in global capitalism. (2003: 21)

Since the early 1960s, Singapore has experienced rapid economic growth and urbanization which has spawned an expanding middle class. This development is evident in far-reaching improvements in people's material lives, which reflect the expansion of global consumerism. New global lifestyles have also emerged among this expanding middle-class. They purchase international designer brands, eat global fast food, and import prestigious cars. In recent years, utilizing improved technological infrastructure and heightened capitalist power, they are able to pursue a global consumerist lifestyle even more easily. Rain's Singaporean fandom is a good example where middle-class Singaporean women pursue such a lifestyle through the consumption of globalized South Korean popular cultural products.

Another scholar, Nirmala PuruShotam, explains that Singaporean women "continuously reproduce a middle-class way of life and society" through many material and ideational choices that they make (1998: 127–62). In addition to their economic capability, PuruShotam also points out the changed socio-political perspective of these women. She explains that in the face of the dominant ideology of the patriarchal family, many of these women have begun to realize their independent capacity to shape Singapore:

> They began making independent judgments rereading their position in the normal family in liberating terms. They sought more and more education; they treated careers seriously and therefore postponed and sometimes refused marriage and children; or they limited the number of children they would bear and raise; they preferred to make time for themselves as [a] person, rather than as a social category tied to husband and child, family and state ... If these new ways of reproducing personal lives take root, the middle class way of life thus reproduced will surely be vastly different. (1998: 160)

These new ways of managing lives exactly describe the trans-pop-consumerist lifestyles of Rain's Singaporean fans. These fans are modern liberated women who have access to an expanded range of material and ideational choices, spend more time, money, and effort on themselves than on others, and prefer spending more time and money on leisure and entertainment. Thus, it is evident that Rain's Singaporean fans are trans-pop-consumers who embody the newly emerging new rich in Asia and who pursue global consumer lifestyles.

Singapore, the City of Advanced Media Technology

The third characteristic of Singaporean fans as trans-pop-consumers is their high technological literacy. The technological capability of these fans is due to Singapore's highly computerized infrastructure, which was constructed according to the National Computerization Plan (1981–1985) and which led to "Singapore's intelligent island vision" (George 2006: 65). Singapore has "a very high household penetration rate of 84.2% [from the result of the 2001 survey] for those who have access to the Internet" (Kau et al. 2004: 152). Four out of five of the fans I interviewed are connected online for more than ten hours per day during weekdays: when they are active, their time is spent being either on MSN (Microsoft Network) Messenger or on general web-surfing. They also spend a minimum of one hour a day on activities related to RainSingapore.com: such activities include producing, circulating, and consuming media content. This highly computerized technological environment allows Singaporean fans to engage in their fandom for Rain daily and virtually. They can be characterized as "media actives," a term suggested by Betsy Frank, executive vice president for research and planning at MTV Networks. According to her, media actives are:

> the group of people born since the mid-70s who've never known a world without cable television, the [VCR], or the [I]nternet, who have never had to settle for forced choice or least objectionable program, who grew up with a what I want when I want it view attitude towards media, and as a result, take a much more active role in their media choices. (quoted in Jenkins 2006a: 244)

This definition of media actives describes the participatory and active attitudes of my interviewees towards new media. Even though two of these interviewees were born before the 1970s, they are able to operate new media technologies as efficiently as the younger generation. This technology-driven participatory fandom of RainSingapore.com is further evidenced in the way in which fan activities in Singapore create news content in South Korea in real time.

On May 30, 2006, every member of RainSingapore.com received an email from its site moderator regarding Rain's twenty-fifth birthday. The email requested members to provide financial support to purchase a birthday gift for him. On June 22, 2006, this "very special gift" was revealed to be "a business class flight ticket" from Seoul to Singapore. Through an MSN Messenger chat, one of the moderators then informed a reporter from the South Korean online news site, JoyNews24.com, of this (M. H. Jeong 2006). Soon after this, an article entitled "Rain's Singaporean fans sent a 'flight ticket' to Rain for his birthday gift" was posted on the main page of South Korea's biggest portal news site, Naver.com (Naver 2006). One hour later, the most influential South Korean cable news channel, YTN, broadcast the same news content (YTN 2006). This example of real-time news posting can be explained through Jenkins's notion of convergence culture, "where old and new media collide, where grassroots and corporate media intersect, where the power of the media producer and the power of the media consumer interact in unpredictable ways" (2006a: 2). Because of the power of new media, cultural content flows across multiple media channels where the news of Rain's birthday gift travels from the emails of his fans to an internet chat, then from this internet chat to a South Korean news site, and finally from this news site to cable television. Thus, it is evident that, by producing transcultural online news, Singaporean fans demonstrate trans-pop-consumerism which is underpinned by Singapore's socio-cultural context of an advanced media technological infrastructure.

RainSingapore.com

In December 2005 and July–August 2006, I interviewed five members of RainSingapore.com at the Takashimaya shopping center in the heart of Singapore's shopping district, Orchard Road. According to my interviewees, the majority of the fan club members are Chinese Singaporeans except for a couple of Malay Singaporean members. They can be categorized as middle-class cosmopolitans because they lead globalized lifestyles based on their English proficiency (for example, the fan site is in English) and financial mobility. Both these factors enable them to cross national and cultural borders freely. In his 1999 National Day rally speech, Singapore's prime minister, Goh Chok Tong, introduced a new pair of terms — "heartlanders" and "cosmopolitans" — to describe Singaporean society:

> [The concept of "heartlanders" refers to] conservative Singaporeans who mostly live in mature public housing estates and whose horizons are generally limited to Singapore's boundaries. They maintain their ethnic character — more comfortable speaking Mandarin ... [they] are seen to be the "keepers" of Asian values and culture. The ideal-typical cosmopolitans, on the other hand, are equipped with world class skills and talent that command internationally competitive salaries; they can live and work quite comfortably anywhere in the world; they export the "Singapore brand" and raise the country's international profile. (quoted in Tan 2003: 411)

Despite Goh's simplistic characterization of heartlanders and cosmopolitans as having mutually exclusive values, it appears that the cosmopolitan Singaporean fans I interviewed still cherish certain Asian values and ideologies. Even though their lifestyles are highly Westernized, they still maintain certain Asian ways of living, as is evident from Fee Lian Kwen's article, "The Nation-State and the Sociology of Singapore," where he argues that the Chinese in Singapore have always, to some extent, practiced Confucian values in their thinking and behavior (1999). One example of the way that Singaporean Chinese maintain Asian ways of living is the fact that the fans I interviewed often use Mandarin to converse with each other rather than English. Chua Beng Huat also explains that the multicultural traditions and everyday practices of Singaporeans have always been mixed with modern Westernized attitudes and commodities, which, together, constitute the complex lifestyles of Singaporeans (2003: 20). Therefore, instead of Goh's binary schema of cosmopolitans and heartlanders, the desires of Singaporean fans must be understood within the framework of their complex and contradictory lifestyles that hybridize Eastern and Western values. Such cultural hybridity is due to the pragmatic and strategic adoption of different cultures and ideologies by a multicultural nation such as Singapore. Thus, cultural hybridity is the first aspect of trans-pop-consumerism, which is demonstrated by Rain's Singaporean fans.

In July 2005, Rain's online fan club site, RainSingapore.com, was launched. According to the interviewees, the major inspiration in starting a Rain fan club was the popularity of the drama, *Full House*. RainSingapore.com has five main boards: "General," "RAINing Spell," "Media Center," "Picture House," and "R&R." The "General" board provides basic information under titles such as "All About Rain" and "Dos and Don'ts." In the "RAINing Spell" board, fans can find the latest news and information about Rain such as his concert schedule or his email letter to the fans. The "Media Center" board has a media library where fans can download most Rain-related media productions such as his television dramas, music videos, television commercials, clips showing his television appearances on game shows, music chart shows, and entertainment news programs, and music files. The site is linked to a South Korean web-storage service, "ClubBox," where fans can find various audiovisual files featuring the early career of Rain as a backstage dancer of JYP to a rather recent news clip where Rain is participating in volunteer work for the Taean oil-spill cleanup.[9] The "Picture House" board is a collection of his photos. The "R&R" board is a discussion board where topics can range from discussing how to order Rain's CD and fan club T-shirts to announcing fan club gatherings. For example, one of the recent postings is "*Ninja Assassin* Special Screening — 18 Nov 2009." This is a fan-organized premiere show of *Ninja Assassin* (2009) in which Rain filmed his first Hollywood leading role. As such, the main function of the online fan club is the sharing and exchanging of information about Rain via the Internet. In particular, because the site is linked to the South Korean web-storage site, ClubBox, the fans can receive the most recent audiovisual data concerning Rain easily and quickly. As observed, it is evident that Singaporean fans are technologically savvy and that their online activities are at the core of the fandom of Rain. These online activities embody the second aspect of trans-pop-consumerism, which is the high technological literacy of the fans.

Another main activity of the fan club is to support Rain by organizing various fan activities. First, the club supports Rain by bulk-buying Rain-related popular products such as CDs, DVDs, photograph books, and T-shirts. Second, the club supports Rain by sending him gifts on special occasions such as his birthday, Valentine's Day, New Year's Day, and Christmas. Fans may also buy costly gifts for Rain; in the case mentioned earlier, where fans bought a business class flight ticket for him, a couple of fans donated US$175. Lastly, and most importantly, the club supports Rain by participating in concerts, fan meetings, and various showcases for the promotion of his newly released albums as well as special screenings of his movies. When his films, *I'm a Cyborg, But That's OK* (*Saibogeujiman Guenchana*, 2006), *Speed Racer* (2008), and *Ninja Assassin* (2009) were released, the fan group organized special premiere screenings. Also, for Rain's various overseas concerts, the fan club purchases concert tickets in bulk for the members, and in many cases, hotels and flight tickets as part of the concert package. Here, it is evident how RainSingapore. com embodies the global consumerist lifestyle of regional trans-pop-consumers, which is enabled by their capitalist ability to purchase leisure and entertainment.

Trans-Pop-Consumerist Singaporean Desire and *Mugukjeok* South Korean Global Masculinity

In the previous two sections, I discussed how Rain became *mugukjeok* and globalized and how Rain's Singaporean fans can be analyzed as trans-pop-consumers. In this section, I focus on three different sets of convergence of the various aspects of Rain's global masculinity that enable this masculinity to resonate with the trans-pop-consumerism of his Singaporean female fans. They are: the convergence between virtual masculinity and actual masculinity; the convergence between *yangban* masculinity and American-pop-idol masculinity; and the convergence between Japanese *kawaii* masculinity and sexy *momjjang* masculinity.

Rain: The Virtually and Actually Consumable Body

Rain's Singaporean fandom depends highly on the fans' use of new media technology such as the Internet and cable television. For example, Rain was first introduced to many Singaporean fans through international music channels such as Channel V and MTV, or through various game shows or entertainment information programs on Taiwanese or Hong Kong cable television. One of my interviewees, Ri, explained how she and her friends searched for Rain-related information on Taiwanese and Hong Kong entertainment news websites. Some fans then watched *Full House* on the pirated DVDs that they had bought from Hong Kong or China while others watched *Full House* on cable television. Finally, five enthusiastic fans launched the online fan club, RainSingapore.com. Their fan activities were not restricted to the virtual or cable world, but also took place in the actual world: for example, they travelled to Rain's television drama locations and to attend his regional concerts. Such fan activities which take place in both the virtual and actual world demonstrate a convergence of the virtual and the actual.

This notion of convergence between the virtual and the actual is explained through Henry Jenkins's concept of "convergence culture," which involves "technological, industrial, cultural and social changes in the ways media [circulates] within our culture" (2006a: 282). He states:

> Some common ideas referenced by the term include the flow of content across multiple media platforms, the cooperation between multiple media industries, the search for new structures of media financing that fall at the interstices between old and new media, and the migratory behavior of media audiences who would go almost anywhere in search of the kind of entertainment experiences they want. (2006a: 282)

In the era of convergence culture, media audiences constantly travel across the borders between the virtual and the actual world to seek entertainment. Regarding this connection between the virtual and the actual, Anthony Fung asks: "could online communities become a nook that substitutes for a geographically bounded community? Does the emergence of the former mitigate the death of the latter?" (2006: 129). Researching online gamers' communities in Hong Kong, he argues that it is impossible to disconnect the cyber world from the real world (2006: 138). My analysis of Singaporean fandom also explores the way that the virtual community merges with real life, rather than the former replacing the latter: in this way, I argue that Singaporean fandom demonstrates the convergence of the virtual and the actual, and exemplifies the complex processes of today's media convergence. As Henry Jenkins states:

> Media convergence is more than simply a technological shift. Convergence alters the relationship between existing technologies, industries, markets, genres and audiences. Convergence alters the logic by which media industries operate and by which media consumers process news and entertainment ... Convergence refers to a process, but not an endpoint. (2004: 34)

As Jenkins argues, convergence alters the relationship between existing technologies and also alters the way in which media consumers process news and entertainment. Jenkins's notion of media convergence helps to explain how the convergence of the virtual and actual in the Singaporean fandom of Rain alters the way that media is consumed, thereby creating trans-pop-consumerism. Singaporean fans, empowered by new technologies and financial capability, freely travel across the virtual and the actual worlds; it is during such travel that South Korean global masculinity is constructed and reinforced.

Participatory Fandom and Reproducing Global Masculinity

My research on the virtual fandom of RainSingapore.com is anchored in Jenkins's concept of "participatory fandom." In the late 1980s and early 1990s, cultural scholars, including Jenkins, depicted "media fandom as an important test site for ideas about active consumption and grassroots creativity" (2006a: 246). According to Jenkins, "fan culture is a complex, multidimensional phenomenon, inviting many forms of participation and levels of engagement" (1992: 2). As such, participatory fandom refers to the active involvement of the fans with various activities such as the creation, circulation, and consumption of cultural products. Over the past decade, new digital media technology has enabled participatory fandom to be more diversified, more active, and able to act faster. Fans have always been early adapters of new media technologies such as the digital camera and new software programs, and they use these technologies to create amateur media content. In the era of digital technology, fans are not only consumers of popular culture but also active producers, as Alvin Toffler has indicated with his term, the "prosumer," which combines the words, "producer" and "consumer" in his book, *The Third Wave* (1980). This combination of consumption and production further illustrates Jenkins's concept of "convergence" within the framework of participatory culture (2006a). Rain's Singaporean fandom is the best example of this.

The virtual fandom of Rain on RainSingapore.com is constituted by various modes of online participation by the fans such as posting, discussing, consuming, producing, distributing, and transforming media content. During these online activities, content travels across multiple media platforms and convergence takes place in various ways between major media corporations and grassroots communities, producers and consumers, and media audiences and travelers. Singaporean fans desire Rain through various forms of online participation on RainSingapore.com, during which they practice convergence culture. RainSingapore.com has become a site of converging desires between the above entities, and the fans' recreation of media content enables the construction of Rain's masculinity. For example, on August 13, 2006, one of the moderators, changed the background picture of RainSingapore.com to an image of a half-naked Rain (Figure 3.2).

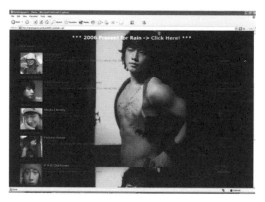

Figure 3.2 The background picture of RainSingapore.com

The background picture of the fan site is taken from a photo shoot that Rain did for a Pepsi Cola television commercial that was shot in July 2006. Due to his regional popularity and commercial influence in Asia, Rain became Pepsi's main model in Asia in September 2005 (J. D. Park 2005). The marketers for Pepsi stated that they chose Rain because his star image fitted the slogan of Pepsi, "dare for more" (ibid.). As observed earlier, his star image is globalized and highly sexualized due to the localization of the sexual elements of the star text of such American pop idols as Usher and Justin Timberlake. The Pepsi commercial employs the sexualized aspects of Rain's globally popular masculinity to reach wider audiences within the region. In the commercial, his sexy masculine body becomes the tool by which a major corporation, Pepsi, extends its global capitalist reach. However, an image of Rain has been taken from this commercial by a fan and turned into a background image for RainSingapore.com with the help of the software program, Photoshop. In relation to this new background image, a fan club member, Eully, posted:[10]

> Hey ... I like the new background ... thanks. Please add in more.. I want more
> ... sexy ... pics of him (August 12, 2006, Eully, fan club member)

In this post, Eully articulates her sexual desire for Rain by requesting for more sexy photos of Rain while the moderator articulates her desire for Rain by recreating and displaying his half-naked photo. The above example demonstrates how fans express their desire for Rain's sexy masculinity by practicing online participatory culture, that is, by recreating, posting, and consuming media content. RainSingapore.com has become a site of convergence between a media corporation (Pepsi) and a grassroot social community (RainSingapore.com) where the capitalist desire of a corporation meets the sexual desire of fans. Through such participatory online fandom, the fans enable the construction of Rain's sexy global masculinity.

The fans also reinforce the construction of Rain's sexy global masculinity through practicing another kind of participatory fandom: the transformation of their cultural location. In each thread under a member's nickname, there is the option of listing one's location, which normally indicates the person's city or country of origin. One of the site moderators describes her location as being "in bed with Jung Ji-Hoon."[11] One member's location is "in Rain's arms" while another member's location is "on Rain's lap." These imagined virtual locations transform the public space to an intimate domestic space; during such imagined transformations, fans fulfill their sexual fantasy of having intimate sexual interactions with Rain. Such acts of transformation demonstrate the way that online fan activities on RainSingapore. com are able to strengthen the sexualized masculine image of Rain through the recreation of media content. It is thus evident that the construction of Rain's sexy global masculinity is reinforced through participatory fandom on RainSingapore. com.

The fans also engage in participatory fandom by producing and distributing homemade media products such as flash animations and moving GIF (Graphics Interchange Format) images. For example, many fans use animated images of Rain's drama characters as their avatars. Fans use image-editing software programs like "Ulead Photoimpact" and "GIF Animator" to edit and recreate these images. Such "recreational" fan activity demonstrates the convergence of producers and consumers through online participation so that these fans become "prosumers." By editing and recreating Rain's images, fans are able to articulate their complex desires for him by enhancing the "cute" or "sexy" aspects of those images. As an example, one of the moderators posted several moving GIF images of Rain, which were originally captured from his concert clip for the 2006 World Concert Premiere, in a web banner. One of the images in this banner emphasizes Rain's sexual use of bodily movements as he repeats pelvic thrusts endlessly. At the same time, next to this sexually explicit *momjjang* moving image is a cute boyish image of Rain that was captured from *Full House*. The juxtaposition of these contradictory images — contradictory because the former image is of a sexual post-adolescent while the latter image is of a non-sexual pre-adolescent — reflects the contradictory desires of the fan for Rain. Such complex desires reinforce the construction of Rain's hybrid global masculinity.

Such sexualized desires of the fans for Rain's global masculinity are also often evident from fan art, which can be found from the "Made in RainSingapore" thread in the "R&B Clubhouse" board. In many images, Rain's sexy *momjjang* body is edited and recreated by fans through their fan art. Using graphic design programs like Photoshop, the sexualized aspects of Rain's exposed upper torso often are enhanced so that the image of Rain becomes a representation of highly sexualized global *momjjang* masculinity. The production and distribution of these Internet artworks reflect the participatory fandom of Singaporean fans. This participatory fandom is enabled by "the increased availability and power of digital technologies ... [which] allow everyone to be a media participant, if not producer ..." (Burgess 2006: 202).

Travelling Fans and the Travelling Global Body

Rain's global masculinity is not only virtually but also actually consumed and strengthened by Singaporean fans. This consumption is enabled by the financial power and mobility of the fans who pursue global consumerist lifestyles. The actual consumption of Rain's global masculinity is evident in the way that Singaporean fans travel around the region to attend Rain's concerts. Ri (52) said, "Basically, we see him every two months." In the interview, Ni (32) confessed that she spent over US$10,000 during the second half of 2005 travelling to various Asian countries to see Rain's concerts. Ni works in the real estate industry and her annual income is more than US$57,000. Another interviewee, Di (38), has travelled to South Korea eleven times in two years to attend Rain-related events such as concerts, showcases, fan meetings, and birthday parties that were organized for him. She owns a restaurant and her annual income is more than US$60,000. Three of my interviewees travelled to Bangkok to see the "Rainy Day" Bangkok concert in February 2006 while four of them travelled to Seoul to see the ING music concert in May 2006 where Rain performed for twenty minutes. Later, in 2006, when Rain held his World Concert Premiere in October, four of them travelled to Seoul. For these fans, they travel to see his concerts even if the concerts are exactly the same as the concerts they have seen before:

> When I saw his MV ... WOW!! And I went to Hong Kong for his concert and I
> saw him in person ... then ... WOW!!!!! ... that's how I came to love him. After
> that I try to go to every single concert ... try ... (Ri, 52, focus group interviewee)

Ri is a director in a marketing company, and her annual income is more than
US$56,000. Thus, it is evident that as middle-class Singaporeans, these fans
have financial power and mobility. They can be identified as typical middle-class
cosmopolitans who "are key agents of the new economy, more globally connected,
knowledge-driven, [and] sexy. They are vital to Singapore's overall economic
wellbeing" (Tan 2003: 411). In this manner, it is clear that financial capability and
technological capability are two significant driving forces behind the participatory
fandom of Singaporean fans. In particular, the capitalist power of the fans enables
them to "actually" cross national and cultural boundaries to engage in participatory
fandom in the real world. This actual border-crossing is one of the major fan
activities.

For instance, when Rain held his "Rainy Day" Bangkok concert in February
2006, more than thirty members of RainSingapore.com flew to Bangkok to see his
concert. In the following year, according to Ni (32), the fan club ordered fifty tickets
for the "Rain's Coming" Bangkok concert held in June 2007. She then added that
"there were others (not sure how many) who got their own tickets and went on
their own." Apart from the Bangkok concert, Ni also attended fourteen other Rain's
Coming tour concerts that were held in different cities including Seoul, Hong Kong,
Singapore, Kuala Lumpur, Ho Chi Minh, Taipei, Tokyo, and Daegu. She even
went to Los Angeles to see the concert there on June 30, 2007. However, the LA
concert was cancelled only two hours before the show was scheduled to begin due
to technical problems at the concert venue. From 2005 to 2009, Ni attended fifty-
eight Rain-related events and had to travel to fifteen different cities in ten countries
to attend these events (see Figure 3.3).

As observed from the case of Ni, some Singaporean fans travel internationally,
to different cities in different countries, to see Rain in real life. Again, such repetitive
travel demonstrates how the economic dynamics have changed in the Asian region
and how these economic changes have affected inter-Asian popular cultural flows in
recent years. This inter-Asian transnational traffic as exemplified by the Singaporean
fandom of Rain points to newly emerging trans-pop-consumerism in Asia. As
observed earlier, trans-pop-consumerists would rather spend time and money on
procuring leisure and entertainment than on procuring material goods. Dlkf June
posted:

> CEO (Rain) is indeed a very expensive hobby–more den half of my salary goes
> to his pocket–(Jan 13, 2006, Dlkf June, fan club member)

Dear Sun,
This is where I've seen him (concerts/fanmeets) apart from stalking him at hotel lobbies, hotel swimming pools and 7-11s. Hahahaha.

25 June 2005 – Birthday Party and Fan meeting (Seoul, South Korea)
3 July 2005 – Album Promo in Hong Kong (Hong Kong)
3 & 4 Aug 05 – Rainy Day Osaka (Japan)
8 & 9 Oct 2005 – Rainy Day Hong Kong (Hong Kong)
29 & 30 Dec 2005 – Rainy Day Taipei (Taiwan)
25 & 26 Feb 2006 – Rainy Day Bangkok (Thailand)
20 May 2006 – ING Concert (Seoul, South Korea)
15 June 2006 – Fan Meeting (Budokan) (Tokyo, Japan)
16 June 2006 – Rain Special Event (Budokan) (Tokyo, Japan)
13 Oct 2006 – Rain World Tour Premiere (Showcase) (Seoul, South Korea)
14 Oct 2006 – MBC Music Core (music show in Seoul, South Korea)
15 Oct 2006 – SBS Music Show Pre-recording (music show in Seoul, South Korea)
15 Oct 2006 – 4th Album Fan Meeting (Seoul, South Korea)
15 & 16 Dec 2006 – Rain's Coming in Seoul (South Korea)
12 & 13 Jan 2007 – Rain's Coming in Hong Kong (Hong Kong)
21 Jan 2007 – Rain's Coming in Singapore (Singapore)
27 Jan 2007 – Rain's Coming in Kuala Lumpur (Malaysia)
3 Mar 2007 - Cloud Fan meeting (South Korea)
10 Mar 2007 – Fans' gathering in Ho Chi Minh (Vietnam)
10 & 11 Mar 2007 – Rain's Coming in Ho Chi Minh (Vietnam)
29 Mar 2007 – Fans' gathering in Taipei (Taiwan)
31 Mar 2007 – Rain's Coming in Taipei (Taiwan)
25 May 2007 – Rain's Coming in Tokyo (Japan)
26 May 2007 – Promo in Bangkok (for Rain's Coming concert) (Thailand)
2 June 2007 – Fans' gathering in Bangkok (Thailand)
2 & 3 June 2007 – Rain's Coming in Bangkok (Thailand)
30 June 2007 – Rain's Coming in LA (the US)
30 June 2007 – Fans' gathering in LA (the US)
27 Oct 2007 – Rain's Coming in Daegu (South Korea)
16 Feb 2008 – Busan Lotte concert (Busan, South Korea)
30 June 2008 - Fanmeeting (Tokyo, Japan)
27 July 2008 - Fanmeeting (Seoul, South Korea)
10 Oct 2008 - 5th album Showcase (Seoul, Korea)
12 Oct 2008 - MBC Music Core (Seoul, South Korea)
21 Nov 2008 - KBS Music Bank (Seoul, South Korea)
22 Nov 2008 - Kim Jung Eun's Chocolate (Seoul, South Korea)
23 Nov 2008 - SBS Inkigayo (Seoul, South Korea)
21 Dec 2008 - SBS Inkigayo (Seoul, South Korea)
23 Dec 2008 - 6 to 5 launching show cum concert
27 Dec 2008 - MBC Music Core (Seoul, South Korea)
27 Dec 2008 - Mini fanmeet (Seoul, South Korea)
29 Dec 2008 - SBS Gayo Dae Jeon (Seoul, South Korea)
30 Dec 2008 - KBS Gayo Dae Chuk Jae (Seoul, South Korea)
6 Mar 2009 - 6to5 autograph session (Seoul, South Korea)
7 Mar 2009 - 6to5 autograph session (Daegu, South Korea)
8 Mar 2008 - 6to5 autograph session (Daejeon, South Korea)

18 April 2009 - Lotte Concert (Seoul, South Korea)
6 June 2009 - Rain's fashion concert (Hong Kong)
27 June 2009- Rain's fashion concert (Macau)
26 July 2009 - Fanmeeting (Seoul, South Korea)
29 Aug 2009 - Legend of Rainism (Tokyo, Japan)
30 Aug 2009 - Legend of Rainism (Tokyo, Japan)
9 Oct 2009 - Legend of Rainism (Seoul, South Korea)
10 Oct 2009 - Legend of Rainism (Seoul, South Korea)
28 Nov 2009 - Legend of Rainism (Hong Kong)
29 Nov 2009 - Legend of Rainism (Hong Kong)
24 Dec 2009 - Legend of Rainism (Las Vegas, USA)
25 Dec 2009 - Legend of Rainism (Las Vegas, USA)

To sum up, for Rainy Day tour - I saw 8 concerts. For Rain's Coming tour – I saw 14 concerts (including the LA one which was cancelled last min). . . . For Legend of Rainism tour – I saw 8 concerts so far. . .

Figure 3.3 An email from an interviewee

Here, Dlkf June's confession of how much she has spent on pursuing Rain as a "hobby" clearly demonstrates how Singaporean fans are able to use their capitalist power to practice trans-pop-consumerism through the purchasing of popular cultural products. Four out of five of the interviewees did not own houses. One interviewee lived in a rental condominium while the other three lived with their parents. Only one of them owned a car. Hence, it is evident that these Singaporean fans epitomize regional trans-pop-consumers who are more concerned about their psychological or spiritual wellbeing and who invest time and money on such intangible goods as travel, leisure, and entertainment:

> I'm single and almost mid thirty. I guess nothing's more important than to keep myself happy and healthy ... That's why I'm doing this [fan club activity]. (Ni, 32, focus group interviewee)
>
> I love travelling overseas and meeting foreign friends ... I met lots of friends through this [fan activity]. (Gi, 32, focus group interviewee)

Ni's and Gi's comments show that by engaging in actual participatory fandom, they are able to add considerable richness to their personal lives. These fans pursue the transnational consumption of a globalized South Korean popular cultural product, Rain, through mobilizing their capitalist power to obtain what they perceive as a healthy and entertaining way of living. Such a way of living is also part of the global consumerist lifestyle that many cosmopolitan Singaporeans aspire to lead. Therefore, the Singaporean actual fandom of Rain demonstrates how Asian trans-pop-consumerism constitutes a newly emerging global lifestyle.

Rain: *Yangban* + Justin Timberlake and the East/West Desires of Singapore

The second convergence of Rain's global masculinity is that of East Asian Confucian *yangban* masculinity and American-pop-idol masculinity. As South Korean scholar Baek Won-Dam argues, "the West has passed through our body [the South Korean's body]" (quoted in Cho Han 2005: 8). Cho Han Hye-Jeong also argues, "the modernization of South Korea is a history of imitation" (2005: 35). She then explains how South Korean popular music imitates the styles of Michael Jackson and Madonna while South Korean television dramas imitate Japanese dramas. In this sense, the star text of Rain — which also has a history of imitation — can be an absolute exemplification of the South Korean popular culture of today. This is a popular culture that has been highly hybridized through the processes of Japanization and Americanization due to the fast, forced, and compressed modernization generated by turbo capitalism. However, Cho Han further points out that transcultural production based on imitation is different from direct copying and emphasizes the importance of recognizing the process of localization that occurs during imitation (2005: 8). In the case of Rain's global masculinity, Cho Han's point of localization can be applied to analyze the convergence of *yangban* masculinity with American-pop-idol masculinity that occurs in Rain's star text.

Fans often see the convergence of *yangban* masculinity (perceived in Rain's drama character) with American-pop-idol masculinity in Rain's stage performances. According to Gi (32), one of my interviewees, "sometimes, [on the stage] he shakes his *eongdeongi* ["hips" in Korean] and shows this obnoxious smile. It's so cute, reminds me of Young-Jae [from *Full House*]." Regarding the "cute" aspects of Rain's stage performances, Lee Gyeong-Hui, chief editor of the *Hallyu* magazine *Platinum*, comments: "I don't think Western audiences would appreciate that kind of funny weird gesture. They might think it's cheesy. It would only please Asian fans who know Young-Jae" (2006). The regional Asian fans see the Asianized image of Rain's character, Young-Jae, in *Full House* when they view his Americanized stage performance. Thus it is evident that Singaporean fans perceive Rain's Americanized masculine image, which overlaps with his already constructed Asianized masculinity. This multi-layered *mugukjeok* East/West masculinity of Rain, it appears, speaks to the complex desires of trans-pop-consumerist Singaporean female fans, which is evident in their pragmatic reception of the culturally diverse masculine images of his drama characters and concert performances.

Transformed *Sadaebu Yangban* and Subversive Desire

In *Full House*, Rain plays a famous actor, Lee Young-Jae, who is arrogant, rude, and obnoxious but is, at the same time, vulnerable and innocent. Young-Jae happens to move into a "Full House" that is owned by a script writer, Han Ji-Eun (Song Hye-Kyo). After returning from her vacation, Ji-Eun discovers that her best friends have sold her house, without her knowledge, to Young-Jae. Young-Jae sees an opportunity to escape a marriage scandal by entering into a contractual marriage with Ji-Eun and the two pretend to be a married couple. In exchange, Ji-Eun has to do all the cooking and cleaning in the house, but she would redeem her house in six months. Despite their promise to keep things as "just business," Ji-Eun starts to fall for Young-Jae even though he, in turn, is in love with his childhood friend, Kang Hye-Won.

As explained earlier, the most significant selling point of *Full House* in the Asian region is the "obnoxious," yet "cute" and "innocent," Young-Jae (ETN 2005). In addition, all my Singaporean interviewees mention that Young-Jae's "obnoxious but cute and innocent" image is what attracts them the most. Here, both the obnoxious and innocent images of Young-Jae embody traditional Korean *sadaebu yangban* masculinity: first, his obnoxious behavior reflects authoritarian South Korean *sadaebu yangban* masculinity; second, his innocent image reflects respect for the Confucian value of chastity within the *sadaebu yangban* class. It is evident that Singaporean fans practice trans-pop-consumerism when they embrace the *sadaebu yangban* masculinity of Rain. Through embracing Rain's *sadaebu yangban* masculinity, they demonstrate ambivalent desires that both subvert and uphold traditional East Asian Confucian masculinity.

Sadaebu yangban was the aristocracy during the Joseon Dynasty, which was influenced by the ancient Chinese class system.[12] *Sadaebu* (사대부, 士大夫) was a dominating class that was consisted of government officials and their families. *Yangban* (양반, 兩班) initially referred to two separate government official groups, *munban* (문반, 文班), the civil functionaries, and *muban* (무반, 武班), the military nobility. Later, the term *yangban* referred to not only the government officials but also to their family and clan. Hence, *yangban* became a concept that describes the dominant class. Usually, because *yangban* officials were from the *sadaebu* class, the combined *sadaebu yangban* has become the archetypal term to describe the dominant class during the Joseon era (D. H. Jeong 2004: 171–72). People from the *sadaebu yangban* class practiced strict Confucian ideology, and restricted and regulated their way of living according to Confucian norms.[13] In chapter 1, I have discussed how South Korean hegemonic masculinity embodies patriarchal authoritarianism where men were traditionally considered to be heads of family and the main providers and this patriarchal authoritarianism is traditionally based on Confucian *yangban* ideology. In *Full House*, patriarchal *yangban* ideology can be seen in Rain's character, Young-Jae.

The obnoxious image of Young-Jae embodies the authoritarian masculinity of the patriarchal *sadaebu yangban*. Patriarchy supports the authority of the males of a household, and it is one of the important institutions of the Confucian society of late imperial China, along with patrimonialism and filial piety (Hamilton 1990: 77). Under significant socio-cultural influence from China, these three Confucian principles also became part of the basic ideological and moral structure of the old Korean dynasties, including the Joseon Dynasty (Cho Han 1999: 72–75). Confucian ethics require a woman's obedience to a man; one of the *samgang* (삼강, 三綱, three basic ethics) decrees that "a wife should respect her husband" (S. J. Kang 2006: 13–14).[14] In *Full House*, Young-Jae and Ji-Eun become husband and wife based on their contract. In order to get her house back at the end of the contract, Ji-Eun must obediently perform domestic chores according to Young-Jae's will. Thus, Young-Jae wields power over Ji-Eun, and Ji-Eun is obedient to her master and head of the household. It is through this power relationship that the Confucian patriarchal relationship is exemplified in *Full House*. For instance, when Young-Jae is angry at her and creates a new rule, she still obeys the rule even though the rule is unrealistic:

> Young-Jae: After nine o'clock, you can't come out of your room. That's the new rule!
> Ji-Eun: (with a dumbfounded face) …
> Young-Jae: … You'd better go to the toilet before nine!

As observed from this conversation, Young-Jae wields the decision-making power in the household, just as a *Sadaebu Yangban* man did in patriarchal Joseon society. In this sense, Young-Jae is a modern version of an East Asian traditional patriarchal male who has the absolute authoritative power in the household. This obnoxious *yangban* masculinity of Young-Jae appeals to Singaporean fans partly because the image is familiar to them; as Mi explained, "there are obnoxious [authoritarian] men everywhere." Then she added, "but no one's cute as he [Rain] is." Conventionally, the authoritarian masculine image has been repeatedly reproduced in many East Asian cultural products. However, it is not simply Young-Jae's authoritarian masculinity that resonates well with Singaporean fans; rather, it is the transformation of this masculinity, so that Young-Jae becomes an obedient love slave, that resonates well with them. After Young-Jae falls in love with Ji-Eun, he transforms from an obnoxious patriarchal male to one who wears an apron, happily cleans the entire house, and prepares breakfast for Ji-Eun. While Ji-Eun is busy with her script-writing job outside the domestic space, Young-Jae takes care of the domestic chores. This changed relationship between Young-Jae and Ji-Eun deconstructs the traditional patriarchal binary of the male-as-provider and the female-as-dependent-housewife. The Singaporean fans identified this dramatic change as one of the key elements of the drama's success:

> The funniest part [of the drama] is how this obnoxious, rude, selfish boy has changed after he falls in love with her. That [dramatic change] was really interesting. (Di, 38, focus group interviewee)

Most of the time, he is mean to her. But after he falls for her, he's become so obedient and caring. Don't we all want that kind of boyfriend? (Mi, 25, focus group interviewee)

Here, Di and Mi explain that this remarkable transformation of Young-Jae endears him to them. Young-Jae's obnoxious image is appealing to them not only because it is familiar to them, as the image implies traditional Confucian masculinity, but also because Young-Jae's patriarchal authoritarianism is finally subverted. This dramatic transformation of Young-Jae fulfills the subversive desires of Singaporean fans for the deconstruction of the ideology of East Asian Confucian patriarchy. It appears that Young-Jae's subverted masculine image, where he becomes a domestic house husband, speaks well to the trans-pop-consumerist lifestyle of the Singaporean interviewees, all of whom are working women who value their activities outside the home such as leisure and travel. Thus, it is evident that Singaporean fans embrace Rain's deconstructed *sadaebu yangban* masculinity, as represented by the domesticized Young-Jae, which resonates well with their trans-pop-consumerist lifestyle.

The fans also mention another aspect of the *sadaebu yangban* masculinity of Young-Jae that resonates well with them: this is that Young-Jae is presented as pure and chaste. This image of Young-Jae reflects the Confucian value of premarital chastity. Upholding sexual chastity is one of the most important Confucian ethics maintained by the *sadaebu yangban* class, particularly for women (Cho Han 1999: 80). This chastity is evident when we consider how Young-Jae and Ji-Eun do not kiss each other until the end of the series. (One exception to this is when Young-Jae forcefully kisses Ji-Eun in order to trick the media into believing that he was going to marry Ji-Eun). They do not even hug each other:

His character is quite conservative in terms of sex and stuff ... I like that kind of innocent image [of Young-Jae]. (Mi, 25, focus group interviewee)

Although we don't say it, [we] still value [Asian] traditional stuff, like [premarital] pure relationship and politeness. *Full House* has those things. (Di, 38, focus group interviewee)

From Mi's and Di's comments, it is evident that some Singaporean fans still value the traditional notion of chastity and that they appreciate the drama's presentation of the pure relationship between Young-Jae and Ji-Eun in *Full House*. In the very last episode, after they decide to get married for real, the couple spends a night together in a tent in their backyard. This scene suggests that Young-Jae and Ji-Eun have engaged in sexual relations. However, sex is not explicitly portrayed so that audiences cannot tell if they actually have sex. The only thing that audiences

Figure 3.4 A scene from the last episode of *Full House*

are able to see is their feet sticking out from under a blanket. Mi explains how such a subtle portrayal of intimacy between the main characters appeals to her:

> [from the very last episode, when they woke up after spending the night together in the tent], he was so shy and couldn't even look at her. That was really cute! (Mi, 25, focus group interviewee)

The above scene, shown in Figure 3.4, well describes the relatively conservative attitudes of Young-Jae and Ji-Eun towards sex, which reflects the Confucian value of premarital chastity. Shim Young-Hee argues that in South Korea, "Confucianism still has a far-reaching effect on many aspects of everyday life, including sexuality" (2001: 134). She also argues that regarding chastity, there is a double standard for men and women. Traditionally, sexual chastity was only required from women. In the case of the *Sadaebu Yangban* class, for women, in particular, losing their chastity outside of marriage could be a valid reason for committing suicide (2001: 134). In the drama, however, maintaining sexual chastity applies to both sexes, as both Ji-Eun and Young-Jae preserve their chastity until after their actual marriage.

The drama portrays the traditional Confucian requirement of upholding sexual chastity; but, at the same time, it subversively entrusts this requirement to a male character. In addition, Young-Jae is the one who is shy and submissive after having lost his virginity. In the morning after they have had sex, Ji-Eun says to Young-Jae, "from now on, you should listen to me well, ok?" and Young-Jae nods in an obedient and bashful manner. This portrayal again subverts the normative gender constructs of the obedient female and the authoritarian male. Through embracing the chaste and obedient Young-Jae, the fans fulfill their desires for liberation from patriarchy. The fans' subversive desire for patriarchal liberation reflects the aforementioned new lifestyle of Singaporean middle-class women where they are able to gain a measure of independence from patriarchal norms and can pay more attention to their own personal wellbeing.

American Pop in an Asian Body and Consuming Asianized Americanized Product

Unlike his drama characters, the images of Rain's stage performances are highly influenced by the West (especially America). As *Time* magazine has described, "Rain's style virtually clones American pop" (Walsh 2006). As observed earlier, many American media tend to evaluate Rain as a blatant imitation of American pop idols; such evaluations ignore the fact that aspects of American popular culture are localized during the process of transculturation. According to the focus group interviews, it appears that Singaporean fans embrace Rain within the framework of glocalized and regionalized masculinity, and not as an example of mere Americanized masculinity. Such embrace is evident through the two ways that fans practice trans-pop-consumerism: first, the fans highlight Rain's "Asian" body rather than the American popular culture that his body represents; second, they pursue complex global lifestyles that allow them to consume Rain as a hybrid East/West popular cultural product.

According to the result of interviews and participant observation on RainSingapore.com, it is obvious that the fans do not consider Rain as an imitation of American pop idols. He is, for them, "unique and so different," as Ni has described. In particular, in more than 2,000 Chatterbox messages, no one mentioned that Rain is an imitation or a copy of American pop idols. On the other hand, all of my interviewees pointed out the fact of his uniqueness; as Gi said, "There is no Asian artist who can sing, dance, and act as well as him." Mi also explained, "Well, when I first saw his live performances, I was very impressed coz I have never seen the likes of it in Asia before." According to Gi and Mi, Rain's uniqueness is rooted in his Asian identity. He is the first and only "Asian" artist who has performed in "such" a way in terms of singing, dancing, and acting. Their comments suggest that Rain appeals to them because he is "an Asian artist," who is able to perfectly recreate American popular culture, and who is as good as American pop idols. This suggests that they recognize that American popular culture is localized in Rain's performances:

> I do see similarities between Usher's tour and Rain's Rainy Day (some [people] say that it was almost blatant copying :P) — but to me, Rain has made his Rainy Day wholly his, just by virtue of his stage magnetism. So, even if he was "copying" certain aspects — if he can surpass the original — that's an accomplishment [in] itself. (Ni, 32, focus group interviewee)[15]

Here, Ni points out that even if he adopts Usher's performance style, Rain creates a new style of performance that is unique to him. In this way, Ni demonstrates an understanding of the glocalization of American popular culture that is evident in Rain's performances. Further, according to Mi, although Rain is Americanized, fans still desire him over many American idols because he is an "Asianized" Americanized product:

> Instead of saying that he copied Usher's moves, I would think a more appropriate description will be that he learnt from Usher instead. to copy is easy, but to adopt that skill & turn it into something of your own is not. let me quote an example of [Taiwanese] variety shows, a lot of their gimmicks are copied from Japanese variety shows, however they [don't] blindly copy, instead they add their own ideas to it and it evolves into a thing which the [Taiwanese] can proudly call their own. and guess what? [Singaporean] variety shows actually copy the improved-ideas from the [Taiwanese] and add on to it. this is a cycle which goes on and on all around the world. (Mi, 25, focus group interviewee)

Mi clearly pointed out that Rain adopts American popular cultural elements and turns them "into his own." Her comments highlight the way that popular cultures flow transculturally and create new forms of culture through cycles of imitation. Mi's point is clearly supported by Ni's further explanation:

> In the Asian countries, many male artistes [especially] TW and HK, have been accused of "copying" Rain by stripping and having similar dance moves on stage. Of course, stripping or wearing very little is nothing new but Rain made [it have] an impact in Asia. He practically owns the stripping act in Asia hahaha. (Ni, 32, focus group interviewee)[16]

Here, Ni explains that, within "Asia," Rain "owns" American popular dance moves and performing styles even though he is not the originator of these styles. Again, her comments emphasize the glocalization of American popular culture in Asia. It seems that fans desire Rain because of his global American popular cultural repertoire that is perfectly represented and recreated by an Asian artist. Rain's Singaporean fandom, in short, is partly due to his highly Americanized image that is articulated in a familiar Asian body. The above comments of the fans demonstrate that when American popular culture penetrates Rain's body, American popular culture itself becomes Asianized.

As an Asianized Americanized product, Rain appears to satisfy the complex trans-pop-consumerist desires of Singaporean female fans as they can pragmatically satisfy their appetite for both global and Asian popular culture:

> Well, I think most pop music (whatever language — Chinese, Japanese, South Korean …) has its roots in American pop culture. Know what I mean? I doubt I'll be listening to Rain if he sang traditional songs. The groove of the music

is important; the language is not (I've listened to Italian, Spanish, Cantonese, Mandarin, English music ...) We are so used to American pop. (Ni, 32, focus group interviewee)

Ni's above comment indicates that Singaporean fans are familiar with global popular culture as epitomized by American popular music. She is able to embrace Rain easily because he is Americanized and familiar. This demonstrates one of the major characteristics of trans-pop-consumers in Asia: they are ready to consume Americanized global popular culture. Singapore is a space well penetrated by American consumer goods, as well as American values and cultures (Chua 2003: 22–23). Hence, the Americanized Rain is able to speak to the desires of trans-pop-consumers for an Americanized and global lifestyle. Nevertheless, as observed earlier, the lifestyles of Singaporean trans-pop-consumers are not merely Americanized but are contradictory, where global cosmopolitan lifestyles are highly encouraged while Asian moral values are simultaneously held to be important. Through embracing American popular culture as represented in Rain's Asian body, Singaporean fans pragmatically fulfill their complex trans-pop-consumerist desires for both Asianization and Westernization. Within Singaporean fandom, Rain's body, as penetrated by American popular culture, becomes a model masculine form of reconstructed South Korean global masculinity that pragmatically combines Eastern and Western masculine elements.

Rain, a Boy in a Man's Body

The last convergence of Rain's global masculinity is that of Japanese *kawaii* masculinity and *momjjang* masculinity. *Kawaii* masculinity is evident from the "cute" aspect of the boyish image of Young-Jae while *momjjang* masculinity is evident from the sexual aspects of Rain's stage performances. The former implies pre-adolescent masculinity while the latter implies post-adolescent masculinity. This sexually ambiguous pre-post-adolescent masculinity of Rain, it appears, resonates with the complex trans-pop-consumerist desires of Singaporean fans. Here, I particularly focus on how this complex trans-pop-consumerist desire is influenced by Singapore's socio-cultural paradigm of pragmatism. As observed, the main operational ideology of Singaporean society is pragmatism. The government often enacts contradictory cultural and media policies to pragmatically fulfill the complex will of the state, which embraces polarized norms and values. The nation's practice of pragmatism is well represented in the contradictory aspects of the government-led social campaign, "Romancing Singapore."

Beginning as a month-long festival in February 2003, "Romancing Singapore" aimed to "celebrate and cherish relationships" by encouraging heterosexual couples to "be more expressive with their partners" (Tan 2003: 404–5). Later, it became a year-long social campaign. "Romancing Singapore" was originally designed to "get people married and procreating" (Hudson 2004). This campaign is evidence of the rational repackaging of the notion of "romance" for the national interests of increasing population, economic success, and prosperity. Chris Hudson argues that by launching such a campaign, "the irrationality of falling in love becomes an instrumentally rational cultural practice linked to the commodification of romance as a consumer goal" (2004). For example, the official "Romancing Singapore" website, RomancingSingapore.com, advertises products and events to help couples create a "romantic mood." Products of the campaign include the Romancing Singapore Eau de Parfum and the Romancing Singapore chocolate truffle cake, "Aphrodisiac." The commercialization of "romance," Hudson says, hits its apex with the reality television program, "Dr. Love's Super Baby-Making Show," where one couple wins US$100,000 if they, out of nine other couples, become the first to have a child. The "Romancing Singapore" campaign and the reality television program demonstrate how the Singaporean government applies extreme pragmatism to the ideology of "romance" to achieve the rational goal of successful nation-building through the maintenance of human reproduction and capitalist productivity.

Besides the aim of increasing rates of child birth in Singapore, there is another aspect of the "Romancing Singapore" campaign that relates to the notion of "sexing up" for the new economy that is driven by creativity, imagination, and innovation. Kenneth Paul Tan argues that the notion of "sexing up" could mean "allowing for a more open, non-repressive and plural environment in which to live, work and play" (2003: 418). The underlying aim of "sexing up" the economy is to revitalize Singapore and to increase its economic output. In other words, the government encourages each individual to become sexually more open in the hope that this sexual liberation could have a positive effect on the economy by stimulating creativity in the workplace. However, according to Tan, "sexing up" also has a contradictory aspect:

> [It] must be read in the context of longstanding attempts, led by the government, to harness the reproductive capacities of Singaporeans primarily for the good of the economy. Ironically, it was precisely this focus on economics that turned Singaporeans into *kiasu* [a Hokkien term that means "afraid to lose out to others"] workaholics who have no time for relationships and family. A medical researcher reports that tired, uptight and stressed Singaporeans suffer from "lifestyle impotency," much preferring sleep to sex. (Soh cited in Tan 2003: 416–17)

While the policy of "sexing up" seems to encourage people to be sexually open, its aim and focus on the economy paradoxically led to "lifestyle impotency" among Singaporeans. This conflict between prioritizing economic development and sexual desire is rooted in the pragmatism of the state.

The government's contradictory attitude is also evident in that it enacts strict media censorship that is directly contradicts the focus on sex and sexuality that underpins the "Romancing Singapore" campaign. Tan claims:

> The government has therefore been more ambivalent about the idea of sex, sexuality and sexiness, continuing in public to frown on "perverted" sex while promoting "normal" procreative sex tied to the family. (2003: 414)

On the one hand, the Singaporean government tries to control the sexual desire of individuals by enforcing a strict media censorship policy while, on the other hand, it encourages each individual to become sexually more open. The focus on sex and sexuality has traditionally been connected with Western culture in the Singaporean context and the Singaporean government, afraid of the "Westoxication" of Singapore by Western individualism and sex, therefore promulgates Eastern values through the "Asianization" campaign. Yet, at the same time, it encourages Singaporeans to become sexually more open, which is, according to the government, based on Western lifestyles and values. This is one example of the way in which the Singaporean government pragmatically uses Eastern and Western values and ideologies for its own purposes of maintaining economic growth and prosperity. These contradictions are evident not only in the policies implemented by the state, but also in the everyday lives of Singaporeans.

The authoritarian Singapore government tries to control the public's sexual desires through the pragmatic employment of "Romancing Singapore" and strict media censorship. In this situation, Singaporean women are burdened with a contradictory societal request: to be sexually more open in a sexually oppressive environment in order to create national prosperity. They are asked to remain sexually pure and innocent in keeping with Asian values; at the same time, they are asked to be sexually more open in order to boost the nation's flagging birth rates. Singaporean women, therefore, face a dilemma: should they be sexually pure or sexually open? By embracing the sexually ambiguous pre-post-adolescent masculinity of Rain, it appears that Singaporean female fans confront this contradictory dilemma.

Kawaii Masculinity and Pre-Adolescent Desire

Rain's sexually ambiguous masculinity is constituted by various representations, such as the "cute" (*kawaii*) boyish image of Young-Jae in *Full House* and the "sexy" performance images in his concerts. *Kawaii* (かわいい) in Japanese means "cute." However, the implication of cuteness in the term *kawaii* is different from the general meaning of the English "cute," which simply implies attractiveness in an adorable way. Since the 1970s, cuteness has become a prominent aspect of Japanese popular culture, entertainment, clothing, food, toys, personal appearance, behavior, and mannerisms. In contemporary times, Japanese cuteness, or *kawaii*, has become a globally known concept that is employed for various popular cultural products as well as for general industrial products. Two of the best examples of globally popular *kawaii* products are "Hello Kitty" and "Pokemon." The Japanese employment of cuteness could be intriguing, and sometimes strange, for non-Japanese because the Japanese employ it in a vast array of situations where, in other cultures, the employment of *kawaii* in those same situations would be considered incongruous, juvenile, or frivolous. For instance, some police stations in Japan have cuddly cartoon mascots. Some Japanese scholars, like Hiroto Murasawa, argue that cute is proof of an infantile mentality, saying that "cute is merely proof that Japanese simply don't want to grow up" (quoted in Kageyama 2006). Thus, it is evident that Japanese *kawaii* cuteness suggests an element of juvenility and childishness that is different from the English "cute," which means attractiveness in an adorable way.

Because of significant pan-Asian influence of Japanese popular culture, *kawaii* cuteness is easily observed in many Asian countries where regional Asian consumers purchase *kawaii* products such as Hello Kitty mobile phone accessories, Pokemon video games, Doraemon shirts, and *kawaii bishōnen* band CDs. As these products repeatedly cross national and cultural borders, the concept of *kawaii* has become *mugukjeok* and globalized. Apart from *kawaii* products originating from Japan, various non-Japanese *mugukjeok kawaii* products are produced, circulated, and consumed particularly in Asia. Hence, in many Asian societies, "cute" is often understood as *kawaii*. When Singaporean fans mention the cute aspects of Rain's character, Young-Jae, in *Full House*, what they are really referring to here is the concept of *kawaii* rather than the English notion of "cuteness."

Full House is based on the best-selling girls' comic (*sunjeong manhwa*), which has teenage fantasies at the core of its plot. One of the main fantasies of the series, with which most Singaporean fans resonate, is Rain's "naughty boy-like" character, Young-Jae. They recognize Rain's cuteness because of his childish and juvenile characteristics:

> When it [*Full House*] was shown on TV everybody was talking about it … from teenage girls to housewives. My daughter is fifteen years old and the whole school was talking about Rain. "He is sooooo cute," that's what I always heard from them. (Ri, 52, focus group interviewee)

> He is also very jealous behind her back. That's very cute and obnoxious … He is such a sweet and childish character. (Ni, 32, focus group interviewee)

Ri mentioned that a broad range of audiences were fascinated by Rain's cute character, Young-Jae. As Ni suggests, most of the fans' discussions about Young-Jae revolve around how "cute" and "obnoxious" he is, and how they are enthralled by his childish behavior. Such descriptions of Young-Jae support the argument that fans embrace Rain's cuteness within the framework of childish *kawaii* cuteness. It is thus clear that Rain's pre-adolescent *kawaii* masculinity appeals to Singaporean fans. His childish behavior is evident from the repeatedly portrayed situation in *Full House* where Young-Jae is actually in love with Ji-Eun, but stubbornly hides his true emotions and, instead, teases her like a pre-adolescent boy who is unable to express his love. The best example is shown in the much-discussed honeymoon sequence in *Full House*. In this sequence, Young-Jae and Ji-Eun go on their pretend honeymoon in Phuket; during the honeymoon, Young-Jae becomes angry with Ji-Eun over a trivial matter and Ji-Eun has to eat packet noodles while Young-Jae enjoys gourmet meals. (Again, the purpose of the honeymoon is to trick the media). At night, Young-Jae kicks Ji-Eun out of the bed and even out of the hotel room, and she ends up having to sleep on the balcony while being bitten by mosquitoes. In this way, Rain is portrayed as a petulant pre-adolescent:

> His cute image is very endearing. Even though you hate him for being a total jerk, you can't help warming up to him because his behavior is so childish. (Ni, 32, focus group interviewee)

Although Ni describes him as "childish" and "a jerk," she also shows a desire to be a part of this childish fantasy when she stresses that she cannot help "warming up to him." Her fantasy highlights a desire for Young-Jae's childish and immature pre-adolescent *kawaii* masculinity. Another interviewee, Gi, supports this claim:

> The way he takes care of her [Ji-Eun] is so sweet and nice even though he is mostly mean to her. He is the one that most of the girls want our boyfriends to be. (Gi, 32, focus group interviewee)

> It's like a fairytale. Obviously he is obnoxious. But he has such a sweet side. He also has a very sad moment. Then we want to comfort him. So he has every single side we girls want. (Ri, 52, focus group interviewee)

As Ri mentioned, Young-Jae's character has a fairytale quality, which reflects a fantasy of heterosexual teenage girls. It is noteworthy that both Gi and Ri use the word "girl," instead of the word "woman," to refer to themselves when they describe their desires for Rain, thus indicating that their adult fantasies are retrospective adolescent desires. In this way, Rain's fairytale-like *kawaii* masculinity resonates with the retrospective desires of Singaporean fans.

Sexy *Momjjang* Masculinity and Post-Adolescent Desire

On the stage, Rain's image is that of a sexually mature adult man. In contrast to the pre-adolescent *kawaii* image of Young-Jae, Rain's onstage performances are full of sex appeal. This representation of Rain's sexy body in his concerts is highly related with his *momjjang* masculinity; this masculinity is one of the most popular global masculine forms that has already been explained in chapter 2 in relation to BYJ's *momjjang* body. Rain's toned *momjjang* body reflects his adoption of globally popular masculine elements and reconstructs South Korean global masculinity as sexy, postmodern, and in line with global wellbeing lifestyles. Among these three elements of globally popular *momjjang* masculinity, BYJ's *momjjang* image emphasizes the aspects of personal wellbeing and postmodernity whereas Rain's *momjjang* masculinity predominantly highlights sexiness. Rain often exposes his half-naked body on the stage by ripping off his shirt and he also often wears low-cut white pants that expose the well-toned muscles framing his lower abdomen. This sexy *momjjang* masculinity of Rain resonates most strongly with Singaporean fans. This is evident in their answers to the question, "Please explain the most significant aspect of Rain, the one which attracts you the most." All five of my interviewees, in responding to this question, mention "his sexy image" on the stage:

> When I saw the concert MV clips for the first time, WOW!! his moving images were so sexy. (Ri, 52, focus group interviewee)

> We've had enough ballad singers in Asia like Jay Chou. But never had anyone like him. I wouldn't like him if he wasn't sexy. (Gi, 32, focus group interviewee)

At the concert, Rain often shows off his half-naked, muscular body and emphasizes the sexuality of his body through sensual dance moves that involve rhythmic gyrations of his pelvis and pelvic thrusts. This performance emphasizes the post-adolescent, muscular, and sexualized body of a fully grown man. Ri says, "It's all about body sell [selling the body]... Somehow it appeals to everybody's basic nature ... We appreciate the [good] body forms." She adds:

Figure 3.5 Rainy Day Hong Kong concert

For the first media showcase he only ripped off his shirt, he didn't take it off. And fans loved it. Then he realized "hey, sex sells." From the next concert he took the shirt off. And for the next one, half naked in white low pants ... then the water falls down. You see almost everything ... see?... He obviously knows what girls are thinking and what girls want. (Ri, 52, focus group interviewee)

As the "Rainy Day" Hong Kong concert clips (Figure 3.5) demonstrate, Rain's performances are highly sexualized. The peak of the sexualization of his performance is the "shower show." Most of my interviewees agree that the "shower show" is the highlight of his concerts. This part of the show refers to his name "Rain." Historically, "cloud and rain" have been the representation in Chinese literature of sexual intercourse. Clouds were interpreted as the "ovum" of earth, and rain as the "sperm" of the sky (Zhang et al. 1999: 583). At the climax of the concert, when the fans reach the peak of their excitement, water (that is, "rain") falls down to simulate ejaculated sperm. The fans, in turn, experience a simulated orgasm. Further evidence of this connection is that according to Rain's official fan site, "all his fans are officially called 'cloud'" (RainSingapore.com 2005). In this sense, the ritual of the shower show between Rain and the entire audience represents an act of sexual intercourse between a man (rain) and a woman (cloud). Here, one can argue that the fans compensate for their possibly desexualized everyday lives by submitting to the simulation of sexual intercourse in the shower show ritual. In the social context of Singapore, where women are faced with the contradictory demands of having to have reproductive sex but yet maintain standards of sexual purity, these fans satisfy the nation's demands by participating in the collective symbolic intercourse offered by the shower show in Rain's concerts.

As the above fans' comments regarding Rain's post-adolescent *momjjang* masculinity indicate, the fans demonstrate open attitudes towards his highly sexualized performances. According to Peter Pugsley, this receptivity is partly because Singaporean women are "completely au-fait with the sexual morals and 'Western values' advocated by TV programs such as *Sex and the City* and transnational magazines ..." (2006). Singaporean fans are already familiar with sexualized depictions and expressions of global popular culture due to the transcultural flows of media content, which is, in part, driven by their trans-pop-consumerist lifestyle. These transcultural flows are also evident from the way in which the sexy image of Rain is influenced by global pop icons such as Usher and Justin Timberlake. As Ni stated earlier, Rain "adopts the stripping act" mainly from American artists and "made an impact with it in Asia." As Ri stated above, "it is about selling the body" and "he knows what the fans want." Ni also explained that after adopting it, Rain "practically owns the stripping act in Asia." These fans' comments demonstrate how Rain actively adopts sexually explicit visual elements of American popular culture to appeal to wider audiences. In this sense, the Singaporean consumption of Rain's post-adolescent *momjjang* masculinity can be conceptualized through the framework of the pragmatic conjunction between two different regional Asian desires for globalization: Rain's globalized desire to adopt the sexy aspects of *momjjang* masculinity from American pop idols and the globalized desire of Singaporean female fans to pursue trans-pop-consumerist lifestyles, by which they can pragmatically consume and perform simulated sex.

As Ri said, "Rain is a little boy in a man's body," where Rain's male body is perceived as containing both an innocent boy's immaturity and a fully grown man's sexual maturity. Rain, with the image of "a little boy in a man's body," satisfies the ambivalent need of Singaporean female fans who are asked to be sexually more open in the sexually oppressive society of Singapore. The above analysis shows that this ambivalent need is fulfilled by the trans-pop-consumerist practice of the Singaporean female fans, where they pragmatically embrace Rain's globally amalgamated *kawaii* and *momjjang* masculinities; it is during such a pragmatic embrace that South Korean global masculinity is constructed.

Conclusion

The Singaporean female fandom of Rain can be conceptualized through the pragmatic conjunction between two different desires for globalization in the region: the desire of the South Korean popular cultural industry for globalization, as exemplified by the manufactured global popular cultural product, Rain; and the desire of the new rich in Asia for globalization, as signified by the trans-pop-consumerist lifestyles of Singaporean female fans. Such a pragmatic conjunction is most evident in the way that Rain's hybrid global masculinity is reinforced by Singaporean fandom based on the mixed cultural practices arising from *mugukjeok* and trans-pop-consumerism.

As observed, due to South Korea's socio-economic context of turbo-capitalism, Rain strategically adopts various global masculine forms such as American-pop-idol, *momjjang*, and Japanese *kawaii* masculinities; through such an adoption, Rain represents hybridized, globalized, and *mugukjeok* masculinity. Singaporean fans, who are typical trans-pop-consumers of the region, also demonstrate complex East/West global characteristics due to the nation's socio-historical contexts such as immigration, colonialism, and rapid social development. Such globalized characteristics of the fans are further evident from the main features of trans-pop-consumerism: cultural hybridity, high technological literacy, and the pursuit of global consumerist lifestyles.

I have discussed how South Korean global masculinity is reconstructed within such trans-pop-consumerist Singaporean fandom: firstly, through the Singaporean reception of the hybrid virtual and actual masculinity of Rain, which reflects the technological and financial mobility of the fans; secondly, through the Singaporean embrace of the hybrid *yangban* and American-pop-idol masculinity of Rain, which reflects their culturally mixed East/West lifestyle; and lastly, through the Singaporean embrace of the hybrid *kawaii* and *momjjang* masculinity of Rain, which reflects their pragmatic pre-post-adolescent sexual desire.

Thus, it is my conclusion that South Korean global masculinity, as represented by Rain, is reconstructed by Singaporean fandom, which is enabled by the transcultural flows that create *mugukjeok* global aspects and by the trans-pop-consumerist desire of the fans that is derived from the newly emerging lifestyle of the new rich in Asia.

4

Oldboy, Postmodern Masculinity, and Western Fandom on Film Review Websites:
Time between Dog and Wolf

As dusk becomes night and the sun slowly wanes between the mountain ridges, this is the time when you cannot tell whether the silhouette that approaches slowly is your faithful dog or a dangerous wolf, the time when friend and foe are indistinguishable. This is the moment when both righteous and errant paths all become crimson.

— Comment from a character in the 2007 South Korean television drama series, *Time between Dog and Wolf* (*Gae-wa Neukdae-ui Shigan*)

Before [I started watching recent South Korean films], my knowledge about Korea was very limited. One is *M*A*S*H*, in which the Korean War seems to never end. Then, some photos of [South] Korean students protesting during the 80s ... [and] of North Korean people in extreme poverty ... [but] Dae-Soo is totally cool ... totally savage but cool ... like Alex from *A Clockwork Orange*.

— Gu, 39, an Australian fan of South Korean films from Melbourne

In 2006, the South Korean action thriller, *Oldboy*, was ranked 118th in IMDb.com's top 250 films (G. C. Yoon 2006). This high ranking is significant when considering the fact that most users of IMDb.com are English-speaking Westerners. Indeed, *Oldboy*'s high ranking on the website reflects the popularity of South Korean genre films overseas and, in particular, in Western countries since the early 2000s. Around that time, South Korean genre films were becoming known on the international film festival circuit and were acknowledged by Western fans on online film-related websites.[1] For instance, since *Oldboy* won the Grand Prix in 2004 at the Cannes International Film Festival with the accompanying praise of Quentin Tarantino, the Cannes jury president, the film has gained a new cult status among genre film fans. This cult fandom is evident on many discussion boards on Western film-related websites where film site users often hail the film's graphic violence and its transgressive themes of abduction and incest. In this chapter, I use the term "Western" to describe the users and film reviewers of the English-language-based film websites that are analyzed here. Even though these websites are mostly established by Americans, many of the users and film reviewers of these websites are native English speakers such as Canadians, Britons, and Australians. Also, I use "web forum," "message board," and "discussion board" interchangeably in this chapter, because each website employs different terms to describe its user forums.

The fans' acclaim for the violent and transgressive content of the film is further evident in their obsessive affection for the main male character, Oh Dae-Soo (Choi Min-Shik). As the quotation from the Australian fan at the beginning of this chapter demonstrates, some viewers clearly express their ambivalent attraction to the South Korean male character, Dae-Soo, who is perceived as "totally savage but cool." This fan explains that he "found a whole new world" through the experience of watching a "strange" South Korean genre film, and in particular, through embracing this "savage but cool" South Korean male character, Dae-Soo. I suggest that this Western affection for Dae-Soo, particularly in response to Dae-Soo's savageness, can be understood within the conceptual framework of the commodification of Otherness, which is explained by bell hooks in *Black Looks* (1992). She argues that the consumption of Otherness offers intense enjoyment that mainstream white cultures often taboo:

> Cultural taboos around sexuality and desire are transgressed and made explicit as the media bombards folks with a message of difference no longer based on the white supremacist assumption that "blondes have more fun." The "real fun" is to be had by bringing to the surface all those "nasty" unconscious fantasies and longings about contact with the Other embedded in the secret (not so secret) deep structure of white supremacy. (1992: 21–22)

White mainstream Westerners desire the taboo-breaking cultural practices that are involved with consuming ethnic difference, hooks explains, as transgressive Otherness can provide sources of unknown pleasures. This desire, according to hooks, is nothing but "a contemporary revival of [Orientalist] interest in the "primitive" with a distinctly postmodern slant" (1992: 21–22). The recent cult fandom of *Oldboy* can be partly explained within this same framework of Orientalist Western longings for primitive Otherness. In particular, the favoring of the transgressive themes and the portrayal of Dae-Soo as savage in *Oldboy* by fans clearly support hooks's argument about what she refers to as the West's "nasty" unconscious fantasies. However, I argue that the Western longing for Dae-Soo is, to some extent, different. The fan, Gu, whose words are quoted above, states that his perceptions of South Korean culture and South Korean men have changed after watching South Korean genre films such as *Oldboy*. Even though his view of Dae-Soo as savage fits in with Orientalist notions of the primitive Other, he also sees Dae-Soo as a "cool" man.

This fan also compares Dae-Soo with Alex, the male protagonist of Stanley Kubrick's crime thriller, *A Clockwork Orange* (1971), and declares that Dae-Soo is as "cool" as Alex. Set in Britain in the postmodern 1990s as imagined by Kubrick, the film follows the life of a teenage boy named Alex de Large who takes pleasure in listening to classic music (especially Beethoven), rape, and violence. He epitomizes a chaotic postmodern society, as he subverts all the conventional virtues that Western culture has valued. According to Susan Fraiman's book, *Cool Men and the Second Sex*, "the cool subject identifies with an emergent, precarious masculinity produced in large part by youthful rule breaking" (2003: xii). Thus, "coolness," which both Dae-Soo and Alex embody, can be conceptualized as the expression of transgressive and dangerous masculinity. Fraiman further explains that this "male coolness" is defined by the modern adolescent boy's alienation from the maternal: within this context of male coolness, the presence of maternal love implies rigid domesticity and, thus, is "uncool" (2003: xii). In this sense, it is evident that the primary notion of male coolness is based on the detachment and isolation from the home and the family, which are identified with "the mother." Hence, because male coolness is anti-maternal, men must detach themselves from the familial realms to remain cool. Such isolation results in masculine loneliness and both these aspects of detachment are distinctive socio-cultural symptoms of postmodernity. Both *Oldboy* and *A Clockwork Orange* contain this narrative of the construction of male coolness. In *Oldboy*, Dae-Soo is mysteriously imprisoned for fifteen years. During this isolation, he becomes a vicious fighting machine and, therefore, a "cool" man. It is also significant that Alex, in *A Clockwork Orange*, often represents a postmodern anti-hero, a "cool" man, because he transgresses all the moral values of Western traditional culture (Feldmann 1976: 15). Both characters represent the postmodern masculinity of "cool" men in terms of demonstrating isolation (loneliness) and transgression. This comparison between Dae-Soo and Alex indicates that the attitudes of Western viewers resonate not only with the primitive aspect (savagery) that is perceived in South Korean masculinity, but also with its postmodernity (coolness). In other words, Western viewers desire the hybrid postmodern South Korean masculinity found in contemporary South Korean genre films that is, in turn, redefined and reconstructed by Western film spectatorship.

The Western desire for Dae-Soo is ambivalent because it seeks the strangeness of Otherness and, at the same time, the familiarity of modern "coolness": hence, I argue that Western audiences of *Oldboy* experience the hybrid "time between dog and wolf," which is the time when they are unable to identify whether Dae-Soo is a "cool" friend or a savage stranger.[2] This "time between dog and wolf" epitomizes the contemporary postmodern era that is ever-fluctuating, an era that has been described as seeing "the demise of the tradition of Aristotelian logic, through which Western society has long defined itself via a series of polar oppositions, the central of which were Good versus Evil, and Us versus Them" (Booker 2007: xv). Jean-François Lyotard discusses this collapse of Western belief as a radical rejection of "totalizing metanarratives" in his influential book, *The Postmodern Condition: A Report on Knowledge* (1984: 37–38). This rejection is based on, among other things, the fact that virtually all aspects of life, culture, and society in the postmodern era have experienced an accelerating rate of transformation and an increasing complexity of narratives due to the rapid, frequent, multi-directional cultural flows made possible by advanced technology. The areas of gender and sexuality, and in particular, South Korean masculinity, are no exceptions to this. Thus, the time between dog and wolf epitomizes the dizzying postmodern time when "multiple masculinities" are actively and diversely produced and consumed (Connell 2000a: 10) and the time when postmodern South Korean masculinity is reconstructed by ambivalent Western spectatorship.

Such ambivalent Western desire of postmodern South Korean masculinity is evident in the mixed practice of *mugukjeok* (non-nationality) and the neo-Orientalism of new cinephiles on Western film websites. The term "neo-Orientalism" used in this chapter differs from the conventional concept of Orientalism: while Orientalism is characterized by Western desires for the Other that is perceived as completely primitive, neo-Orientalism is characterized by ambivalent Western desires for the hybrid postmodern Other that is perceived as not quite primitive. In the Western reception of postmodern South Korean masculinity, the practice of *mugukjeok* is evident in the way that audiences resonate with Dae-Soo through their comparisons of *Oldboy* with other Western genre films. In particular, fans frequently compare Dae-Soo with Tyler Durden (Brad Pitt), the main protagonist of *Fight Club* (1999), and this indicates the audiences' acknowledgement of a "cool" postmodern South Korean masculinity that is characterized by isolation (alienation) and psychic fragmentation. Another aspect of the Western reception of postmodern South Korean masculinity, neo-Orientalism, is evident in the way that Western audiences objectify and fetishize transgressive South Korean masculinity. Using the framework of "techno-Orientalism," as suggested by David Morley and Kevin Robins, I analyze how viewers fetishize South Korean masculinity through their enthusiastic consumption of the representations of Dae-Soo as "machinic." Such techno-Orientalist desire is evident from the Western embrace of three aspects of the machinic Dae-Soo — Dae-Soo as the human-hammer-machine, his eating of a live octopus, and his transgression of the incest taboo.

In this chapter, I use the term "Euro-American" interchangeably with the term "Western." I also use the term "the West" to refer to the websites and their users after spending a considerable amount of time participating in and observing these websites. This term describes the origins and backgrounds of the users of these sites where they are mostly English-speaking Euro-Americans. From conducting participant observation on these websites, I also discovered that the majority of the fans of *Oldboy* were male. This was evident from the demographic breakdown of the voters who rated *Oldboy* on IMDb.com (Figure 4.1). Of all the voters for *Oldboy*, 42,738 were males while 4,103 were females. This fact is further supported by the comments of Christian Were, who is a brand manager at Madman, a film and DVD distribution company in Melbourne that specializes in Asian cinema. Were said "more than 95% of the consumers of Asian extreme genre films are men between their early 20s and mid-30s" (personal interview). It can thus be argued that this particular fan group of *Oldboy*, which I examine in this chapter, consists of Western males in their twenties and thirties. Thus, the gender dynamics between the fans and the star in this chapter are different from those dynamics existing between the fans and the star in the previous chapters of this book. Hence, regarding the Western reception of *Oldboy* in general and Dae-Soo in particular, it can be argued that this Western fandom signifies an ambivalent phenomenon between the West's Orientalist desire for the primitive Other and Western male identification with South Korean cool masculinity.

Rating Breakdown

Demographics			
• All votes	8.3		52,561
Males	8.4		42,738
Females	7.8		4,103
• Aged under 18	7.9		1,053
Males	8.5		896
Females	4.6		156
• Aged 18-29	8.5		34,013
Males	8.5		31,093
Females	8.5		2,796
• Aged 30-44	8.0		10,143
Males	8.1		9,172
Females	7.4		893
• Aged 45+	6.8		1,532
Males	6.9		1,295
Females	6.0		224
• Top 1000 voters	6.5		441
• US users	8.2		11,808
• Non-us users	8.4		34,957

All votes		
10	37.5%	19,702
9	25.2%	13,234
8	17.8%	9,335
7	8.2%	4,311
6	3.7%	1,928
5	1.8%	954
4	1.0%	534
3	0.7%	392
2	0.7%	347
1	3.5%	1,824
Arithmetic mean = 8.4		
Median = 9		

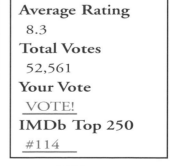

Average Rating
8.3
Total Votes
52,561
Your Vote
VOTE!
IMDb Top 250
#114

Figure 4.1 Demographic breakdown of *Oldboy* voters on IMDb.com

South Korean Genre Films beyond South Korea

In 2003, several South Korean genre films achieved commercial and critical acclaim in the domestic market. In the year-end forum of the influential weekly film magazine, *Cine21*, Jeong Seong-Il, Kim So-Young, and Heo Moon-Young point to the popularity of "well-made" genre films as one of the remarkable phenomena of the year (2003).[3] Among these well-made genre films, Park Chan-Wook's *Oldboy* and Bong Joon-Ho's *Memories of Murder* were chosen as two of the best South Korean films of the year by many film critics and industry professionals (S. W. Lee et al. 2003; S. H. Kim 2004). These films were commonly acknowledged as combining, in an ideal manner, genre film aesthetics and social commentary. *Oldboy* sold more than 3.1 million tickets while *Memories of Murder* sold over 5.2 million tickets nationwide (Korean Film Council 2003). Their popularity has further expanded to foreign markets, particularly to Western markets. The Western popularity of South Korean genre films is evident in the international film festival circuit and on film-related websites.

Oldboy and *The Host* on the International Film Festival Circuit

In 2004, *Oldboy* won the Grand Prix at the Cannes International Film Festival, which is an exemplary indication of overseas recognition. Due to the reputation it garnered at Cannes, *Oldboy* was welcomed at numerous international film festivals, including the Melbourne International Film Festival in Australia and the Toronto International Film Festival in Canada. *Oldboy* also won many other foreign film festival awards, especially from festivals dedicated to fantasy and horror genre films such as the Sitges International Film Festival in Spain and the Oporto International Film Festival (also known as Fantasporto) in Portugal. The film was also commercially well received in many Western countries, including the UK, France, and the US. Even though *Oldboy* was released through only twenty art-house cinemas in the UK, in eight weeks, following its first screening on October 15, 2004, it earned more than US$539,000, (H. L. Kim 2004). The film has been sold in forty-one different countries worldwide, and in 2007, was considered for a Hollywood remake by Universal Pictures, who bought the film's rights for the remake at the American Film Market in 2004 (C. W. Park et al. 2005: 10–11; B. G. Kim 2004).

Bong Joon-Ho's *Memories of Murder* was also recognized in many foreign countries. The film won several film festival awards, including those at the Tokyo International Film Festival in Japan, the San Sebastian International Film Festival in Spain, and the Cognac International Thriller Film Festival in France (Kofic 2003). Although *Memories of Murder* achieved critical recognition at various film festivals worldwide, it was not until 2006 that Bong Joon-Ho truly obtained broad foreign acknowledgment as a South Korean genre maestro through his monster horror film, *The Host* (*Gwoemul*). This film made history in South Korean cinema. Selling more than 13 million tickets, it "monstrously" broke the box office record of 12.3 million tickets, which had been held briefly by the 2005 historical drama, *The King and the Clown* (*Wang-ui Namja*) (Kofic 2006). Like *Oldboy, The Host* was also first acknowledged by foreign audiences at the Cannes International Film Festival. Although it was invited to Cannes as a Directors Fortnight entry rather than an Official Selection, the film was acclaimed by many world media critics (H. I. Kim 2006). The film has gained overseas recognition through the festival circuit, including such venues as the Melbourne International Film Festival, the Toronto International Film Festival, and the New York Film Festival: the total four screening sessions of *The Host* at the New York Film Festival were sold out (J. H. Yang 2006); when *The Host* was invited to the Vancouver Film Festival, the influential Canadian newspaper *The Vancouver Sun* introduced the film as one of the top ten "must see" movies in the festival (R. Oh 2006). It has been released in the mainstream cinema circuit in many countries such as the UK, France, the US, Singapore, China, and Australia, and has achieved both commercially remarkable results and critical acclaim. In France, for instance, the influential film magazine *Cahiers du Cinéma* selected *The Host* as the third best film in 2006 after *Private Fears in Public Places* (*Coeurs* 2006) and *The Sun* (*Solntse* 2006) (S. Moon 2007a). In China, the film reached the box-office number one spot for the first two weeks, and it has become one of the best-selling Asian movies in Australia (S. Moon 2007b; H. J. Kim 2007). Finally, at the American Film Market in 2006, the rights to *The Host* were sold to Universal Pictures for a Hollywood remake (S. Moon 2006). Besides the international film festival circuit and overseas box office sales results, the global popularity of *Oldboy* and *The Host* is further evident in the cult fandom on many film websites.

The Online Cult Fandom of *Oldboy* and *The Host*

On various Western film websites, many users discuss *Oldboy* and *The Host* under the "Asian cult" genre category. Asian genre films — horror films, in particular — have become synonymous with Asian cult among many Western viewers. J. P. Telotte defines the cult film this way: "[I]t is a type marked by both its highly specified and limited audience as well as a singular pleasure that this audience finds in the film's transgressions" (1991: 7). In the edited book *The Cult Film Experience*, Tellote and other authors describe the broad field of cult films by locating two poles: the classical cult film and the midnight movie. Telotte, however, points out that because film types and film viewing practices are constantly changing, there ought to be varying definitions and recognition of different kinds of cult film (1991: 1–3). Timothy Corrigan, one of the book's contributors, describes the cult moviegoer as a kind of "accidental tourist" who finds great pleasure in the casual encounter with a cultural terra incognita. He states:

> Cult movies are always after a fashion foreign films: the images are especially
> exotic; the viewer uniquely touristic; and within that relationship viewers get
> to go places, see things, and manipulate customs in a way that no indigenous
> member of that culture or mainstream filmgoer normally could ... Cultural
> distance allows for the textual transformation of cult audiences. (1991: 27)

What Corrigan emphasizes here is that it is the "strangeness" of cult films that
fans long for. Susan Stewart, in *On Longing*, suggests that such films "allow one
to be a tourist in one's own life, or allow the tourist to appropriate, consume, and
thereby 'tame' the cultural other" (cited in Corrigan 1991: 27). Both the arguments
of Corrigan and Stewart support the point that the genre of Asian cult addresses
Western audiences' need for the Other by providing images that are perceived as
foreign, strange, and transgressive.

The overseas cult fandom of South Korean genre films first become evident
in 2003, when a popular film review website, AintItCool.com (*Ain't It Cool News*),
selected *Oldboy* as one of the best ten films of the year. This site is considered to be
one of the most influential film review websites available that specializes in reviewing
science fiction, fantasy, horror, and action films. The founder of the site, Harry
Knowles — also an online film critic — describes *Oldboy* as such:

> Park is a deft director, able to convey scenes of raw emotion, raw fury, and
> pure pain ... Park is unflinching, showing the moments where most filmmakers
> would look the other way. When Oh Dae-Soo tortures an employee by pulling
> his teeth with a claw hammer, Park shows it (And holy shit was it painful to
> watch). (Knowles 2003)

Knowles praises the director's ability to convey scenes of "raw" emotion, "raw" fury,
and "pure" pain. In particular, his words clearly show that he was enthralled by
some of the purely graphic scenes, for example, pulling the teeth out with a claw
hammer even though it "was painful to watch." He also suggests that Park handles
this rawness in a strange way, a way that most filmmakers would not have chosen
to use. For a cult film fan such as Knowles, the obsessive inclination for such raw
depictions of violence and strangeness in the film reflects his cult taste for violent
action and gore movies. It appears that the strange "rawness" of *Oldboy* appeals to
the cult taste of the site users and this further suggests that the users of this site share
Knowles's cult tastes. In conjunction with winning the Grand Prix at Cannes, this
acknowledgement by AintItCool.com boosted the online fandom of *Oldboy*.

After it incited passionate discussion on AintItCool.com, *Oldboy* attracted
critical attention from other horror, fantasy, and science-fiction film websites, such as
BeyondHollywood.com, Moria.co.nz, Bloody-Disgusting.com, and HorrorReview.
com. Many of these sites selected *Oldboy* as one of the top ten films of the year and gave
outstanding reviews of its horror and gore aspects (Moria.co.nz 2003; Horrorreview.

com 2005a). For instance, the film received five skulls out of five on the "horror meter" at Bloody-Disgusting.com and three out of four stars for its "scary factor" from HorrorReview.com. Horror Bob, a reviewer and webmaster of HorrorReview. com, states that "so far, *Oldboy* is the best film I've seen in this year ... It's a must for all fans of Asian horror films and Asian films in general to see" (HorrorReview.com 2005b). Another reviewer, Mr Disgusting from Bloody-Disgusting.com, writes that "*Oldboy* is pure shock cinema that would have Takashi Miike on his knees. Director Chan-Wook Park is quickly making a name for himself in the Asian cult cinema community ... the blood level is intense and the use of gore is frightening" (Bloody-Disgusting.com 2005).[4] The film was first recognized by genre film sites due to its gore and horror aspects, and gained online popularity especially among Asian horror and Asian cult film fans. Later, as the film was released in cinemas in many countries and gained the attention of wider audiences, its online popularity expanded and it reached mainstream major film sites such as IMDb.com and RottenTomatoes.com. The film received 8.3 out of 10 from the "user rating" at IMDb.com, and a 82% rating from the "User Tomatometer" of RottenTomatoes.com (IMDb.com 2003; RottenTomatoes.com 2005). As observed, *Oldboy* was the first South Korean film to spawn online fandom among Western audiences.

Three years later, Bong Joon-Ho's *The Host* followed almost the same footsteps as *Oldboy* in gaining online fandom. Firstly, the film was largely acknowledged by Western audiences through the Cannes International Film Festival. Then, just like *Oldboy*, *The Host* was also selected as one of the best ten films in 2006 by AintItCool.com. In AintItCool.com, Knowles posts: "*The Host* is the best full on monster movie since *Jaws*" (Knowles 2006). Because it became known as the first blockbuster scale South Korean film belonging to the "monster horror" genre to gain overseas popularity, various horror film sites besides AintItCool.com soon paid attention to it. At the end of 2006, many reviewers writing for these sites selected *The Host* as one of the top ten films of the year. In BeyondHollywood. com, a reviewer writes, "An old-fashioned monster movie with an Asian twist. This Korean genre entry deftly balances horror and gore with comedy and family values" (Gopal 2007). Another reviewer for the same website writes: "a monster rises out of the Han River and attacks Seoul, South Korea like *Godzilla* armed with really good special effects ... a thrilling popcorn selling horror movie in the tradition of *Jaws* that even echoes the post-Watergate politics of Spielberg's film with its own post-9/11 vibes" (Holcomb 2006). Many horror film sites recognize *The Host* mainly through its similarities with classic monster horror films such as *Jaws* and *Godzilla*, or through its classification as "Asian horror." Through these horror film sites, *The Host* has established its cult fandom, especially among Asian horror fans.

After *The Host* was officially released in many Western countries such as the US, France, and Australia, its online popularity expanded to wider audiences. In particular, since the film was introduced at the American Film Market in November

2006, it has come into the spotlight in some major US media such as the *LA Times*, due to its controversial anti-American aspects (MBC 2006). This publicity attracted the attention of many audiences in the US, the biggest film market in the world, and initiated online critical debates among web-users. In March 2007, *The Host* was commercially released on 116 screens in fifteen different cities of the US; the film had indeed reached mainstream audiences in addition to the cult fan audience of Asian horror films (E. J. Kang 2007; H. L. Kim 2007).[5] Mainstream audiences began discussing the film on general film sites such as IMDb.com and RottenTomatoes.com. The expanded online fandom of *The Host* is evident from these major film sites where the film gained high viewer approval ratings; it obtained a rating of 7.4 out of 10 from IMDb.com and 7.7 out of 10 from RottenTomatoes. com (IMDb 2006; RottenTomatoes.com 2007). As observed, *The Host* had indeed expanded the online popularity of South Korean genre films among the Western audiences that *Oldboy* had initially reached.

Film Review Websites

Film review websites mainly contain film reviews, film-related news, and audience responses, and occasionally contain material related to DVDs, video games, and books. Some major film websites are operated by media entertainment corporations. For example, IMDb.com was acquired by Amazon.com in 1998 and RottenTomatoes.com was acquired by News Corporation in 2005. However, many of the film review sites are established and operated by individual film fans who also write the reviews. I have chosen to focus on two major websites — IMDb. com and RottenTomatoes.com — and three fan-operated review websites — AintItCool.com, BeyondHollywood.com, and TwitchFilm.net. These sites are generally well-known to the Western viewers who seek additional information about South Korean genre films on Internet websites. In particular, the three fan-operated websites are explicitly dedicated to genre films such as horror, thriller, fantasy, and foreign (particularly Asian) genre films. Many of these fan-operated websites have indeed become a site to acquire new cultural capital as they are the first to obtain the latest news about Asian genre films. Because they hold such valuable information and are accessed by many users everyday, these film sites have become more and more powerful in the fields of film criticism and film marketing. For instance, a number of Asian film distribution companies in the West consult the reviews and opinions on these websites. Even though most of the founders of these websites established these sites as fans of genre and/or Asian films, many of them are now considered to be genre or Asian film experts or online film critics. This slippage between fans and professional reviewers occurs partly because of media convergence: the grassroots merge with conventional media and the distance between the two parties diminishes or even vanishes (Jenkins 2006a: 1–3; Slevin

2000: 74–75). It shows how an individual film fan/reviewer can wield as much power as large media institutions because the Internet has redefined and blurred the boundaries of the conventional producer and receiver dichotomy.[6]

Five Film Review Websites

This section explicates the characteristics of five popular film review websites — IMDb.com, RottenTomatoes.com, AintItCool.com, BeyondHollywood.com, and TwitchFilm.net — to show their substantial significance for demonstrating the Western fandom of contemporary South Korean genre films.

First, IMDb.com is an online database of information about movies, actors, production crew personnel, television shows, and video games. Because the site consists of the largest accumulation of user-based data about films online, it has become the primary site of choice for fans to collect and share information. In addition, the site has an active message board system. There are message boards found at the bottom of the webpage for each film entry in its database. Many of these are actively maintained through the discussion of each movie by its users. For *Oldboy* and *The Host*, there are active discussions on each message board that contain numerous user postings. In particular, on the *Oldboy* page, there are almost 600 user comments, with more than a thousand user postings on the message board; among these, some threads consist of more than 200 replies, demonstrating the active and varied discussions incited by this film (IMDb.com 2003). Hence, the user comments from IMDb.com provide some of the richest and most diverse audience responses to *Oldboy*.

Second, RottenTomatoes.com contains reviews, information, and news of movies and video games that are contributed by various commentators ranging from amateurs to professionals. It is one of the biggest film databases worldwide, as it holds more than 127,000 titles and 644,000 reviews with 5.4 million readers each month. At the bottom of each webpage in the site is a section for user ratings and reviews. Directly below that section is a message board where site users discuss the particular film. Through these user ratings and discussions, it is possible to assess the general overseas popularity of *Oldboy* and *The Host*. However, the message board is not as active as that of IMDb.com since there are less than a dozen threads for each film. Although it does not provide a range of opinions from audiences, this site is useful for analyzing professional film reviews. There are 221 such reviews and articles for *Oldboy* and 175 such reviews and articles for *The Host* (RottenTomatoes.com 2005; 2007). In particular, some major film reviewers such as Roger Ebert (*Chicago Sun-Times*), Desson Thomson and Stephen Hunter (*Washington Post*), Derek Elley (*Variety*), and Lisa Schwarzbaum (*Entertainment Weekly*) are listed in a sub-listing called "Cream of the Crop" that compiles their reviews. Hence, I mainly use this site as a source of professional comments on the films. Apart from these reputable film reviewers from major media companies under "Cream of the Crop," there are various minor media reviewers (mostly online) such as DVDTalk.com, Reel.com, and SciFiMoviePage.com. As I explained earlier, some of the reviews of these online reviewers are relatively amateurish and can probably be considered web-users' comments. Therefore, I will regard the comments of these minor online film reviewers as coming from ordinary site users.

Third, AintItCool.com is, as mentioned above, a popular website founded and run by the online film critic, Harry Knowles. The site is dedicated to news and reviews of upcoming films and television programs with an emphasis on science fiction, fantasy, horror, and action genre films. This emphasis means that the site targets fans with more specific interests than IMDb.com or RottenTomatoes.com. The site contains film news, reviews, and internet chats, with more than a dozen site contributors posting articles and reviews. "Readers Talkback," which is located below each posted page, allows the site users to critique the review and article offered. The site — where film buffs and "geeks," including "the head geek," Knowles, participate in lively debates — is often criticized by many conventional media for its low standard of attempting to confirm and spread rumor and gossip. Despite such charges of having low standards, this site is essential for examining the internet fandom of *Oldboy* and *The Host*. Not only was it the first of the film sites to introduce both films to genre film fans in the West on a large scale, it is also a site that is dedicated to horror and fantasy films and is therefore a rich site to examine the Western cult fandom of South Korean horror films.

Fourth, BeyondHollywood.com offers movie reviews of non-American films for the English-reading public, with a major emphasis on Asian films. Significantly, BeyondHollywood.com contains a collection of reviews of Asian, foreign, independent, and genre, and especially horror, films that are rarely reviewed elsewhere. In particular, this site pays special attention to rare titles of South Korean cinema. For example, they have reviews of internationally less known 1980s South Korean films such as *Wanderer in Winter* (*Gyeoul Nageune* 1986), *Gagman* (*Gaegeumaen* 1989), and *The Black Republic* (*Geudeuldo Uricheoreom* 1990). The main home page is also linked to web sites on South Korean cinema via a Google advertising program. This site is relatively less organized and poorly maintained, compared with the aforementioned websites. In fact, it is difficult to search for films by genres or any other features because the site has a crucial problem in classifying the titles it holds. This problem perhaps arises because the site is largely operated by a web-master, who is also the main reviewer, with minor help from a few contributors. It also seems difficult to find user opinions because there is no separate forum or message board on this website. Nevertheless, BeyondHollywood.com is useful for demonstrating the current online fandom of South Korean genre film among Western audiences due to its vast archive of South Korean films.

Fifth, TwitchFilm.net is, according to the site's introduction, "a film news, review, [and] discussion site that pays particular attention to independent, cult, foreign, and genre films." Specifically, this site is dedicated to foreign horror and gore films. Unlike many other horror and cult film sites, which mainly focus on Japanese horror or Hong Kong action films while including South Korean films as more of an adjunct, TwitchFilm.net predominantly focuses on South Korean horror films as well as other South Korean genre films. Among the thirty-six official contributors, there are four South Korean film specialists, more than the average number of film specialists that TwitchFilm.net has for any other country (TwitchFilm.net 2007). They update South Korean film news on the website almost at the same time as the South Korean local media. For general user comments, there is a separate discussion forum. Because this site started later than the above four sites (2005), there is only a small number of postings on its discussion board. In particular, there are very limited discussions on *Oldboy* because the site was launched only after the film had already achieved global and online popularity. However, compared with the users of the aforementioned sites, the users of TwitchFilm.net are well informed and display a rich knowledge of South Korean genre films. In addition, they show an awareness of new media technologies. For instance, one of the users posted a report on the different picture qualities between the limited edition *Oldboy* HD-DVD and the ordinary *Oldboy* DVD. Therefore, TwitchFilm.net is valuable for looking at the new technology-driven cinephiliac cult fandom of *Oldboy*.

Additional South Korean Cinema–Related Websites

Among the above mentioned five websites, the two most recently launched ones, BeyondHollywood.com (2003) and TwitchFilm.net (2005), provide relatively rich information on South Korean cinema. In particular, TwitchFilm.net holds the most up-to-date and detailed information about South Korean genre directors and their works. These websites reflect the emerging Western cult fandom of South Korean genre films. Such Western cult fandom is also evident from another group of film websites which explicitly use the terms, "extreme Asia" and "Asian cult," to categorize South Korean genre films: for example, AsianCultCinema.com, AsianCultCinema. co.uk, and AsiaExtremeFilms.com. The first two are mainly DVD sales websites, selling rare titles from some of the most well-known Asian countries that produce genre films. For instance, on AsianCultCinema.co.uk, there are separate DVD categories for the four main countries it deals with, namely, Hong Kong, Japan, South Korea, and Thailand. AsianCultCinema.com seems to have originated from the similarly named off-line magazine, *Asian Cult Cinema*, published by Vital Books Inc. According to the website, "Vital Books Inc. is not only the publisher of various books and *Asian Cult Cinema* magazine, but also a leading importer of rare DVDs from all over the world. These DVDs play on any American machine and are English friendly."[7] Hence, it is clear that this website is operated by a US company that mainly targets the US fans of Asian cult films. However, I do not examine in detail these two websites because they only focus on DVD sales, and do not contain reviews or viewer comments. AsiaExtremeFilms.com, on the other hand, does contain some reviews. However, I do not consider this website because it has very few reviews. I only refer to these websites to demonstrate the current cult fandom of Asian films in the West.

As well as the abovementioned websites, there are several older websites dedicated to South Korean cinema such as KoreanFilm.org and HanCinema.net. However, these are South Korean–based English-language websites whose major focus is on providing South Korean film news and data to non–South Korean audiences. In particular, HanCinema.net is dedicated to South Korean television dramas rather than movies, thus targeting the regional *Hallyu* drama fans rather than Western viewers. KoreanFilm.org was launched in 1999 by Darcy Paquet. The site has been considered to be the best database and a quality source of contemporary South Korean film information for non–South Korean filmgoers. However, in this chapter, I will not discuss KoreanFilm.org in depth because the site is more likely to show insiders' views, rather than the emerging interest of global (mostly Western) audiences. Even though this website still contains transnational and multicultural content (e.g., a discussion board), I excluded it because of its different provenance. Therefore, in this chapter, I mainly cite user comments on *Oldboy* from the five film websites: IMDb.com, RottenTomatoes.com, AintItCool.com, BeyondHollywood. com, and TwitchFilm.net.

Site Users, New Cinephiles

The main characteristic of these site users can be conceptualized through David Desser's idea of "the new cinephilia" (2005: 205–21). *Cinephilia* is a term derived from the combination of the words *cinema* and *phile* (a Greek word for *love*) and refers to the love of cinema. This term has been used to describe the cinema-going phenomenon among young people and university students that first became visible in the 1950s in France. In her seminal article, "The Decay of Cinema," Susan Sontag explains:

> [Cinema's] forum was the legendary film magazine *Cahiers du Cinéma* (followed by similarly fervent magazines in Germany, Italy, Great Britain, Sweden, the US and Canada). Its temples, as it spread throughout Europe and the Americas, were the many cinémathèques and clubs specializing in films from the past and directors' retrospectives that sprang up. The 1960's and early 1970's [were] the feverish age of movie-going, with the full-time cinephile always hoping to find a seat as close as possible to the big screen, ideally the third row center. (1996)

Paul Willemen, in *Looks and Frictions*, finds evidence of an earlier cinephilic movement by examining the term *photogénie*, which appeared in the writings of Riciotto Canudo, Louis Delluc, René Schwob, René Clair, and Jean Epstein; they use the term to describe the French "impressionist" cinema that flourished between 1918 and 1928 (Bordwell cited in Willemen 1994: 124). "*Photogénie* was promoted as 'the law of cinema' (Delluc), and as 'the purest expression of cinema' (Epstein)" (1994: 124). Broadly speaking, it was explained as a mysterious and indefinable something present in the cinematic image which differentiated cinema from all other art forms and therefore "constituted the very foundation of cinematic art" (1994: 124). Willemen observes that *photogénie* is closely related to a viewer's aesthetic, as the term "mobilized to demarcate one set of viewers — those able to 'see' — from others" (1994: 126). He argues that the origins of cinephilia are to be found in those who believed that *photogénie* is the quintessence of cinema. In a word, cinephiles are said to be those who are sensitive enough to perceive what others cannot see, namely, the essence of cinema.

The notion of cinephilia is anchored on the sense of superiority that is based on being able to see what others are unable to see. This sense of superiority, however, is not only derived from the ability to tell the difference "between ordinary and extraordinary" but also from the access to the extraordinary. According to David Desser, this accessibility is enhanced by the development of new media technology, access to which is a fundamental requirement for the new cinephiles. He writes:

> Festival screenings, videotape, DVD, VCD, Internet sales sites and web-based discussion groups have facilitated the transnational flow of films. In particular, the introduction of the VCR in the early 1980s and the VCD in the mid-1990s may be marked as those moments where the new cinephilia took root. In both instances Hong Kong cinema was at the heart of this new global network of cinephiles. (2005: 209)

The new cinephilia, according to Desser, took root in the development of new media technologies, such as DVDs and the Internet, that enable global audiences to access extraordinary, non-Hollywood films. Desser further argues that the cult popularity of John Woo, in particular, and Hong Kong action cinema, in general, is the driving force behind the new cinephilia. He then explains that VCD, DVD, and commercial sales websites enable globalized (particularly Euro-American) audiences who prefer action and horror genres to become web-based cinephiles.

Desser's description of the new cinephiles as globalized and driven by digital technology can be further elaborated using Henry Jenkins's concept of "pop cosmopolitanism" (2006b: 152–72). Jenkins argues that a "pop cosmopolitan" is one who embraces global popular culture as an escape from the parochialism of her or his local community (2006b: 152). Pop cosmopolitanism refers to "the ways that the transcultural flows of popular culture inspire new forms of global consciousness and cultural competency" (2006b: 156). He explains:

> Much as teens in the developing world use American popular culture to express generational differences or to articulate fantasies of social, political, and cultural transformation, younger Americans are distinguishing themselves from their parents' culture through their consumption of Japanese anime and manga, Bollywood films and Bhangra, and Hong Kong action movies. (2006b: 156)

Jenkins also uses the term "Asiaphilia" to describe the globalized consumption of Asian popular culture by Euro-American fans. According to him, the Asiaphiliac pop cosmopolitan "walks a thin line between dilettantism and connoisseurship, between [O]rientalistic fantasies and a desire to honestly connect and understand an alien culture, between assertion of mastery and surrender to cultural difference" (2006b: 164). His explanation suggests that Westerners ambivalently practice Orientalism and globalism in consuming Asian popular culture. This notion of "pop cosmopolitanism" clearly relates to the aforementioned concept of the "time between dog and wolf" during the contemporary hybrid postmodern era, when Western audiences embrace *Oldboy* and its character of Dae-Soo with a blend of Orientalist fantasies and the desire for "cool" alien culture.

Extreme Asian Cinema Fans: The Orientalist Point of View

Western Orientalist fantasies are evident in the frenetic online cult fandom of *Oldboy*, where film site users predominantly favor the film's transgressive and violent content. Underpinning this frenetic reception of *Oldboy* is the recent Western fandom of Asian horror genre films, which are also often categorized as "extreme Asian cinema." According to Steve Neale, genre categorization is frequently employed for marketing purposes; as he states, genres serve as "basic and convenient units" to ensure the maximum capacity in producing profit (cited in Watson 2007). It is a useful method for attracting the existing audiences of certain genres. South Korean genre films are no exception. There are several examples of "extreme Asian" film categorization.

The first example is found from a separate label of "Tartan Asia Extreme" on the website of the UK DVD sales company, Tartan Video. Tartan Asia Extreme, which promotes films from Hong Kong, Japan, South Korea, and Thailand and mainly focuses on horror, thriller, and action genres. The site, however, also introduces Asian melodramas, comedies, and even European art-house films, all of which have nothing to do with "extreme" features. This looseness in the classification of films suggests that the website regularly uses the term "extreme" to attract existing Asian genre film fans. The best example occurs in the section of the Asia Extreme Collection webpage of the website where the title of the film, *In the Mood for Love* (2000), an art-house film by Hong Kong director Wong Kar Wai, first appears.

Another example of how films are loosely classified under the label of "extreme Asian films" is found in the promotion trailer for the television broadcast of a series of movies by an Australian television company, SBS (Special Broadcasting Service). In October 2007, SBS hosted a movie series that was called "Korean Extreme," which consisted of *Oldboy, Memories of Murder, A Good Lawyer's Wife*, and *Spring Summer Fall Winter and Spring*. In fact, apart from *Oldboy*, none of these movies contain features that could be described as "extreme." This is a good example of the way the West conventionally uses an "extreme" title for any Asian film to target the existing cult fans of Asian genre (mostly horror) films. *Memories of Murder* is a crime thriller and contains only mild depictions of violence. *Spring Summer Fall Winter and Spring* is a meditative "Buddhist-themed" film and not extreme at all except during the moment when a boy is shown torturing a frog. *A Good Lawyer's Wife* is a melodrama that contains many sex scenes that also do not contain any extreme features. Nevertheless, the television trailer presents the movie series as extreme by extracting and creating a collage of the most striking and sensational sequences from the films with big red Korean characters.[8] From the above two examples of *Tartan Asia Extreme* and the presentation of the SBS "Korean Extreme" series, it is evident that the label of "extreme" is strategically employed to target the cult film fans of the West.

Another example of the categorization of Asian films as "extreme Asian" is seen in the ways in which Asian filmmakers are titling their own genre films. Some Asian producers and directors make heavy use of the label of "extreme Asia" to market their works to Western fans. For example, as the cult boom of Asian horror continues to infiltrate Western markets, some ambitious producers have put together an anthology featuring three of the key instigators of the cult horror trend in three Asian countries: the film *Three Extremes* (*Saam Gaang Yi* 2004) contains short works by Hong Kong's Fruit Chan, Japan's Miike Takashi, and South Korea's Park Chan-Wook. Each segment depicts events of horror and fantasy in everyday life.[9] *Three Extremes* achieved widespread recognition in the West, as is shown by the fifty-nine reviews by media critics and a high rating of 86% from the Critics Tomatometer on RottenTomatoes.com. *Three Extremes* is a sequel to an original attempt, *Three* (*Saam Gaang* 2002), which features short films by Hong Kong's Peter Chan, Thailand's Nonzee Nimibutr, and South Korea's Kim Ji-Woon. Even though *Three* preceded *Three Extremes*, it was released under the title of *Three Extremes 2* in the West in 2006, four years after its initial release in Asia. This re-titling is further evidence of the way the label "Extreme Asia" is strategically used to target Asian cult film fans in the West.

The last example of the categorization of Asian films as "extreme Asian" is found from a film collection box set, the *Asian Cult Cinema Extreme Horror Collection*. This is a collection of four Japanese horror movies: *Organ* (1996), *Evil Dead Trap* (1988), *Entrails of a Virgin* (1986), and *Entrails of a Beautiful Woman* (1986). The DVD distribution company, Synapse Films, deploys every marketing term — such as "Asian cult," "extreme," and "horror" — used in advertising Asian cult films to appeal to existing Western fans of the genre. Due to such strategies, it is almost always the first title to appear on DVD sales websites when users attempt to search for films using the keywords "Asian cult," "Asian horror," or "extreme Asian movies." As the four film titles suggest, this film collection contains appalling depictions of organ-harvesting, gang rape, gore, and dismemberment. These graphic contents illustrate what the fans expect from extreme Asian titles. These fans specifically look for elements of transgression that are not generally available in mainstream Hollywood films.

In his article, "Cult Fictions: Cult Movies, Subcultural Capital and the Production of Cultural Distinctions," Mark Jankovich argues that cult movie fandom often derives from a sense of subcultural identity originating in the fans' supposed difference from the mainstream (2002: 318–19). Here, a film gains cult status when it displays cultural differences that deviate from the mainstream values of Hollywood productions. Therefore, fans identify themselves through a subcultural identity that is defined "against the supposed obscene accessibility of mass culture" (Thornton cited in Jankovich 2002: 309). The exclusive knowledge of the fans and their consumption of films perceived to be inaccessible to the mainstream strengthen their sense of difference from the mainstream. In other words, the notion of cult fandom involves a rejection of the commercial mainstream and a predilection for the rare and the exclusive. Another way to define cult fandom could be as an "alternative," "subversive," and "transgressive" subculture. Even though Jankovich states that cult film fans "do not share a single, and certainly not a uniformly oppositional, attitude towards legitimate culture," there is a clear indication of an inclination towards a transgressive subcultural ideology among cult film fans (2002: 314). He explains that the origin of cult movie fandom started during the 1950s with the spectatorship of art films in New York, where the most lauded films were foreign and contained "themes and materials which were supposedly unavailable or even taboo within [the] Hollywood product" (2002: 316). In this sense, it is possible to say that the Western cult fandom of extreme Asian cinema can be explained through the socio-cultural framework of the consumption of "difference" and "transgression." For these fans, difference and transgression are often the two most important factors in assessing the status and value of a cult film.

It is evident that Western fans value *Oldboy* for these two factors. Firstly, the difference factor is evident in that film site users claim that *Oldboy* is a good movie because it is different from mainstream Hollywood productions. A user decisively states that "You cannot compare this masterpiece with Hollywood crap" and many users express similar opinions. Cksdayoff, from IMDb.com, writes: "Let's not put *Kill Bill* ... in the same sentence as *Oldboy*. *Kill Bill* ... [is a] garbage flick ..." (posted on July 10, 2007). Under a thread titled, "Better than Transformers," another user, mjensen-3, writes:

> No offen[c]e, but you just created one of the most idiotic comparisons of all time. Look, *Transformers* is a great pop-corn flick. It's something to watch, and to be entertained by. Nothing to take seriously. *Oldboy* is a serious, dramatic, epic, and completely character driven. It is [a] masterpiece. If you can't tell the difference between two films, th[e]n you're a dumbass. (posted on July 28, 2007)

Mjensen-3 writes that the Hollywood action blockbuster, *Transformers*, is a great pop-corn flick while *Oldboy* is a serious epic masterpiece and that they are two "different" kinds of film. S/he then declares that anyone who cannot tell the difference deserves to be called "a dumbass." This statement implies that s/he draws a clear distinction between her/himself, a cult film fan who can tell the difference, and "you," the mainstream film viewer, who is unable to make this distinction. This quote reflects the way that Asian cult film fans construct a sense of difference to distinguish themselves from mainstream audiences.

Secondly, the transgression factor is another quality film site users commonly invoke to identify themselves as cult fans of extreme Asian cinema. Because they are supposed to be fans of transgressive and taboo-breaking materials, the users display their subcultural tastes for the exotic by demonstrating their relaxed acceptance of these materials. Many of them indeed claim that the transgressive content of *Oldboy* — the violent scenes and the incestuous theme — is not shocking at all; rather, they insist that these transgressive elements enhance the film. For example, a user, Liain, started a thread in IMDb.com entitled, "Disgusting!!!!" (May 7, 2007) and explains that s/he was disgusted by the ending when the truth of the incestuous relationships between brother and sister and father and daughter is revealed. There are almost sixty replies attached to the thread, mostly arguing against Liain. One of them says, "The ending made it better no matter how 'gross'" (July 19, 2007, Rosebud16). Another poster, truheart 1, writes:

> This is a great movie that I've shown others and they always want to see it again. The ending is a complete shock to everyone who sees it. It's not shock for shock[']s sake. It's a completely engrossing story that throws you in so many different directions that by the time you find out the truth it is not what you expected at all. This is what a good movie should do. Watching this movie is almost like reading a great book because no matter how strange it gets you just have to know what comes next. (July 3, 2007)

The user, employing affirmative words like "good" and "great," explains that the transgressive theme of incest makes the film more engrossing. S/he then declares that watching this transgressive movie is almost like reading a "great" book because its strangeness evokes the suspense of waiting for what has to come next. Here, the user suggests that strangeness and transgression form the quintessence of a good cult movie.

Western audiences construct the cult fandom of *Oldboy* through the cultural consumption of difference and transgression, which appears to have nothing to do with Orientalism at first glance. This particular cult fandom of *Oldboy*, however, is based upon a new form of Orientalism — neo-Orientalism — where Western audiences fetishize and desire the different and transgressive modern aspects of *Oldboy* as "Asian extreme cinema." In *The Turbulence of Migration: Globalization, Deterritorialization and Hybridity*, Nikos Papastergiadis argues that, given the predominantly Eurocentric environment of contemporary art, many non-Euro-American art practices, which display a complex negotiation between tradition and modernity, are often relegated to the margins and labeled as "ethnic art" or "neo-primitivism" (2000: 133–34). He also points out that this Eurocentric perspective locates non-Euro-American artworks elsewhere, in the field of "the Other," and that it fetishizes the artist from the margins (2000: 133–34). His comment clarifies the way Western audiences fetishize *Oldboy* by relegating the film to the margins and labeling it as "extreme Asian cinema." This classification highlights the Western perception of *Oldboy* as harboring an alien presence, a film whose unfamiliar Otherness is paradoxically greeted with enthusiasm by Western audiences. The film's main qualities of difference and transgression, which are the preconditions by which it achieves cult status, become the qualities of the fetishized Other. A good example is found in the user comments section of IMDb. com. One of the users, Teebs2, posts:

> *Oldboy* (2003) is the latest, and possibly most critically acclaimed, of a series of films to come out of Asia, which are best described as "Extreme." They are all very slick, stylish, violent and taboo-breaking to an almost self-conscious level ... In terms of sensation and brutal violence such films as Takashi Miike's cartoon-like *Ichi the Killer* (2001) or the brilliant *Audition* (1999) are unsurpassed by any Western cinema. *Oldboy* comes close with much tooth-pulling, hammer battering, tongue cutting and live octopus eating, but nothing which quite matches the sadistic, absurd violence in Miike's films. (June 9, 2005)

Another user, Joe3_98, posts, "[Asian films] such as *Battle Royale*, *Oldboy* and *Infernal Affairs* have been nothing but immature, violent, embarrassing efforts" (June 10, 2007). Mapet6, from the same website, also posts, "Every Asian film I've seen ... has one or two ludicrous violent scenes thrown in, like without them it wouldn't signify an Asian film" (May 10, 2007). These three viewers explicitly point out that *Oldboy* is "violent," just as other Asian films are. They fetishize *Oldboy* and other so-called extreme Asian movies by highlighting only their transgressive features of violence and gruesomeness. Instead of looking at the various cinematic qualities the film possesses, for example, the theme that revenge (violence) is dangerous and that it gets people nowhere, these users focus only on the violent aspects of the film.

In particular, Teebs2's comparison of *Oldboy* and other extreme Asian films directed by Miike Takashi is exclusively based on their level of "sadistic and absurd" violence. From the posting, it is evident that the only aspect of *Oldboy* that this user focuses on is its "violent content." The film's other qualities, such as its genre, themes, characters, editing, music, and set-design, do not appear to have any significance for this user. The only feature that is focused on is the film's degree of violence because *Oldboy* is fetishized as extreme Asian cinema. As audiences highlight and only focus on its violence, the film becomes a fetishized object; this narrow focus exemplifies the cult fantasies of audiences. By cult fantasies, I mean the alternative narratives and scenarios engendered about Asian (and in particular, South Korean) culture by the cult imagination of Western cult film fans as fed by neo-Orientalism.

Global Pop Consumers: The New Media Technology Point of View

In the earlier section, I referred to David Desser's and Henry Jenkins's analysis of the recent Euro-American (Western) fandom of Asian popular culture within the framework of global popular cultural flows. Desser argues that in consuming genre films from Asia, new and young cinephilic Western audiences complement their desires for Asian cinema with digital technology that is capable of consuming and retransmitting these desires on the web (2005: 213). This notion of new cinephiles as cosmopolitans driven by advanced technology is also supported by Barbara Klinger. In *Beyond the Multiplex*, Klinger suggests that the emergence of the contemporary cinephile is related to the development of new media technologies such as home theaters and DVD markets (2006: 54–90). Klinger writes:

> Seated in front of the television set, today's [film] collector is a member of a corps of impassioned film devotees who are, like Metz's cinephile, "enchanted at what the machine is capable of," that is, mesmerized by the machines of reproduction that deliver the cinematic illusion. However, the mesmerizing apparatuses in this case are not the camera, projector, and screen related to the exhibition of celluloid, but the accoutrement[s] associated with cinema playback in the home. The contemporary film collector's romance with various technological aspects of the films and machines that make up the experience of cinema in domestic space suggests that cinephilia has been broadened to encompass the "forbidden" territories of television and the home. (2006: 55)

Focusing on newly emerging DVD collectors and home theater owners, Klinger argues that the obsession of this new group of film collectors with technology demonstrates that the desire for cinema is inextricably linked with the desire for the newest and best technology. Like Desser, she also points out that this new group of collectors is fascinated by rare titles and imported cult titles. Unlike Desser, who emphasizes the obsession of globalized youth fans with Asian genre films (specifically, Hong Kong action films), Klinger emphasizes these fans' passion for hardware, the home theater system, and the DVD collection.

Her point is evident in a thread on the TwitchFilm.net forum, where web-users discuss adapting HD television and HD-DVDs under the title, "Have you made the jump to HD/Blue-Ray?" Collin A, one of the forum users, says, "We're running both HD formats at home (both through video game systems) on a 37" display that tops out at 1080i ... HD-DVD seems a might[y] bit sharper" (July 27, 2007). Another user, Nemo, writes:

> I have HD DVD add on for XBOX 360 and PS3 for BR, Netflix already has decent selection (200+) both formats. having 700+ DVDs I only replacing a few (Gilliam, Burton, Kubri[c]k) ... Just got *Fountain*, *The Host* and ordered *300* ($15 from Columbia House). I was very impressed with an amazing transfer of old movie's [sic] (*Casablanca*, *The Thing*, *Forbidden Planet*). With HDDVD player for $238 (Amazon) and 5 free movies, it is a must buy for every HD TV owner. (July 27, 2007)

These site users freely discuss the most up-dated information about HD television and HD-DVDs, using technological jargon and demonstrating their knowledge of new media technology. The above postings also show that they are early adapters who are quick to take up high technology. Both users encourage other users to adapt these new devices, saying that "it is a must buy" or "it seems sharper." Most importantly, they actively utilize such newly adapted technologies and related knowledge to maximize the enjoyment of their movie-watching experience. Such web discussions demonstrate that the acquisition of new technology and the skills to be able to manipulate this new technology contribute to the construction of the new cinephilia, along with the global cosmopolitanism of the site users.

The privileged accessibility of these new cinephiles to new media technology often creates elitism. The cinephiles commonly show an attitude which implies, "I know something you don't know." This elitism is based on their special knowledge of relatively unknown Asian cult films, a knowledge acquired through watching many movies, reading magazines and reviews, obtaining rare DVDs, and participating in online community postings. As explained earlier, some site users convey this sense of superiority over ordinary film viewers. For example, one of the users, kyle-morrison-1, from IMDb.com, compares *Oldboy* with *Saw* (2004), a Hollywood slasher movie; another user, truejordan, argues against this comparison by posting: "I feel like your friend that's comparing it to *Saw* is really missing something ... The kind of [disturbing] situation presented goes back to Sophocles' Oedipus and these kinds of situations still resonate just as powerfully today as they did in ancient Greece (Shakespeare later played with similarly horrifying revelations in 'Titus Andronicus')" (July 23, 2007). Truejordan's elitism is evident in this response to the less well-informed kyle-morrison-1. Truejordan may have collected in-depth information about *Oldboy* through reading various reviews and articles from internet film sites. Another example of the elitism of new cinephiles is found in another posting of pmathewson from IMDb.com:

> "You see, they say that people shrivel up because they have an imagination. So, don't imagine anything, you'll become brave as hell" [quoted from *Oldboy*].
>
> You gotta love the irony of that line in a film where not much gore or sex is shown yet people imagine more horror than was actually presented. Disgusting? Sure but no more disgusting than many Greek tragedies. This film is masterful and yet I found it a challenge to really embrace it due to some of the "disgusting" bits. Personally, I find any film that challenges me like that earns my seal of approval. Usually I don't watch movies with a twist ending more than once but it was executed so masterfully that I've made an exception for *Oldboy*. That's saying a lot. (August 7, 2007)

At the beginning of the post, pmathewson quotes the words of the owner of the private prison in *Oldboy* and states that he finds the quoted line ironic. The irony arises because while the quote espouses the idea that one can become braver by not imagining anything, the film itself actually causes viewers to become less brave because they are led to imagine more by the film's selectiveness in presenting certain elements of gore and sex that stimulate the imagination. By quoting a detailed line from the film, this user demonstrates that s/he knows *Oldboy* better than other users. For the same reason, this user also refers to Greek tragedies as relevant to the film's main plot. The exact quote and information might have been gained from "*Oldboy* Three-Disc Ultimate Collector's Edition," possibly bought from an online DVD sales website or maybe even from a pirated DVD rented from a grocery shop in a Korea town. The user then conveys how difficult it is for a film to obtain her/his "seal of approval" as a film worth watching, emphasizing the mastery required to discover a good film, and implying the possession of a special skill which differentiates her/him from ordinary audiences. Such postings show the elitism of new cinephiles, possibly driven by their globalized pop consumer lifestyles.

Further evidence of the globalized consumption practice of site users is seen in their understanding of and familiarization with South Korean culture. Transcultural new media flows diminish the distance between "us" (Western site users) and "them" (South Korean culture), and construct a new order of global interaction where users perceive South Korean culture as something desirable and consumable. For example, many users explain that they have become fond of South Korean cinema and its characters ever since they began watching the films. A user from IMDb.com, NickNaylor, says "I really want to see more Korean films because I think they're fantastic!" Under this thread, many other users declare that they are now big fans of "kickass" and "awesome" South Korean films. By using these expressions of approval, these users demonstrate their new taste for South Korean cinema, and possibly South Korean culture, on the internet. As the quotation from the Melbourne fan, Gu, at the very beginning of this chapter clearly showed, some of the users may have had negative impressions of Korea previously, created largely by narrow media images of Korea as being characterized by the Korean War, fierce student protests, and extreme poverty. The approving expressions of the site users on IMDb.com, however, show that they now have a positive desire for South Korea and South Korean culture. This desire arises from their construction and sharing of a notion of Koreanness as "fantastic" through the buying, watching, and online discussion of South Korean films.

In particular, the comments of some users exemplify the way that they identify with the new South Korean masculinity that is represented by *Oldboy*'s male protagonist, Dae-Soo. It appears that such identification is largely related with their gendered specificity as young males. Under the thread title of "Top #5 Coolest Characters" on IMDb.com, Alex_DeLarge_666 nominates Dae-Soo along with four other "super cool" Hollywood characters: Tyler Durden from *Fight Club*, Riddick from *Pitch Black*, Vincent Vega from *Pulp Fiction*, and Tony Montana from *Scarface* (August 18, 2007). Another user, amina456, states, "*A Bitter Sweet Life* really kicks ass and the lead actor is just totally hot." This posting is a clear indication that Western male viewers now harbor a new longing for South Korean masculinity. Described as sexually "hot" and "cool," Western male viewers, to some extent, seem to identify themselves with this desirable image of South Korean masculinity. Again, as the earlier quotation from the Melbourne fan, Gu, shows, the image of the "cool" Dae-Soo character diverges sharply from pre-existing images of Korea and Korean culture. In other words, due to the global cultural flows that are enabled by postmodern pop consumerism, Western audiences now consider South Korean masculinity, once undesirable because marginalized, as "totally consumably hot and/or cool." This newly manifested Western desire for South Korean masculinity constitutes a characteristic of the new web-based cinephiles, whose views are influenced by technology-driven global pop consumerism.

Oldboy and Western Ambivalent Desires for South Korean Postmodern Masculinity

Park Chan-Wook's *Oldboy* was first released in 2003 in South Korea. Since 2004, it has gradually been released in forty-one countries worldwide (Park et al. 2005: 10–11). The film's local and global releases created controversy because of the film's themes of incest and graphic violence. At the film's beginning, Oh Dae-Soo, a middle-aged office worker, who is also the film's main protagonist, disappears on a rainy night. He has been kidnapped by unseen and unknown captors and will be held captive for fifteen years in a private prison cell. In the cell, his only "companion" is a television set and while watching it, he learns that he is wanted for the murder of his wife. After failing to commit suicide a couple of times, he starts writing diaries to examine his past, hoping to discover the reasons for his present confinement. He develops extraordinary fighting skills by undergoing a rigorous physical training regime, and gradually becomes an unfeeling fighting machine. Suddenly released on the eve of staging his own breakout, he receives a wallet full of cash and a mobile phone. His tormentor, Woo-Jin, calls him and makes a deal with Dae-Soo: if Dae-Soo can determine in five days the reasons for his imprisonment, then Woo-Jin will kill himself, but if Dae-Soo fails, then the people that Dae-Soo loves will die. With the help of Mi-Do, a female chef whom Dae-Soo meets at a sushi restaurant on the night of his release, Dae-Soo slowly figures out why he had been imprisoned from various clues and discovers the tragic truth: Mi-Do, the woman whom Dae-Soo falls in love with, is his own daughter. This tragedy, indeed, is Woo-Jin's ultimate revenge: Because Woo-Jin believes that Dae-Soo's gossip had caused Woo-Jin's sister's suicide, Woo-Jin manipulates Dae-Soo into having an incestuous relationship with his own daughter, as Woo-Jin had had with his own sister.

This confronting tragedy portrays Dae-Soo as a Kafkaesque hero who rages against fate and who takes such violent revenge that it becomes transgressive. It is evident that the transgressive and ultra-violent Dae-Soo resonates with fans within the framework of the West's ambivalent consumption of South Korean masculinity that is "savage but cool." This section examines two ways in which the ambivalent desire of Western viewers redefines and reconstructs South Korean masculinity: these ways are the desire for the primitive and the desire for the postmodern. As a neo-Orientalist practice, the former desire fetishizes the transgressive violence of Dae-Soo. As a *mugukjeok* practice, the latter desire seeks the familiarity of Dae-Soo's postmodern "coolness." The contrasting aspects of *mugukjeok* and neo-Orientalism in the Western identification with Dae-Soo show the ambivalent desires of Western viewers towards South Korean masculinity in postmodern time; this is the time when it is impossible to tell whether Dae-Soo is a familiar friend (dog) or a dangerous stranger (wolf).

South Korea, the Capital of Information Capitalism

Postmodern South Korean society is characterized by information capitalism. Information capitalism occurs when media communication technology is grafted onto a global capitalist system and when "information" has replaced manufacturing as the foundation of the economy (McChesney 1998: 1–26). As global capitalism enters a new era, new information technology plays an important role in capitalist economies as it provides access to skill, work, services, and commerce at a much lower cost and thereby generates greater economic profits. On the other hand, the application of electronic technology within the framework of capitalism could exacerbate capitalist exploitation of the poor and worsen social polarization (Davis et al. 1997: 3). In *Oldboy*, such exacerbated capitalist exploitation is exemplified by the ways the entrepreneur, Woo-Jin, torments the ordinary office worker, Dae-Soo. Woo-Jin, whose capitalist power enables him to employ advanced technological devices, is a perfect embodiment of capitalist South Korean information society. This embodiment is governed by two aspects of information capitalism: media communication technology and cybernetic technology.

Examples of Media Communication Technology

Surveillance cameras constitute the first example of media communication technology in *Oldboy*. In Dae-Soo's prison cell, for instance, surveillance cameras record Dae-Soo's movements twenty-four hours a day for fifteen years. These surveillance cameras, as well as the multi-screen displays that are linked to the cameras, are symbolic metaphors of Woo-Jin's capitalist supremacy as there is a high financial cost associated with building and maintaining a private prison cell with such advanced technology. It is this capitalist supremacy that gives Woo-Jin what seems like omnipotent control over Dae-Soo. From Dae-Soo's point of view, the cameras contribute to his almost-complete subjugation by Woo-Jin because he cannot even commit suicide without the prison guards' knowing. This situation of relentless surveillance exemplifies a postmodern technologically driven South Korean society where people can be easily exploited by the use of phone, digital, and surveillance cameras in public places.[10] An article (November 8, 2007) in the *Hankyoreh Shinmun* observes that more and more schools in South Korea have installed surveillance cameras for the purpose of preventing violence and theft (O. Y. Hah 2007). The article points out that "CCTV in schools is against human rights and violates the privacy of students." It can be argued that the cinematic reference to the use of surveillance cameras to monitor Dae-Soo twenty-four hours a day in *Oldboy* signifies the ways in which people in contemporary South Korean society are exploited by advanced media technologies.

The second example of media communication technology in *Oldboy* is the technological gadgetry in Woo-Jin's penthouse. The penthouse is furnished with advanced technology such as medical equipment, automated wardrobes, and a fully remote-controlled home theater system. In one of the scenes, Woo-Jin's personal doctor examines his health using the high-tech medical equipment in the penthouse as Woo-Jin watches pre-recorded video clips of Dae-Soo in the prison cell on a large ceiling television screen. At the same time, a computerized audio system is delivering real-time sound transmissions of Dae-Soo's actions and conversations to Woo-Jin via a bug in Dae-Soo's shoes. These multimedia devices allow Woo-Jin to penetrate and gain valuable information about Dae-Soo's past, present, and future, and demonstrate how Woo-Jin's capitalist power enables him to completely control Dae-Soo's life. Woo-Jin's penthouse, which is fully equipped with advanced media technology, illustrates contemporary South Korean society where multimedia contents from super-speed internet, MP3 players, and hundreds of cable television channels ubiquitously infiltrate the everyday lives of people.

The third example of media communication technology in *Oldboy* is the mobile phone. Near the end of the film, Dae-Soo finally finds out where Woo-Jin lives and the two men meet at Woo-Jin's penthouse. There, Woo-Jin reveals how he manipulated Dae-Soo into falling in love with Mi-Do by hiring the hypnotist, Mrs. Yoo, to hypnotize Dae-Soo and Mi-Do:

> Ever heard of posthypnotic suggestion? You suggest something during hypnosis and then it's acted out in your wakened state. Still haven't figure it out? ... We hypnotized both of you. One very fortunate thing was that both of you were highly receptive to hypnosis compared to others ... Your first suggestion was to go to that restaurant after your release. Next, to react to the mobile phone's melody. When you heard this, you were to say something ... And Mi-Do was to react to the man who were to say this. When she grabs your hand, your reaction would be ...

Then the film shows the previous scene of Dae-Soo where he suddenly collapses at the Japanese restaurant where he met Mi-Do for the first time. Here, Woo-Jin's revelation of the central role that the mobile phone played in his revenge against Dae-Soo can be interpreted in relation to the fact that South Korea holds the world's top mobile phone distribution rate where more than 40 million users out of the total population of 49 million owns a mobile phone (S. Y. Lee 2006; wirelessfederation. com 2006). South Korea is also acknowledged as having one of the most advanced mobile phone network systems in the world. Because South Korea is so saturated with mobile phones and mobile phone networks, extensive mobile phone use has become part of the iconic imagery of postmodern South Korea. Hence, when Dae-Soo is released from his prison in *Oldboy*, he is given a wallet full of cash and a mobile phone. Here, the "cash and mobile phone" symbolizes the capitalist information system of South Korea where more and more people appear to be excessively attached to such advanced communication technology as the mobile phone to the point of addiction. According to the research report produced by Bun-Dang Seoul University Hospital, 30% of high school students in South Korea show symptoms of mobile phone addiction which is also known as "mobile syndrome." These students feel anxious when they do not have a mobile phone with them. Ten percent of these students even experienced "text message injury" which is a condition caused by the excessive use of text messages and/or games where muscle pains are experienced in the shoulder and wrists (Y. J. Chang 2004). In this sense, the mobile phone given by Woo-Jin to Dae-Soo signifies postmodern South Korean society where Dae-Soo, an ordinary office worker, bears the cost of information capitalism.

Examples of Cybernetic Technology

In *Oldboy*, postmodern South Korea's technologically driven capitalist system is also evident from the depiction of cybernetic technology in the cyborg bodies of Woo-Jin and Mr. Park, the owner of Dae-Soo's prison cell. Donna Haraway, in her article "A Manifesto for Cyborgs," states that the cyborg is a cybernetic organism which is a hybrid identity of machine and organism (1991: 149–81). The idea of the cyborg deconstructs such binary oppositions as the control and lack of control over the body, object and subject, and nature and culture. The blurring of binary oppositions is one of the main aspects of the conceptual paradigm of postmodernity; therefore, cyborg subjects, by blurring binary oppositions, are postmodern identities. In *Oldboy*, Woo-Jin, whose "artificial heart" has been transplanted in the US, is a cyborg subject because his body is kept alive only by a motor (machine). This cyborg body is constructed through Woo-Jin's capitalist power which enables him to procure the artificial heart transplant. He whispers mockingly to Dae-Soo, "Know what I asked the doctor? 'Dr, Hopkins, give me a remote control to turn that motor off ... So that I can kill myself easily at anytime. I'll give you $100,000 more.'" Here, Woo-Jin is able to exert his capitalist power to gain a prodigious and costly (remote) control over life and death. Woo-Jin's artificial heart, the life span of which can be negotiated within the framework of the market economy, exemplifies the institutionalized capitalist system of contemporary South Korean society. Woo-Jin's cyborg identity is an exact embodiment of a postmodern South Korea where advanced technology is able to blur the boundaries between machines and human beings.

Another reference to cybernetic technology in *Oldboy* is found in the cyborg body of Mr. Park, who has artificial teeth and an artificial hand. After Dae-Soo is released from his prison, he tries to find out who and where his captors are. When Dae-Soo finally discovers where the secret prison is, he brutally tortures Mr. Park by forcibly extracting his teeth with a claw hammer to coerce Mr. Park into divulging information about Woo-Jin, who has engaged Mr. Park's services to imprison Dae-Soo. However, even after losing five to six teeth, Mr. Park refuses to reveal his client's information but tells Dae-Soo instead that "in our 7.5 floor business, our clients' info is top secret." Here, it is clear that Mr. Park has chosen to prioritize client confidentiality over his teeth. Seen in this way, Mr. Park exchanges his body parts, specifically his teeth, for economic profit. This gruesome exchange indicates the ways in which the global market economy can exploit people to generate profits. Mr. Park's cyborg subjectivity is also evident from his other prosthetic body part: an artificial hand. At the end of the film, Woo-Jin reveals how he tricks Dae-Soo: "Mr. Park's hand? You moron … know that new prison of his? He said he had to move, so I gave him that building for his hand!" Here again, Mr. Park has exchanged one of his body parts for real estate, a kind of economic capital. His cyborg body, easily exchangeable for economic capital, signifies the dehumanization of postmodern South Korean society where the boundaries of the human body can be easily transgressed for the sake of economic profit.

Through the analysis of the two aspects — media communication technology and cybernetic technology — of the information capitalist society of South Korea as depicted in *Oldboy*, it is evident that Woo-Jin's capitalist control demonstrates how Dae-Soo, an ordinary office worker, bears the cost of information capitalism. *Oldboy* illustrates how South Korea's postmodernity can, to some extent, create the dehumanization of human subjects and lead to the control of people via technology. These aspects of dehumanization and control are exemplified through Dae-Soo's imprisonment. Further, this imprisonment produces two psychological reactions in Dae-Soo that are archetypal symptoms of postmodernity: isolation and psychic fragmentation.

Postmodern Symptoms: Isolation and Psychic Fragmentation

On many film sites, *Oldboy*'s Kafkaesque set-up, Hitchcockian thriller plot, dark beautifully shot visuals with a touch of film noir, and twisted Greek-tragedy-inspired ending, are often discussed. These descriptions by film site users are good examples of genre formulae that demonstrate *mugukjeok* in the Western reception of *Oldboy*. Indeed, the above genre conventions in *Oldboy*, also typically found in such genre films as the thriller or film noir, are familiar to Western viewers. The popularity of *Oldboy* in the West is partly due to these shared genre conventions that are globally popular and non-national. Such *mugukjeok* elements are evident from the frequent references by film site users to globally established authors, directors, and genres such as Kafka, Hitchcock, and Greek tragedy.

In particular, by referring to Tyler Durden from David Fincher's *Fight Club*, it appears, these users seek the familiarity of postmodern coolness in Dae-Soo by identifying it in Tyler. In fact, Fincher is one of the most frequently mentioned names by film site users in their discussions of *Oldboy*. A reviewer from IndieWire. com, Jeff Reichert, writes: "Both directors [Fincher and Park] seem concerned with presenting a hyper-stylized aesthetic coherence that's seductive (both physically and intellectually) yet repulsive" (2005). An unknown user from TheLastCandle.

net writes, "*Oldboy* reminds me most of the dark-dry humor and kinetic, brutal thrill of David Fincher's *Fight Club*." Another user, Funnyman1235, from IMDb. com writes, "*Oldboy* recalls Fincher in its CG-assisted flourishes and doom[-] ridden themes." Many reviewers and film site users continue to compare *Oldboy* to Fincher's film because of their aesthetic and plot similarities, such as dark noir aesthetics and twisted plots. Although these users make many types of comparison between the two films, my analysis here specifically focuses on the comparison made between the two male leads, Dae-Soo and Tyler Durden. This particular comparison demonstrates the ways in which Western viewers desire South Korean masculinity within the framework of *mugukjeok* "cool," which is a coolness often interpreted by these viewers as transgression and violence. This *mugukjeok* cool masculinity can be characterized by two postmodern symptoms: isolation (alienation) and psychic fragmentation.

Isolation

Dae-Soo is imprisoned for fifteen years. During this period, his wife is murdered, and he is subsequently framed for it, while his daughter is adopted by a Swedish family. Throughout this entire period, the only means of staying in touch with the outside world for Dae-Soo (and the audience) is via a television set. As the fifteen years pass, the television shows the major events occurring in the outside world to Dae-Soo: for example, the South Korean presidential elections, the 2002 Korea/Japan World Cup, and the 9/11 attack. This is shown in the film as a series of montage footage of television news clips. However, there is a telling omission in this television footage: there is no news of the disappearance of Dae-Soo, a man who is also a husband, a father, a colleague, and a friend. Indeed, it is as if the film is suggesting that Dae-Soo's disappearance has affected or changed nothing. In the film, no one seems concerned about where Dae-Soo is or how he is, except the police who merely want to lock him up in a bigger prison. Therefore, it is clear that Dae-Soo is not only physically but also emotionally and psychologically isolated from his family, friends, and society in general. His isolation is well summarized by the phrase written on a painting hung on a wall of his prison cell. Under a grotesque portrait of a hairy middle-aged man are the first lines of Ella Wheeler Wilcox's famous poem, *Solitude*: "Laugh and the world laughs with you. Weep and you weep alone." Throughout the movie, this phrase is repeatedly used to describe Dae-Soo's alienated situation.

A site user, "MH and THE MOVIES," on a message board at Rotten Tomatoes. com writes: "[H]is prison cell resembles a hotel room, complete with a bed, television and maids who straighten up." (April 6, 2005). This user's comment explains that Dae-Soo's prison situation seems even more terrifying because the way that Dae-Soo lives during this period of absolute confinement resembles normal everyday life; in a way, Dae-Soo's prison life is even more comfortable than normal everyday life because there are "maids who straighten up." Through the window(-

like picture frame), he can even see beautiful(ly painted) green scenery. Because the audience's view of what looks like an ordinary cheap hotel room in fact turns out to be a bizarre prison cell, the audience becomes even more fearful. This fear can be understood through Sigmund Freud's concept of "the uncanny." According to Freud, the German word for uncanny, "*unheimlich*," refers to something unfamiliar and is the opposite of *heimlich*, which refers to the homely and the familiar (1955: 220). "*Unheimlich* is what was once *heimisch* (familiar)" and "the uncanny (*unheimlich*) is something which is secretly familiar ..." (1955: 245). It is evident that Dae-Soo's isolation incorporates this uncanniness where the familiar and safe home-like environment is, in actual fact, the unfamiliar and alienated environment of the prison cell.

Fight Club also depicts a man's isolation. The central character is a narrator, Jack (Edward Norton), who is a somnambulistic insomniac. To find the emotional release that allows him to sleep, he attends various support group meetings each night of the week for every affliction imaginable. This strategy works until Marla Singer (Helena Bonham Carter), a chain-smoking fellow "support-group tourist," ruins his plan. "I can't cry if there's another faker present!" Jack exclaims. His insomnia returns. His life takes a dramatic turn when he meets Tyler Durden (Brad Pitt), an eccentric, flamboyant soap salesman. After a mysterious explosion in his apartment, Jack moves into Tyler's dilapidated house. Together, they form the "fight club," and discover the joys of pain. Fighting makes Jack feel alive again. The fight club soon evolves into an underworld organization, and Jack's life spirals out of control. Although Jack is "not physically" isolated, the film clearly shows that he is psychologically isolated from society and other people before he moves into Tyler's house. Before the fight club was established, Jack was a depressive insomniac drone whose monotonous job as a recall coordinator for a major automobile company exemplifies the purposelessness of modern American corporate culture and consumerism. Jack's life is completely governed by American consumerism. In one scene, as Jack confesses that he is a slave to IKEA, the layout of his condominium is transformed into the pages of IKEA's furniture catalogue, complete with names and prices. Impassively walking around his condominium, now furnished like an IKEA showroom, it seems as if Jack is trapped in this shopping catalogue and alienated from the real world. It is American consumer culture that isolates Jack within his high-rise condominium where the perceived necessities of a consumer existence have emptied his life of all meaning and feeling so that he becomes numb and soulless. It could even be said that Jack's condominium is nothing but a classier version of Dae-Soo's private prison cell.

In both *Oldboy* and *Fight Club*, both Dae-Soo and Jack are released from isolation to find their boring drone-like lives transformed into transgressive thrilling ones that violently break all social rules. Many male film website users identify these transgressive violent traits in Dae-Soo and Jack as being associated with "coolness."

For example, a user, bohlonuts, from IMDb.com writes, "[Dae-Soo] beats up 20 dudes with a knife stuck in his back, and that is cool no matter who you are." This notion of "cool," as deployed by this user, is similar to the transformed meanings of what bell hooks has referred to as "black male cool." According to hooks, "Black male cool was [once] defined by the ability to withstand the heat and remain centered" (2004: 147). However, due to the misreading of the term according to stereotypes of black male violence, the term has altered its meaning. hooks explains:

> [Todd] Boyd's definition of cool links it to the state of being lifeless, to necrophilia: "Cool is about a detached, removed, nonchalant sense of being. An aloofness that suggests one is above it all. A pride, an arrogance even, that is at once laid back, unconcerned, perceived to be highly sexual and potentially violent." This definition of black male cool rearticulates the way unenlightened white male hipsters read black masculinity. It is a fake stereotyped notion of cool, that denies the history of the "real cool," which was not about disassociation, hardheartedness, and violence ... (2004: 152)

Here, hooks argues that "coolness" is now commonly identified with stereotypes of black male violence. As observed earlier, Dae-Soo and Tyler are often described by film site users as the coolest characters in cinema. Among the many lists posted by these users under the thread entitled "Top #5 Coolest Characters" on the IMDb.com message board, most of the characters that are mentioned are transgressive and violent: Mr. Blond from *Reservoir Dogs*, Jules Winnfield from *Pulp Fiction*, and Kakihara from *Ichi the Killer*. These user-compiled lists of the coolest male characters in film support hooks's account of a stereotyped notion of "cool" that focuses mainly on violence.

Susan Fraiman, considering the case of *Pulp Fiction*, explains that such violence is "driven by an interest in exploring male vulnerability, along with an only partly self-conscious compulsion to restore men to a state of cool imperviousness" (2003: 3). In both *Oldboy* and *Fight Club*, male vulnerability is characterized by the alienated situations of Dae-Soo and Jack. Freud famously makes the link between male vulnerability and alienation in his theory on the child's game of "Fort!/Da!" (gone/there). By playing the game, Freud argues, a boy symbolically shows his anxiety, and by implication, his vulnerability, about abandonment and being separate from his mother (Freud 1961). Expanding on Freud's insight, Fraiman argues that "modern Western masculinity is shaped by an especially urgent mandate to depart and distinguish itself from a primary female figure. Boys may therefore have a heightened investment in the task of separation" (2003: 9). Using Fraiman's argument, the "cool" modern masculinity of Dae-Soo can be read as having its root in the male vulnerability he experienced after being abandoned by and separated from the maternal which largely signifies home and family. Dae-Soo's transgressive violence is an effort to conceal that vulnerability by the restoration of his "male cool imperviousness." Dae-Soo represents the coolness of modern masculinity that requires the narrative transmutation of male isolation into male transgressive violence, passive male vulnerability into active male mastery. It is thus evident that the social, physical, and psychological isolation that is imposed on Dae-Soo operates as a driving force for him to construct his transgressive violent masculinity. It is this type of masculinity, similar to the masculinity of Tyler Durden, that Western male fans identify as signifying postmodern "coolness."

Psychic Fragmentation

The psychic fragmentation of Dae-Soo suggests another key aspect of the reconstruction of postmodern "cool" South Korean masculinity. The film's narrative structure clearly shows the ways in which Dae-Soo experiences fragmented identities after his imprisonment. During his fifteen years of imprisonment, Dae-Soo, an ordinary middle-aged family man, creates an alter ego named "*monseuteo*" (a monster). His *monseuteo* identity is first evident after he is stabbed in a fight and leaves the fight without showing any pain or fear. He laments, "Now I have become a monster. Can I possibly return to Oh Dae-Soo after finishing this revenge?" Another clear evidence of his *monseuteo* identity is shown at the very end of the film when despairing Dae-Soo asks Mrs. Yoo, the hypnotist, to remove his intolerable memories about the truth of his incestuous relationship with his daughter, Mi-Do. Mrs. Yoo compassionately agrees to help and hypnotizes him: "Now you are in Woo-Jin's penthouse. When I ring my bell, you'll be split into two persons. The one who doesn't know the secret is Oh Dae-Soo. The one who keeps the secret is *monseuteo*." It is allegorically remarkable that this scene of the splitting of Dae-Soo's identities into two by the hypnotist is carried out in Woo-Jin's penthouse, also a symbol of information capitalism. As mentioned earlier, the imprisonment of Dae-Soo itself, which triggers Dae-Soo's psychic fragmentation, is also enabled by Woo-Jin's capitalist power. The conceptual connection between capitalism and the splitting of identity can be understood in terms of Frederic Jameson's argument that in the postmodern era, the level of "alienation" of individual subjects is continually increased under capitalism, so that the individual subject experiences a "psychic fragmentation" (Jameson 1991: 90). Thus, I suggest that Dae-Soo's alter ego, *monseuteo*, is a by-product of postmodern capitalism.

Regarding the cinematic representation of psychic fragmentation, David Eastman, a user from IMDb.com, mentions that *Oldboy* is similar to Western films that are "always involved with some sort of identity problem, e.g., *Seven*, *Fight Club* and *Memento*" (June 15, 2006). As the user points out, the theme of fragmented identity is also seen in *Fight Club*. At the film's end, we discover that Tyler is, in fact, an alter ego of Jack who serves as a proxy via which Jack acts on his desires. Jack is able to use his alter ego to act on his innermost desires because Tyler possesses what Jack lacks — charisma, a strong masculine body, and a soul free from the constraints of consumer-driven society. As with Dae-Soo's psychic splitting, Jack's isolation and subsequent creation of his alter ego occurs in relation to capitalism, since Jack is attempting to free himself of his consumerist lifestyle by creating Tyler. The notion of an alter ego in both films fits in with the conceptual framework of postmodern schizo-fragmentation. Schizophrenia is characterized by delusions of reference, grandeur, and persecution. Jameson suggested:

> This differentiation and specialization or semiautonomization of reality is then prior to what happens in the psyche — postmodern schizo-fragmentation as opposed to modern or modernist anxieties and hysterias — which takes the form of the world it models and seeks to reproduce in the form of experience as well as of concepts ... (1991: 372)

Jack's somnambulistic insomnia is a by-product of modernist anxieties and hysterias. Hysteria is clearly depicted in the very first sequence of *Oldboy*: a drunken Dae-Soo, held in custody at the police station, blurts out random words, attempts to urinate, and screams to be released. This hysterical behavior is an externalization of the anxieties of modern office workers in South Korea, whose automatic daily adherence to tedious nine-to-five work routines can only be interrupted and enlivened through such frenzied behavior. In the next scene, Dae-Soo is shown confined in a private jail (which represents a schizoid reality) where he gradually creates his double — *monseuteo*. Hence, it is by separating from the tedious reality of his everyday life that Dae-Soo develops his postmodern alter ego.

When Western fans profess their appreciation for the cool postmodern masculinity represented in both *Oldboy* and *Fight Club*, what they are really referring to is the masculinity of the alter egos, *monseuteo* and Tyler, and not that of Dae-Soo and Jack. A notable point here is that the alter egos of Dae-Soo and Jack are transgressive and violent while their true selves are conventional and weak. One day, after six years in the prison cell, Dae-Soo obtains one extra metal chopstick that he uses to excavate a hole in the wall. Hoping to escape through this hole, he stops trying to commit suicide. He begins physical training by punching an imagined enemy drawn on the concrete wall. Soon, however, his fists become bloody and painful and he writhes in agony. The next scene shows Dae-Soo tattooing one line for each year of incarceration on the back of his left hand. It is through such transgressive violence as "fighting" (with an imagined enemy) and "wounding" oneself (from tattooing) that the *monseuteo* Dae-Soo proves his "self" in order to escape from his alienated situation, a situation that the conventional and weak Dae-Soo can do nothing about. His self-inflicted violence is a transgression against his body and this wounded body signifies the powerful fearless *monseuteo*. In other words, Dae-Soo's fragmented identity, which is evident from his monstrous wounded and tattooed body, represents his transformation into transgressive masculinity. Such fractured identity, commonly recognized by fans in the case of Tyler, is one of the reasons for the identification of the *monseuteo* Dae-Soo as a "cool" man by many Western viewers. In this way, the *monseuteo* Dae-Soo embodies the postmodern "cool" masculinity as underpinned by transgressive violence and psychic fragmentation.

Dehumanization of Dae-Soo: A Transgressive Machine

As argued in the earlier section dealing with film site users as fans of extreme Asian cinema, Western viewers satisfy their Orientalist desires by categorizing *Oldboy* as extreme Asian cinema and by predominantly focusing on and consuming violent and transgressive images of Dae-Soo. According to Edward Said's well-known theory of Orientalism, the West exaggerates and selectively consumes certain aspects of Eastern culture to fit in with their Orientalist fantasies (Said 1978: 49–73; Reck 1985: 84). By selectively focusing on and consuming the transgressive characteristics of the *monseuteo* Dae-Soo, Dae-Soo becomes a fetishized object through which Western viewers fulfill their Orientalist desires. However, this desire is different from the classical concept of Western Orientalist desire towards a primitive Other. Rather, the desire for the *monseuteo* Dae-Soo is a desire for the new hybrid postmodern South Korean masculinity that is "savage but cool" and which is derived from the postmodern symptoms of isolation and psychic fragmentation. This new form of desire — neo-Orientalist desire — should be distinguished from the classical concept of Orientalist desire.

The Western neo-Orientalist desire is clearly shown from the ways in which viewers enthusiastically embrace the representations of Dae-Soo as dehumanized and machinic in *Oldboy*. The Western neo-Orientalist desire for a "machinic" Dae-Soo can be conceptualized within the postmodern framework of "techno-Orientalism" as suggested by David Morley and Kevin Robins in their influential book *The Spaces of Identity*. They argue that "Western stereotypes of the Japanese hold them to be sub-human, as if they have no feeling, no emotion, no humanity" and that the Japanese are seen as automated Others (1995: 172). According to Morley and Robins, these Orientalist stereotypes are founded upon the contemporary global circulation of advanced Japanese technologies within the paradigm of technology-driven postmodern capitalism. The notion of techno-Orientalism describes this conflation of Orientalism with the rise of Eastern technology. In the case of Dae-Soo, it is the isolation and psychic fragmentation that was imposed upon him by Woo-Jin that dehumanizes Dae-Soo to the extent that he becomes a machinic body. In this sense, the machinic body of the *monseuteo* Dae-Soo can be understood as an "automatized Other" that is controlled by Woo-Jin, who exemplifies the operations of a technology-driven postmodern capitalist system. In *Oldboy*, the automatized Dae-Soo demonstrates three different examples of transgression that resonate well with film site users: the transgression of becoming a "human-hammer-machine," the transgression of eating a live animal, and the transgression of committing incest.

Transgression of a Human-Hammer-Machine

Oldboy is a revenge thriller in which graphic violence and bloodshed predominate as Dae-Soo retraces the steps that led to his mysterious capture and confinement. The film shows how an ordinary middle-aged man becomes a dehumanized avenger when he undergoes fifteen years of isolation and the subsequent experience of psychic fragmentation. Western viewers appear to be enthralled by his dehumanized violent actions. The scene where he extracts the teeth of Mr. Park is often pointed out as one of the most appalling. In this scene, Dae-Soo brutally tortures Mr. Park, the prison owner, and extracts his teeth with a claw hammer in order to obtain information about Woo-Jin. Dae-Soo, without revealing his pain or anger, informs Mr. Park impassively, "I'm going to pay you back all fifteen years. Each one I yank out will make you age one year." A claw hammer is shown in a close-up shot pressing against Mr. Park's front tooth where blood soon begins to flow. This is followed by a shot of Dae-Soo's emotionless face with a twitching cheek as he wrenches the hammer. The next shot shows five to six extracted teeth lying on a bloody computer keyboard. Dae-Soo again quietly and impassively asks Mr. Park, "Ready to talk?" This sequence of cross-cutting between the bloody hammer, the teeth, and Dae-Soo's emotionless face emphasizes his dehumanization. Such editing highlights Dae-Soo's machine-like psyche, which is driven solely by the goal of bloody vengeance.

This tooth torture scene is preceded by the corridor fight scene, which is often described by many fans as one of the most authentic and well-choreographed action scenes. A user, Matt Layden from IMDb.com, writes, "Park shows his talent in this film as he shows us a beautifully choreographed corridor fight scene, with no cuts." Another user, Jiggy Joey 2k3, also writes, "The violence is sparingly used and beautifully done especially in the long corridor scene." In this scene, Dae-Soo, armed with a hammer and with a knife sticking out of his back, defeats a couple of dozen vicious enemies. In this seven-minute sequence, he is portrayed as a ruthless machinic man who does not scream at all even when he is stabbed during the long and bloody fighting. Dae-Soo's machinic identity was one that was created during his fifteen years of isolation, a period in which he lost his human identities as a father, a husband, and an ordinary office worker. After the loss of all these identities, only the need for revenge remains in his well-trained machinic body which does not seem to experience human pain. This notion of the amnesiac-machinic identity is explored at length in Toshiya Ueno's article, "Japanimation and Techno-Orientalism," where he discusses the "puppets (cyborgs) without ghost (soul)," and the "Puppet Master" who controls them, in the Japanese animation *Ghost in the Shell* (2001: 223–31). Without human memories, Dae-Soo has become "a puppet without ghost." Woo-

Jin, then, is the puppet master who controls the machinic Dae-Soo. It is Woo-Jin's capitalist and information-gathering power that enables the incarceration, surveillance, hypnotization, and anesthetization of Dae-Soo; this is also the power that transforms Dae-Soo into a dangerous human-hammer-machine.

Dae-Soo's image of a dangerous human-hammer-machine is further reinforced in the way the US media links the Virginia Tech incident with *Oldboy*. On April 16, 2007, the tragic shooting incident at Virginia Tech occurred. Thirty-two people were killed by a gunman, Cho Seung-Hui, a Korean American who had migrated to the US at the age of eight. Soon after the incident, many US media, including some film websites, started suggesting that Cho had been inspired by *Oldboy*. First, April 18, 2007, Paul Harrill, a writer and filmmaker, and also a professor at Virginia Tech, alerted a *New York Times* blog "The LEDE" of "the striking similarity between one of the photographs the shooter sent to NBC, and a shot from *Oldboy*" (Nizza 2007). Soon, US media frantically started reproducing Harrill's personal guess, turned almost into factual news under the sensational titles: "VT Killer's Hammer Pose Resembles Movie" (ABCnews.go.com, Boston.com), "VT Killer's Hammer pose linked to South Korean movie" (USAToday.com), "Virginia Tech Murderer Mimicked Movie" (DeadlineHollywoodDaily.com) (Coyle 2007a; Coyle 2007b; Finke 2007). Jake Coyle, from USAToday.com, writes "The similarities have prompted speculation, especially in online forums, that Cho's entire massacre may have been inspired by *Oldboy*" (2007b). On BeyondHollywood.com, an anonymous writer posted an article, "Did Cho Seung Hui Copied [sic] Park Chan-Wook's *Oldboy*?" (April 19, 2007). The writer observed that Cho's poses in the pictures that he had sent to NBC news are exactly the same as some of Dae-Soo's poses in *Oldboy*.[11] The US media repeatedly showed two juxtaposed images: one is a photo of Cho, holding a hammer; the other is an *Oldboy* movie poster where Dae-Soo holds a hammer. Along with these sensational media reports, there was much debate among US critics and audiences on many film websites. One of the most active debaters, Primemover, from IMDb.com writes:

Figure 4.2 A scene from *Oldboy*

> In respect to those 32 dead children in America ... my boyfriend and I
> DESTROYED our copy of the *Oldboy* DVD. We mashed it up into tiny pieces.
> Anyone else on here BRAVE enough to take ACTION against these wretched
> movies? It's about time film makers started acting RESPONSIBLY. (April 27,
> 2007)

Instead of considering whether the educational, political, and social institutions in the US may have played a major role in causing the tragic incident, commentators, such as Primemover, simply shift the blame onto a single foreign action thriller. However, as Donald Black argues, violence, unpredictable as it is, does emerge from precise social configurations:

> Violence might appear to be an unpredictable outburst or unexplainable
> explosion, but it arises with geometrical precision. It is unpredictable and
> unexplainable only if we seek its origins in the characteristics of individuals
> (such as their beliefs or frustrations) or in the characteristics of societies,
> communities, or other collectivities (such as their cultural values or level of
> inequality). But violent individuals and violent collectivities do not exist:
> No individual or collectivity is violent in all settings at all times, and neither
> individualistic nor collectivistic theories predict and explain precisely when and
> how violence occurs ... Violence occurs when the social geometry of a conflict
> — the conflict structure — is violent. (2004: 15)

Following Black, I suggest that it is the conflict structure of the US in particular, and the whole world in general, that is responsible for the tragic incident at Virginia Tech, not Cho's individual frustration nor a single action thriller. Nevertheless, by juxtaposing photos of Dae-Soo with those of Cho, the US media has identified the dangerous Other as embodied in the figure of a Korean American mass murderer on the one hand, and in a violent South Korean action film on the other. Due to this juxtaposition, it can be argued that Dae-Soo's hammer acquires the connotation of societal destruction, which is reinforced by the parallel imagery of Cho's demolishing weapon. It is significant that in his multimedia manifesto, Cho angrily railed against the wealthy people of the establishment:

> You had everything you wanted. Your Mercedes wasn't enough, you brats. Your
> golden necklaces weren't enough, you snobs. Your trust fund wasn't enough.
> Your vodka and cognac weren't enough. All your debaucheries weren't enough.
> Those weren't enough to fulfill your hedonistic needs. You had everything.
> (MSNBC.com quoted Cho as saying)

Cho's angry words clearly indicate the target of his hammer: the economic elite who are the chief beneficiaries of capitalism. Yet, because of the connotation of social destruction that is implied by the juxtaposition of Cho's and Dae-Soo's photos, Dae-Soo's hammer has become a weapon to destroy Western capitalism. The juxtaposition of Dae-Soo with Cho — a mass murderer perceived by the media to be inhuman, irrational, and savage — reinforces the perception that Dae-Soo embodies a dangerous Other who ignites and realizes the subversive violence enacted upon it. The plea of the film site user, Primemover, to participate in the "action" by "boycotting" the film and "destroying" the DVD demonstrates her paranoia of this dangerous Other. Primemover's "action" of "mashing it up into tiny pieces" — which, ostensibly, did actually take place — appears to be a symbolic ritual performed by her to prevent this dangerous Other from encroaching into her life. The majority of the more than 260 replies to Primemover's post argue against her idea of banning *Oldboy*. In response, Primemover created another thread entitled "Why are you ALL in denial about how DANGEROUS this film is?" Despite Primemover's strong appeal to boycott the film, many of the subsequent responders still maintain that the violent content of the film "has got nothing to do with the VT incident" and that the film is not dangerous but "cool" and "beautiful." Unlike Primemover, it is evident that many film site users believe that the character of Dae-Soo, despite his menacing hammer, is rather entertaining and harmless.

It can be argued that the positive stance held by many film site users towards Dae-Soo is partly due to his representation in the film as an automatized puppet who is programmed and operated by the puppet master, Woo-Jin. A good example of Woo-Jin's absolute control over Dae-Soo is the scene where Dae-Soo and Mi-Do stay overnight in a motel room during their attempted escape from Woo-Jin's relentless surveillance. As they sleep, gas is discharged into their room through a chink in the door. Woo-Jin, wearing a gas mask, walks into the room and, without any word or action, lies down next to Dae-Soo and Mi-Do, and watches them sleep. This scene illustrates Woo-Jin's ubiquitous presence and omnipotent God-like power, as a site user, asdj_bassett, from IMDb.com observes (April 24, 2005). In this scene, Woo-Jin's omnipresence and his use of sleeping gas symbolize the puppet master's absolute control of the automaton Dae-Soo, who loses his consciousness and his soul. Dae-Soo's transgressive violence, such as his aggressive use of the hammer, is only allowed with Woo-Jin's tacit permission. Because of this automatized aspect, the character of Dae-Soo evokes only transgressive pleasure, not real fear, in viewers. That is why many film site users express the fact that the human-hammer-machine Dae-Soo is harmless and rather enjoyable. This is despite efforts by the media to suggest that the character of Dae-Soo may have inspired Cho's killing spree at Virginia Tech. The embrace of the human-hammer-machine Dae-Soo by Western viewers demonstrates the ways that they fulfill their techno-Orientalist fantasy for transgressive South Korean masculinity.

Transgression of Eating a Live Octopus

The techno-Orientalist desire for a transgressive Other by Western viewers is also evident in their fervent response to the live-octopus-eating Dae-Soo. On being released from his prison, Dae-Soo goes to a *sushi* restaurant where Mi-Do works. With an impassive face, he tells her, "I want something alive." When Mi-Do serves Dae-Soo a live octopus, he eats it alive without any hesitation or expression (Figure 4.3). Here, the film is perhaps illustrating the fact that after spending fifteen years in a prison cell eating the same kind of food (fried dumplings) that is completely dead day in and day out, Dae-Soo's desperate desire to regain his feeling for life leads him to consume the octopus alive. However, many Western viewers merely see this live-octopus-eating Dae-Soo as a horrifying Other. Patrick Galloway, in his book *Asia Shock*, describes this scene as such: "[Dae-Soo] proceeds to eat the wriggling thing, causing US critics to scream like schoolgirls and blow the scene out of all proportion in their reviews" (2006: 100). In fact, many Euro-American critics and reviewers have described how shocking and sensational the "octopus" scene is. However, an interesting fact to bear in mind is that few Koreans consider eating a live octopus shocking because a Korean meal often includes a live octopus as a dish. A live octopus is one of the most popular side dishes in Korea; it goes well with Korean traditional alcohol. Koreans are familiar with eating live octopuses, although they usually do not swallow them whole as Dae-Soo does in the film. Hence, one of the writers of *Oldboy Book*, Kim Ji-Eun seems mystified: "I don't know why many Western critics are terrified by the scene. Does eating a live octopus look so violent and vicious?" (2005: 30).

In the *Washington Post*, Desson Thomson begins his article by confessing his timorousness. He says, "Call me a wimp ... although I can slurp sushi with the best of them, I tend to cringe when someone gnaws a live octopus while the poor creature writhes and flails away" (2005). In *The New Yorker*, Anthony Lane also begins his review by describing how Dae-Soo swallows a live octopus and how it squirms

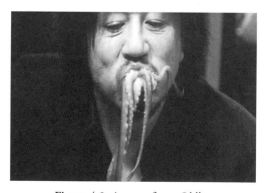

Figure 4.3 A scene from *Oldboy*

around his mouth (2005). Lane then uses almost half of his article to analyze this scene. Peter Bradshaw, from *The Guardian*, also gives a very detailed description of how Dae-Soo gobbles a live octopus down "as the unfortunate beast writhes and slithers around his chin" (2004). Surprisingly, many media critics and reporters, including Michael Atkinson from the *Village Voice*, Ty Burr from *Boston Globe*, and Derek Elley from *Variety*, commence their articles by describing how shocking the scene is (Atkinson 2005; Burr 2005; Elley 2005). The Western readings of the live octopus scene in *Oldboy* show how a familiar element in one's culture can appear unfamiliar and take on different meanings in a different cultural context. In other words, the above comments of Euro-American critics demonstrate how the cultural practice of eating live octopuses, encoded in Korea as being part of normal food culture, has been decoded in the West as a practice that can be categorized under the label of "extreme horror."

Such misinterpretation contributes to the dehumanization of Dae-Soo — who appears to be unable to empathize with the position of the live octopus — in the West where many empathetic reviewers view the live octopus as "poor" and "unfortunate." In these reviews, Dae-Soo is perceived as a dehumanized Other who transgresses the moral and ethical boundaries of established Western values regarding animal welfare. Dae-Soo, emotionlessly grabbing and gnawing a live octopus, embodies a transgressive machine, a machine that has been created and is controlled by Woo-Jin. Indeed, Dae-Soo's dehumanized machinic trait is evident from the way he desperately consumes something "alive." Paradoxically, while Dae-Soo's desperate consumption of the octopus highlights his dehumanization as a machine, such consumption is also a way for Dae-Soo to merge with something "alive" to compensate for his lack of humanness. Dae-Soo's regaining of his humanity by eating this live octopus would then enable his resistance against Woo-Jin's similarly dehumanized control over him. Such an attempt also suggests that Dae-Soo may be able to transgress institutionalized Western norms regarding animal welfare. The Western response of shock towards the live octopus scene demonstrates their fear of the transgressive Other.

However, as soon as Dae-Soo consumes the live octopus, he collapses, as had been programmed by Woo-Jin, due to the hypnotic suggestion that he had received. This sudden collapse is significant because it suggests that Dae-Soo fails to restore his humanity; despite consuming a live creature, he still remains a machine. His collapse also signifies that he is not able to transgress Western norms and moral values. This is why many Western viewers express the fact that they find the live-octopus-eating Dae-Soo frightening yet amusing. For instance, Fritax, from IMDb.com, remarks that the scene is "kinda gross but mostly funny." Another user, Funnyman125, writes that the scene is "done with such unabashed verve that you'll be as compelled as you are repulsed." Thus, for Western viewers, the live-octopus-eating Dae-Soo is repulsive yet innocuous. This is because his failure at restoring his humanity means that he remains a machinic and soulless identity who is ultimately still safely controlled and contained by Woo-Jin, an agent of the capitalist system which is also the system that Western viewers safely live in. The Western resonation with the live-octopus-eating Dae-Soo is therefore based upon a techno-Orientalist fantasy of a transgressive South Korean masculinity which offers the thrilling and taboo-breaking pleasures of eating something alive but yet is completely innocuous.

Transgression of Incest

Finally, further evidence of the techno-Orientalist fantasy of Western viewers is their enthusiastic embrace of the *Oldboy*'s representation of the transgression of incest. Dae-Soo's transgression reaches its apex in the scene where he has incestuous sex with Mi-Do, who is later revealed to be his own daughter. Notably, Dae-Soo's transgression in this scene is enacted in a dehumanized and machinic manner. When Dae-Soo and Mi-Do meet at a *sushi* restaurant, they fall in love with each other because both of them have been hypnotized to do so. Their falling in love is part of Woo-Jin's plan to manipulate Dae-Soo into having an incestuous relationship with his own daughter and thereby exact his revenge. Thinking that they have escaped from their tormentors, Dae-Soo and Mi-Do spend a night in a motel room. A tracking shot by a hand-held camera along the red-lit corridor of their motel cuts away directly to a shot in which Dae-Soo penetrates Mi-Do without any foreplay or dialogue. Significantly, Dae-Soo's piston-like movements are machinic. Dae-Soo's machinic sexual manner is emphasized by the specific positioning of the two lovers where Mi-Do's placing of her legs on Dae-Soo's shoulders minimizes physical contact but maximizes the depth of genital penetration. In contrast to Dae-Soo's emotionless lovemaking, Mi-Do displays human emotions, painfully saying to Dae-Soo, "*Ajeosshi* [Dae-Soo], it really hurts. But I'm enduring ... I want to be good to you."[12] This is the moment that Dae-Soo's machinic manner is augmented: Dae-Soo disregards Mi-Do's moans of pain, and continues his mechanical piston-like movements. With minimal emotional expression and an almost-acrobatic posture that requires very little human physical contact, Dae-Soo is portrayed as a machine, rather than a human man, making love.

Many Western viewers appear to approve this portrayal of machine-like sex implicitly, as critical objections to Dae-Soo's machinic manner in the scene are rare. Many viewers indeed show disapproving responses to the scene in relation to the portrayal of the incestuous relationship. However, these reactions are to the incest, rather than to the representation of sex itself. Some, to a certain extent, show positive responses to the scene. Boyle0798, from IMDb.com, writes that the scene is "freaking hot," while mtvguidee points out that it is "one of the most stimulating sex scenes." Another user, bobbydik3, writes, "It is tantalizingly erotic." However, these positive responses turn negative as soon as Dae-Soo recovers from his machinic state and regains his humanity in the film. At the end of the film, Woo-Jin reveals the truth about the father-daughter relationship between Dae-Soo and Mi-Do. Realizing that his sexual relationship with Mi-Do is in fact an incestuous one, Dae-Soo becomes very distressed and begs Woo-Jin not to tell Mi-Do the truth. Weeping bitterly, Dae-Soo begs:

What has she done wrong? ... please leave Mi-Do alone ... [Then he suddenly changes his voice tone to yell and threaten Woo-Jin.] If Mi-Do finds out the truth, you asshole! I'll rip your whole body apart, and no one will be able to find your body anywhere. WHY? Because I'm going to chew it all down. [Then again, he bitterly weeps and begs, and crawls towards Woo-Jin.] Woo-Jin! I made a mistake. Please forget what I said. Please! Sir! Boss! ... I'll do whatever you want. I'll do anything. If you want me to be a dog, I will! I'm Lee Woo-Jin's dog from now on! I'm your puppy!

Dae-Soo even barks and wags an imaginary tail. This sequence is significant in terms of the aforementioned machinic Dae-Soo who has lost his human memories and emotions. In this scene, he finally recovers his original human identity and becomes able to feel fear, repentance, and pain again. His memory of being a father is also restored and he even severs his own tongue for the sake of his daughter. Here, Dae-Soo's machinic desire for vengeance becomes transformed into human concern for his daughter. The transgressive violence in this scene, which occurs when Dae-Soo cuts off his tongue, now signifies his paternal feelings and not vengeful ones. The restoration of his humanity is even reinforced by his mimicking an animal — a dog. This animal mimicry arises from basic human fear and anxiety and from a father's intense love for his daughter. Dae-Soo's mimicking of a dog suggests that he has reconstructed his humanity even as he deconstructs the machinic state that had plagued him before.

Some viewers, however, respond negatively to Dae-Soo's transformation from machine to human. One of the users on IMDb.com, andrewthezeppo, posts a thread, "Anybody else hate dog bit at the end?" He writes, "I just found it drastically out of character ... how do you go from a revenge seeking killer to begging, barking and licking somebody's feet so quickly? I really wanted Oh Dae-Soo to torture his captor like he did everybody else" (June 27, 2007). This user finds it difficult to accept Dae-Soo's ability to feel human fear and pain at the end of *Oldboy*; rather, s/he appears to prefer that Dae-Soo remain a machine only capable of seeking revenge and inflicting torture. The user's clear opposition to Dae-Soo's regaining of humanity suggests that there is a Western desire for the dehumanized transgressive Other as a fetishized object.

Donna Haraway states, "[B]asically machines are not self-moving, self-designing, autonomous. They could not achieve man's dream, only mock it. They were not man, an author to himself, but only a caricature of that masculinist reproductive dream" (1991: 69). In such a techno-Orientalist fantasy as andrewthezeppo's, Dae-Soo cannot be a subject who can achieve self-actualization — that is, a Western man — but should remain a fetishized machinic object in order to be convincing. This fetishized Othered object is transgressive, hyper-masculine, and dangerous. Without feeling fear or guilt, it performs transgressions and breaks various taboos present in Western culture such as taboos against torture, terror, and incest. This transgressive machinic South Korean masculinity becomes the West's masculinist dream — the West's techno-Orientalist fantasy. This fantasy enables Western viewers to vicariously enjoy the transgressive pleasures of the machinic father-daughter incestuous masculinity that Dae-Soo represents without having to bear the twin burdens of fear and guilt.

Conclusion

The Western cult fandom of *Oldboy* can be conceptualized as the West's ambivalent reception of postmodern South Korean masculinity, which is exemplified by the "savage but cool" Dae-Soo. Such ambivalent Western reception is evident in the mixed practice of *mugukjeok* and the neo-Orientalism of new cinephiles on Western film review websites.

As observed, the practice of *mugukjeok* is evident in the way in which Western male fans identify with Dae-Soo through acknowledging the cool South Korean masculinity which is evident from two postmodern characteristics of Dae-Soo: isolation and psychic fragmentation. These are also the postmodern characteristics that define the globally well-known cool masculine icon, Tyler Durden, the male protagonist of *Fight Club*. Through examining how Western male fans embrace the two postmodern aspects of Dae-Soo, I have shown the ways in which postmodern, global, and cool South Korean masculinity has been constructed within Western spectatorship.

Another aspect of the construction of postmodern South Korean masculinity is found in the neo-Orientalist reception of the West, which is evident in the way in which Western audiences desire the transgressive Dae-Soo as a machinic Other. As observed, the site users resonate with three machinic aspects of Dae-Soo — the human-hammer-machine, live-octopus-eating, and father-daughter incest — based on their techno-Orientalist fantasy. By examining the Western reception of the machinic Dae-Soo, I have shown the ways in which postmodern Korean masculinity is reinforced by the Western techno-Orientalist desire for the transgressive Other.

I have examined how Western audiences ambivalently embrace South Korean masculinity by identifying with its *mugukjeok* coolness as well as longing for its techno-Orientalist Otherness. Most importantly, unlike the previous two chapters, this chapter has examined the ways in which Western male fans identify with South Korean masculinity, where the gender dynamics between the fans and the star differ from the gender dynamics that drive the female fandom of BYJ and Rain.

This chapter concludes that due to the ever-fluctuating postmodern popular cultural flows, Western audiences experience the hybrid "time between dog and wolf" when they view *Oldboy*: the time when contemporary postmodern South Korean masculinity, as epitomized by the "savage but cool" Dae-Soo, is reconstructed within ambivalent neo-Orientalist Western spectatorship.

5

K-Pop Idol Boy Bands and Manufactured Versatile
Masculinity:
Making *Chogukjeok* Boys

[I can now tell that] cultural content can be more powerful than guns and swords … After I've been travelling around the world, I realized that "the world is big and there's lots to do" like the book title written by Kim Woo-Jung, the former chairperson of Dae-Woo Group. Then, it came to my mind that I should become a powerful (cultural) product which can represent the made-in Korea brand in the global cultural content market … I also realized that the most Koreanized is not necessarily the most globalized. Representing things overly Koreanized often can be a reason of failure. Thus, the best solution I found is the amalgamation between something Korean (Asian) and something global.

—Rain, from an interview with G. H. Lee
on January 3, 2010

In this concluding chapter, I look at some of the most recent developments in South Korean popular culture, using the example of idol boy bands and their manufactured versatile masculinity. I argue that, in addition to *mugukjeok* or the effort to make South Korean stars Asianized and/or globalized and to play down their Korean specificity, another characteristic is increasingly demanding of attention. This is *chogukjeok* (cross- or trans-national[ity], 초국적, 超國籍), or the tendency to retain national specificity while deploying it as part of a transborder and multinational cultural figuration. It appears that such tendency is widely practiced and eagerly developed in the South Korean popular entertainment industry that is driven largely by its capitalist desires for globalization.

In 2009, the year-end South Korean popular music (K-pop) festivals and awards were filled with pretty boys disguised as girls.[1] At the SBS Music Festival (*Gayo Daejeon*), some of the top idol boy bands — Super Junior, SHINee, 2PM, 2AM, B2AST, MBLAQ — re-interpreted and re-presented the 2009 hit songs and dances of idol girl groups. Not only boys mimicking girls, but girl bands also performed the hit repertoires of boy bands. Such transgender role-playing practices among idol girl and boy groups were a huge trend in the K-pop scene in 2009, due mainly to the phenomenal success of many idol — particularly girl — groups in South Korea.[2] In many game shows and music programs, wearing wigs and miniskirts, idol boy group members repeatedly imitated girl group performances. Two of the most popularly mimicked pieces are *Gee* by Girls' Generation (aka. SNSD) and *Abracadabra* by Brown Eyed Girls. In particular, the parody music video of *Abracadabra* by 2PM and 2AM has gained enormous recognition inside as well as outside South Korea, and has rewritten the history of the K-pop parody genre. One of many uploaded video clips on YouTube drew a total hit count of more than 1,150,000 (February 3, 2010). One of the performers, Jo Kwon, a leader of 2AM, has become the queen of the girl group mimickers and has conquered the South Korean entertainment industry by way of dizzily re-presenting all kinds of — sexy and cute — girl group performances on various television programs.[3] In a game show, *Quiz to Change the World* (*Sebaqui*), after watching Jo Kwon's performance, a veteran actor even remarks, "this is my first time to feel like being with a man [to be attracted to a man] after twenty-something years of my acting career" (broadcast on February 20, 2010). Not only the girl-mimicking feminized pretty boys, but the tough-looking boys, who show off their fully masculine features, have also attracted the nation's attention in the year. Since late 2008, a few idol boy bands that claim to embody "beast-like" masculinity, such as 2PM, B2AST, and MBLAQ, have made their debuts. 2PM was unquestionably at the center of the nation's feverish embrace of beast-like masculinity.

2PM, a six-member South Korean idol boy band, from JYPE debuted with their single, *10 Points Out of 10* (*Sipjeom Manjeome Sipjeom*), in September 2008.[4] Since their debut, 2PM has been displaying dynamic acrobatic and b-boy dance styles, maximizing their tough manly images. Following their image of wild masculinity, the local media and netizens have nicknamed the group *jimseungdol*. *Jimseungdol* is a coined term that is a combination of a Korean word, *jimseung* (짐승, animal or beast), and *dol* from the word "idol". Due to the increasing variety of idol girl and boy band branding, it has become a trend to give nicknames labeling characteristic features to different types of idol groups. This new trend, to some extent, reflects how idol bands in South Korea have become more colorful, skillful, and multi-talented these days (S. H. Lee 2010). Among many, the *jimseungdol* phenomenon led by 2PM swept the entire nation. Unlike the pre-existing Korean idol boy bands — e.g., SS501, TVXQ, SHINee, Super Junior — who practically emphasize their pretty boy (*kkonminam*) features, 2PM, from the beginning, claims to be a tough, manly, and beast-like idol group. Their stage performances exemplify total wildness and manliness. In particular, the various versioned endings of the performance of *Heartbeat*, the title song of their first full-length album, show a vicious, beast-like masculinity. Taec-Yeon fiercely tears his shirt off; Nichkhun brutally rips Taec-Yeon's — symbolic — heart out; and Chan-Sung, fiercely breathing, lifts Nichkhun over his head. In fact, different versions of the *Heartbeat* performance have become sensational hits that are serially showcased on the four major K-pop music programs: KBS Music Bank; MBC Show! Music Core; SBS

Popular Music; and Mnet M Countdown. According to Bae Gook-Nam from *My Daily*, the two main driving forces behind the *jimseungnam* (beast-like men) phenomenon are "the commodification of the male body" and "the expansion of women's right to express their sexual desires" (G. N. Bae 2010b). As Bae suggests, many female viewers fanatically and repeatedly consume such beast-like masculine images of 2PM.

Like Rain, 2PM's stage performances demonstrate sexy and tough masculinity by often showing off their well-toned muscular bodies. At the same time, in many game shows, they often cross-dress and perform cute dances of girl groups, where they exercise feminized soft masculinity. Most of all, in reality shows on cable television such as *Idol Show* and *Wild Bunny*, by performing as immature and obnoxious boys, they practice *kawaii* masculinity. It is thus evident that 2PM's hybrid masculinity has been constructed through exercising different masculine forms via different media channels. The construction of 2PM's hybrid masculinity as a result of exercising different masculine forms utterly reflects Judith Butler's concept of "gender performativity" which was discussed in chapter 1. Butler argues that sexuality and gender are culturally constructed through the repetition of stylized performances of gender in time (1988). Such an aspect is also well supported by Jane Thumim's notion of the construction of a star persona. She describes how a star persona derives from the performances and utterances of the person and is constructed through a variety of media agents (Thumim 1986: 71, 76). 2PM's star persona — and the masculinity it embodies — has been constructed through performing various masculine forms such as beast-like, *kawaii*, and soft, through diverse media agents including music programs, reality shows, and game shows.

2PM demonstrates multi-layered features of masculinity through exercising different images, gestures, and voices. They are an exact embodiment of what I call "manufactured versatile masculinity" often represented by South Korean idol boy bands. It is multi-layered, culturally mixed, simultaneously contradictory, and most of all strategically manufactured. From my observation, the example that best fits this description is a member, Taec-Yeon. He is a *kawaii* cute boy in a sexy beast-like man's body. For sex appeal, Taec-Yeon would not hesitate to fiercely rip his shirt off on stage, revealing his well-toned muscular chest and a six pack.[5] On the other hand, in a number of episodes of the aforementioned reality shows on cable channels, he often exercises "cute gestures (애 교, *aegyo*)," making girly and sweet facial expressions and voices. Moreover, this 186-centimeter-tall muscular boy often transforms into one of the girl group members, wearing a navy cap with a big pink ribbon or bright orange-colored tight skinny jeans. His masculinity is flexible, transformable, and hybridized. As such, 2PM is the best representative of versatile masculinity often exemplified by the contemporary South Korean idol boy bands. The versatility of 2PM is also evident from the way it consists of culturally mixed members: the former leader, Jae-Beom, is a Korean American; Taec-Yeon migrated to the US for seven years before he came back to Korea for his entertainment career; most of all, Nichkhun is an American-born Thai Chinese. Unquestionably, Nichkhun is considered the most successful and well-known foreign artist in the South Korean entertainment industry thus far. With a prince-like *kkonminam* appearance, his *jimseungdol* image with a well-toned body has made him a national iconic figure of the male idol star regardless of cultural barriers (D. H. Hong 2010). Because of Nichkhun, 2PM was able to gain instant recognition among Thai viewers (Figure 5.1). One industry professional explains, "Thai people rather easily accept 2PM because of their own Nichkhun. Currently, 2PM is one of the top idol groups in Thailand" (quoted in D. H. Hong 2010). On July 3, 2009, having been invited to represent the government-led tourism campaign, "I Love Thailand," 2PM even had the chance to meet Abhisit Vejjajiva, the prime minister of Thailand. The invitation reflects the local popularity of 2PM who have swept the Thai music charts with their hit songs, in addition to the nation's enthusiastic love for Nichkhun (Y. B. Moon 2009). Some media point out that JYPE's marketing strategies, which enable the breaking of cultural and language barriers through recruiting a foreign member, suggest the future direction of maintaining the *Hallyu* phenomenon in the global popular culture market (SBS 2009). The success of 2PM in Thailand signifies the ways in which culturally hybridized features reinforce popular products' transcultural border-crossing.

Figure 5.1 2PM Thai fan gathering

Transcultural hybridity is one of the most significant aspects of contemporary South Korean popular culture in the postmodern era and is the main driving force behind its overseas popularity. This book has investigated how transculturally hybridized South Korean masculinity travels freely across cultural boundaries due to its *mugukjeok* aspects. It has also examined how the hybridization of South Korean masculinity is reinforced by the diverse cultural practices of different regions, during which South Korean masculinity is reconstructed. In chapter 1, I have contextualized the hybridization dynamics of transcultural South Korean popular culture on the one hand, and the conceptual background of the reconstruction of *mugukjeok* South Korean masculinity on the other. In chapters 2, 3, and 4, I have analyzed the empirical case study results obtained in relation to the Japanese middle-aged female fandom of Bae Yong-Joon, the middle-class Singaporean female fandom of Rain, and the Western online cult fandom of *Oldboy*. I have shown how the local specificities of regional audiences in Japan, Singapore, and the West — characterized as post-colonialism, trans-pop-consumerism, and neo-Orientalism respectively — have combined with *mugukjeok* to create mixed cultural practices. Within these different cultural contexts, I have demonstrated how South Korean masculinity is reconstructed to give rise to soft, global, and postmodern masculinities respectively.

These varied forms of South Korean masculinity exemplify the crucial finding of this book: contemporary South Korean popular culture is constantly deconstructed and reconstructed within the multifarious transcultural practices of globalization and localization during which contemporary South Korean popular culture becomes *mugukjeok* and globally consumable. It is evident from the importance of local specificities — post-colonialism, trans-pop-consumerism, and neo-Orientalism — in relation to the reconstruction and consumption of South Korean masculinity, that in addition to *mugukjeok*, local specificities are also the key to understanding the transcultural flows of contemporary South Korean popular culture. Lastly and most importantly, I hope to have demonstrated that such transcultural flows are enhanced by global consumerist lifestyles and advanced technology. Thus, this book has concluded that *mugukjeok*, the local specificities of regional audiences, and technology-driven global consumerism are the keys to understanding the multidirectional transcultural flows of contemporary South Korean popular culture in the ever-fluctuating postmodern era. While I was preparing this concluding chapter, I began to think that, other than *mugukjeok*, a new theoretical paradigm is needed to specifically describe the manufactured versatile masculinity of South Korean idol boy bands. This is because the versatile masculine features they represent are not only culturally odorless but also culturally transformable. Thus, here, instead of *mugukjeok*, I suggest the notion of *chogukjeok* (cross- or trans-national[ity]) to describe the transcultural production and consumption of the hybridized Korean popular culture signified by idol boy bands. I choose *chogukjeok* because it not only refers to how popular cultural flows enable the "mixing" of various cultural elements (both specific and global), which then causes those particular cultural elements to lose specificity, but it also implies how hybridity and non-nationality enable such products to be culturally "transformable" and to easily "cross" national borders (Jung 2010).

The recent increased overseas popularity of K-pop idol boy bands exemplifies such multidirectional transcultural flows of *chogukjeok* contemporary South Korean popular culture. Elsewhere, I explained how the *chogukjeok* elements of TVXQ, another top K-pop boy band, enable them to easily travel even to the non-Asian countries like Mexico, Switzerland, and Spain (S. Jung 2009; 2010). In the case of 2PM's success in Thailand, JYPE highlights the group's *chogukjeok* features by having Nichkhun to lead the group in Thailand, particularly — due mainly to the language barrier of other members — in interviews with Thai media. 2PM is often described as "Nichkhun's 2PM" among Thai media and its viewers. It is also their sexually ambiguous features which draw Thai viewers' enthusiastic attention. This aspect is observed from the significant number of video clips featuring 2PM's versatile masculine images posted by Thai users on YouTube. It is, thus, clear how the sexually and culturally hybridized versatile features of 2PM are able to fulfill the complex desires of contemporary pop-consumers with various cultural backgrounds. In fact, such versatility, which empowers the transcultural border crossing of 2PM, signifies the well-planned globalization marketing strategies of the South Korean entertainment industry. As mentioned in chapter 3, it is now a common practice among South Korean entertainment management companies to make their trainees learn foreign languages and/or recruit foreign artists with the aim of conquering the broader overseas market (D. H. Hong 2010). Beginning with Asian — such as Japanese and Chinese — members, such practice has now expanded to recruit American — mostly Asian American — members to target the US market in particular, and the English-speaking market in general. It is also well known that the K-pop traineeship requires a long period of generally three to four years.[6] During such a long training period, these young idol star-wannabes learn not only to be skillful singers but also to be multi-entertainers.[7] Thus, idol stars often cross the boundaries between diverse entertainment media platforms: for example, acting in television drama series and movies, hosting popular music programs, and guest appearing in game shows and reality shows.

In particular, appearing in reality shows is considered crucial for rookie idol groups because it enables them to reveal their seemingly genuine selves to the audiences, which greatly enhances the connections between the viewers and the idol groups. Such an aspect is evident from the ways in which many viewers often express that they have become fans of certain K-pop stars after they have seen the stars' true personalities in reality shows. On Yahoo! Answers Philippines, a user, niyaw, asked "Why do they love K-pop?" to which another user, Rachel, replied "… K-pop artists always appeared in variety shows and reality shows, which reveals their true self and personalities to the fans …"[8] The idol group members are seen to reveal their trivial daily routines and private lives in reality shows, which "reinforces the fans' familiarity with them while reducing their curious mystique as idol stars" (G. N. Bae 2010a). While many viewers embrace such familiar images as the genuine selves of stars, some media critics point out that the images displayed in reality shows are nothing but the fabricated popular products empowered by the capitalist desires of their management companies. A film producer, Hwang Jeong-Hyeon, criticizes the thoroughly capitalist-driven nature of reality shows featuring idol stars:

[Today's the so-called "idol real variety shows" on cable television are] the "jointly manufactured products" which have been created by the mutual needs between the gigantic [entertainment] management business industry and the broadcasting industry. These products are created approximately based on a number of strategies: idols, who have been trained for several years, demonstrate their well-trained dancing and singing abilities and their bodies; and each member achieves her/his own "mission" based on her/his manufactured character. Each idol member, even from the very beginning, occupies her/his unique character [or role] in the group. Such an aspect of the "manufactured" characters of idols perfectly meets the core needs of real variety shows, which is showing [various interesting] "characters" … The Korean cable channels' "idol real variety shows" are nothing but the easily consumable manufactured products created by a factory called the "South Korean media industry," which is a result of the combination between the worsened broadcasting environment, the power of the gigantic entertainment management companies, and the individual desires of general public. (J. H. Hwang 2010)

According to Hwang, the so-called "idol real variety shows" are a site where the manufactured idol characters empowered by the capitalist desires of major entertainment companies meet the individual desires of general public, plus the practical and economic needs of the cable television industry. Here, as is evident from the aforementioned K-pop fan's comment on Yahoo! Answers, it is important to note the ways in which practicing "manufactured idol characters" — not only in reality shows but also in various other media programs — reinforces the construction of the "idol star persona." In one of the game shows, *Strong Heart* (*Gangshimjang*), Taec-Yeon explained that he has become the wildest *jimseungdol* among the 2PM members due to their manager and producer, JYP's instruction. Taec-Yeon said, "JYP always asks me to express the utmost rage whenever we practice. That is why I have to perform an angry man flying into the utmost rage whenever we do album jacket photo shoots and stage performances. [That is the reason I even ripped off my shirt]" (broadcast on February 16, 2010). In short, an idol star persona is constructed based mostly on the well-planned marketing strategies of her/his management company. Unlike Hwang's view though, some local media personnel observe the positive sides of diversely manufactured idol images. According to Lee Su-Hyeon from *Star News*:

These days, one can easily find idol stars from various media channels all around the year; yet, no one seems to get tired of them because they now show a variety of images in different programs … Idols used to be considered as singers who simply depend on their appealing appearances. Today's idols, however, have been significantly upgraded being armored with the well-trained singing and dancing skills which have been carefully developed under the systemized [management] system. (S. H. Lee 2010)

Lee's positive view emphasizes how manufactured idol images appeal to a broader viewer demographic as they are multilayered. Although the above two views address the contradictory — negative and positive — aspects of manufactured idol stars, they both highlight the way in which idols continuously perform different characters through various media channels that reinforces the construction of their versatile idol star personae.

Recently, K-pop related media content has been dynamically circulated in the bigger popular culture market beyond Asia through new media technologies such as fan blogs, social networking websites, UGC websites, and P2P websites. For instance, a search for "K-pop" on Google yielded 300,000 German language websites, while 320,000 results appeared in French (September 11, 2010). Among many others, a range of video clips featuring K-pop idol boy bands have gained noticeable recognition on globally well-known UGC websites as YouTube, and have been eagerly consumed and reproduced by global pop consumers with different cultural backgrounds. There are over 880,000 "Super Junior" related video clips and over 410,000 clips of "TVXQ" found on YouTube (September 11, 2010). As described in Rain's remarks quoted at the beginning of this chapter, these idol boy bands can be an exact embodiment of the well-planned South Korean popular culture products that are carefully manufactured to target a broader consumer demographic. The culturally mixed and versatile features of idol boy bands enable them to travel easily across cultural and national borders. This reflects Rain's comment on the significance of the amalgamation between the Koreanized and the globalized — in other words, culturally hybridized *chogukjeok*. The dynamic transcultural flows of South Korean idol boy bands exemplifying versatile masculinity demonstrates how well planned, carefully manufactured, and culturally hybridized *chogukjeok* popular products meet the complex desires of global mass pop-consumers. Although almost unimaginable as recently as five years ago, it now appears a distinct possibility that in the near future, a family in the US may have their dinner on Saturday night while watching an "idol real variety show" on Fox, featuring *chogukjeok* K-pop idol boys.

Appendix

Breakdown of Nationality of Imdb.com Users Who Posted Comments about *Oldboy* (Number of Users)

Afghanistan(1)	Malaysia (1)
Arab Emirates (2)	Malta (4)
Argentina (1)	Mexico (3)
Australia (12)	Nepal (1)
Austria (1)	Netherlands (10)
Bangladesh (1)	New Zealand (6)
Belgium (3)	Norway (4)
Brazil (3)	Philippines (2)
Canada (32)	Peru (1)
Chile (2)	Poland (4)
China (2)	Portugal (1)
Columbia (1)	Puerto Rico (2)
Croatia (1)	Romania (2)
Czech Republic (1)	Russia (1)
Denmark (6)	Serbia (1)
Egypt (1)	Singapore (1)
Finland (2)	Slovenia (1)
France (8)	South Africa (1)
Germany (8)	Spain (3)
Greece (8)	Sweden (10)
Hong Kong (3)	Switzerland (1)
Hungary (2)	Thailand (1)
India (9)	Turkey (7)
Indonesia (1)	Ukraine (1)
Ireland (4)	Venezuela (1)
Israel (2)	Yugoslavia (1)
Italy (4)	UK (117)
Japan (1)	US (226)
Korea, South (6)	Unknown (52)

Based on the user comment page of *Oldboy* which can be found on
http://www.imdb.com/title/tt0364569/usercomments
(accessed on September 19, 2008)

Notes

Chapter 1

1. The term "ours" is a direct translation of the Korean word "우리 것" (*uri geot*) which is used to refer to "Koreanness" in Kim Gyeong-Wook's book *The Fantasy of Blockbuster, Narcissism of Korean Cinema* (2002: 18–21).

2. While the concept of *Hallyu* was originally used to refer to the popularity of South Korean popular culture within Asia, it can also refer to the circulation of South Korean popular culture outside Asia. Such a usage would point to the global popularity of *Hallyu*. Indeed, some South Korean media and cultural studies scholars have already used the term *Hallyu* to refer to *Hallyu*'s global popularity. In this book, however, I employ *Hallyu* in its original sense in order to distinguish the regional Asian popularity of South Korean popular culture from the Western cult fandom of South Korean genre films. This is because unlike the phenomenal mass popularity of South Korean television drama series and pop stars among Asian audiences, the recent Western popularity of South Korean genre films is typified by the tendency towards cult fandom by a limited number of Western film fans.

3. The term *Hallyu* began to be used in Chinese-speaking countries such as Taiwan, China, and Hong Kong since the late 1990s. According to Lee Ji-Gun, the CEO of Insrea Production in Taiwan, the term originated from the Chinese phrase 夏日寒流 (*xiari hanliu*: a strong cold flow in a summer day), which was a marketing phrase used to promote South Korean popular music and TV dramas. Later, as South Korean popular culture gained regional popularity, the media began to associate the term *Hanliu* [*Hallyu*], with 韓 (Korea) instead of 寒 (cold) (H. M. Kim 2003).

4. According to Park Jeong-Yeon from AGB Neilsen Media Research and Han Ji-Sook from Digital Times, "television audience share" refers to the percentage of televisions which are tuned into the particular program out of all panel televisions with "people meters," the individual viewer reporting devices (J. Y. Park 2008; J. S. Han 2006).

5. For the term television drama series, hereafter, I use the Korean terminology "television drama" or "drama." I chose the shortened form mainly to avoid excessive repetitions throughout the book.

6. *Oricon* (オリコン *Orikon*), also known as *Oricon Style*, is a Japanese company that provides information related to the music industry. It is best known for the music charts it produces, similar to those published by *Billboard Magazine* in the U.S. On February 27, 2008, BoA's sixth album, *The Face*, was released in both South Korea and Japan and reached the top of the *Oricon* chart again. Currently, all of BoA's six albums (or "regular

albums," as full-length albums are called in Asian countries) have reached the number one spot on the chart. These albums are *Listen to My Heart, Valenti, Love & Honesty, Outgrow, Made in Twenty, The Face,* and the special compilation album, *Best of Soul.* Apart from her albums, a number of her singles have also reached the number one spot on the *Oricon* daily chart. These include the ninth single, *Shine We Are;* the fifteenth single, *Do the Motion;* the nineteenth single, *Seven Colors of Tomorrow;* and the twenty-first single, *Winter Love.*

7. The commercial success of *Winter Sonata* in South Korea has enormously influenced the entertainment and tourism industries. The profit for South Korea and Japan alone is a total of US$2.7 billion (Yu et al. 2005: 20).

8. For example, in the Philippines the drama's highest audience share reached 50.5% on April 17, 2005, while in Thailand it reached 64% when the drama's last episode was broadcast in August 2005 (T. E. Kim 2006; E. J. Lee 2005).

9. In South Korea, the drama was first aired in September 2003 on MBC (Munhwa Broadcasting Corporation) and its domestic audience share reached 57.8%, the highest in South Korean broadcasting history (M. H. Lee 2004; S. M. Jeong 2007). When the drama was broadcast on the national TV channel 2 in Iran, audience share of Dae-jang-geum reached 86%, the highest in Iranian television history (W. J. Yoon 2008; S. M. Jeong 2007).

10. Indeed, some Asian movies such as *Crouching Tiger, Hidden Dragon (Wo Hu Cang Long* 2000) have become mega-hits in the global market. Thus, one might point out that the newspaper article cited here is inaccurate as *Crouching Tiger, Hidden Dragon* has sold more than *Oldboy* in the UK. Nevertheless, I have cited this article to support my argument because, I believe, the reporter seems to focus on pure Asianness when s/he referred to the bestselling "Asian" cinema. In other words, *Oldboy* is produced exclusively by South Korean producers, while *Crouching Tiger, Hidden Dragon* is not produced solely by Asian producers. For example, a US production company, Good Machine International, is one of the production companies of *Crouching Tiger, Hidden Dragon.*

11. Elsewhere, I use the term *chogukjeok* (trans- or cross-national[ity]) to describe such *mugukjeok* and hybrid aspects of South Korean popular culture. The term not only refers to how popular cultural flows enable the "mixing" of various cultural elements (both specific and global), which then causes those particular cultural elements to lose specificity, but it also implies how hybridity and non-nationality enable such culturally mixed pop culture products to easily "cross" national borders (Jung 2010). I will further explain the concept of *chogukjeok* in chapter 5.

12. On the other side of hybrid South Korean masculinity, it is also evident that South Korean femininity is hybridized and reconstructed through media cultural flows and is transculturally embraced because of its hybridity and *mugukjeok.* Such new South Korean femininity is apparent in many popular cultural products such as female characters of the romantic comedy film *My Sassy Girl,* the gangster comedy *My Wife Is a Gangster,* the historical drama series *Dae-jang-geum,* and South Korean female singer BoA. However, due to the limited scope of this book, I only focus on hybrid South Korean masculinity.

13. I recruited my interviewees and questionnaire respondents through personal contacts and Internet fan club sites. I then planned and organized interviews via email and phone.

14. Due to the commercial success of these blockbuster films, the Korean domestic film market share has steadily increased. Since *Shiri*, the Korean domestic film market share has increased from 35.15% in 2000, to 50.15% in 2001, 48.34% in 2002, and 53.49% in 2003. Finally, in 2004, the domestic market share of Korean films reached 59.33%. Considering that the market share of the Hollywood film industry is over 85% of the global film market, 59.33% is an impressive figure. However, the Korean domestic film market share has slightly decreased since 2004 — 58.71% in 2005, 63.83% in 2006 (the momentary increase in 2006 is mainly due to the mega-hit of two blockbuster films, *The Host and D-War*), 50.8% in 2007, and 42.1% in 2008 (Korean Film Council 2008).

15. Korean *haan* can be understood within a broader and more common pattern of modern national history. For instance, Rey Chow uses the concept of "the logic of the wound" to describe the historical trauma of China. She explains that after having gone through the 150 year history of humiliation that officially began with the Treaty of Nanking, Chinese people show "the paranoid tendency to cast doubt on everything Western and to insist on qualifying it with the word Chinese," which she calls "the logic of the wound" (Chow 1998: 5–6).

16. In the US, when *Taegukgi* was released during the first weekend of September 2004, it earned US$12,565 per screen for the first four days. It was the highest revenue per screen and 2.28 times more than Zhang Yimou's *Hero* (US$5,513), which was ranked number one at the North American box office for the first two consecutive weekends after it was released on August 27, 2004 (Cine21 2005).

17. Alvin Toffler's term combining producer and consumer comes from *The Third Wave* (1980).

18. According to the conscription policy in South Korea, all able-bodied men are required to serve a mandatory twenty-one months of military service.

19. The term "cultural proximity" refers to cultural similarity across history. In chapter 2, this term is used to describe certain aspects of cultural similarity between South Korea and Japan that have been produced through transcultural flows of popular culture.

20. Expanding on Chua's research on the new rich in Asia in terms of materialistic consumerism, I argue that the regional popularity of Rain can be understood through the new consumption lifestyle of emerging "cultural Asia." As Asia's economic power and technological infrastructure are increasingly developed, there are complex and varied social implications that result from the new cultural practices of the new rich. One of the implications is evident in the practice of transnational consumption of various popular cultures within Asia. I call this group of people "trans-pop-consumers." This term emphasizes the group's key characteristic, which is that they engage in the transnational consumption of Asian popular culture through mobilizing capitalist power to obtain leisure and entertainment rather than material goods and social services.

21. The expression "the time between dog and wolf" is originally derived from the French phrase "l'heure entre chien et loup." It refers to the twilight hour when day is not quite night. In chapter 4, this phrase is metaphorically used to describe this postmodern era

of cultural hybridization and multicultural flows, where Western audiences ambivalently embrace *Oldboy* (Dae-Soo), while they do not know whether it (he) refers to the primitive or the postmodern, and familiarity or strangeness.

22. It is difficult to collect specific data from a demographic breakdown of online users. For example, a demographic breakdown of IMDb.com users, in particular their nationalities, is not specifically addressed on the website. Even IMDb Pro, where the fee-paying users can access professional and detailed data about films, only offers very limited information about the nationality of the site users — the proportion of US to non-US users is approximately 40% to 60%. Thus, in order to obtain a more specific breakdown of nationality of the users, I counted the number of the users from each different country, who posted comments on *Oldboy*. As a result of the counting, out of 542 comments, where the users' nationalities are detectable, 226 are from the US, 117 are from the UK, 32 are from Canada, and 12 are from Australia. Also it is evident that many users are from Western European countries such as Denmark (6), France (8), Germany (8), the Netherlands (10), and Sweden (10).

Chapter 2

1. Ages of fans are inserted where available. Some fans like Gan do not specify their age on the questionnaire.

2. In this chapter, the term "middle-aged women" refers to the Japanese fans who are in between thirty and seventy. This categorization is based on the age range of the sample group who has participated in the interviews and questionnaires. In his article "*Winter Sonata* and Cultural Practices of Active Fans in Japan," Yoshitaka Mori uses "middle-aged" to refer to women, roughly between thirty and seventy years old. He then explains that "here I would deliberately call even seventy-year-old women middle-aged, because they looked much younger than I had expected and I am hesitant to call them 'old ladies'" (Mori 2008: 272). As Mori also experienced, the over-sixty-year-old women I interviewed look young enough to be categorized as middle-aged. In addition, they act young which is evident from their energetic fan activities. Most importantly, when the media and cultural scholars discuss the Japanese middle-aged female fandom, they tend to include these old-aged women in the group of middle-aged fans (Heo and Ham 2005; Yoo et al. 2005; J. W. Cho 2004b).

3. There were about 1,500 fans gathered at the airport when Beckham visited Japan in June 2002 (Y. C. Park 2004).

4. NHK (Nippon Hoso Kyokai, 日本放送協会, Japan Broadcasting Corporation) is Japan's public broadcaster and the most influential Japanese broadcasting company. It operates two terrestrial television services (NHK General TV and NHK Educational TV), three satellite services (NHK BS-1, NHK BS-2, and NHK Hi-Vision — High-definition TV), and three radio networks (NHK Radio 1, NHK Radio 2, and NHK FM).

5. *Winter Sonata* was first broadcast at 10 p.m. every Thursday in April 2003 by NHK BS. The average audience share was about 1.1%. Considering the fact that NHK BS was a satellite service, this share was relatively high (Mori 2008: 130).

6. Considering that it was aired at midnight and that the average audience share is about 10% even during prime time (7 p.m.–10 p.m.), the share was very high (Mori 2008: 130). On the day of the Olympic Games, although the program was broadcast at 2 a.m., the share was just more than 10%.

7. Here, the Korean term "정 (*jeong*)" is translated as "sentiment." The meaning of "정" is peculiar to Korea. It refers to feelings such as compassion, love, affection, and sympathy. 정 is largely driven by the sense of sharing traditional family values and community values, and is thus opposed to individualism.

8. The phrase "Seoul (South Korean) Now" is a direct translation of "지금의 서울 [한국]," which is a phrase Hirata uses to refer to contemporary South Korea.

9. In this book, I mainly focus on the notion of Japan's counter-coeval gaze towards Korea, examining Japanese fandom of BYJ around 2005 and 2006. Nevertheless, thanks to the rapidly changing global cultural market environment, it is evident that recent Japanese consumption of Korean popular culture somewhat demonstrates a rather coeval gaze of the Japanese audiences. This is well portrayed through the phenomenal success of K-pop girl groups among young female fans in Japan since late 2010.

10. According to Baek, one of the examples of the glocalization process, in terms of South Korean popular culture consumption in Vietnam, is found from the case of the Vietnamese and South Korean co-production sitcom *Love Flower Basket* (*Sarang-ui Kkotbaguni* 2005). Baek explains that this co-production project, prepared with the carefully pre-conducted industry/market research, shows the ways in which the South Korean popular culture sector finally attempted to find the drama content and forms which would most suit the local condition. She further elaborates that such a project represents the actual [g]localization of South Korean popular culture because it acknowledges both the commonality between and cultural specificity of Vietnam and South Korea, while it also guarantees improvement of the local production technology and development of drama content in Vietnam (2005: 167–68).

11. The notion of sexual neutrality, as used by Kuroiwa and other Japanese fans to describe BYJ, is different from the concept of being androgynous. For Japanese fans, such neutral traits are still perceived as masculine attributes. Therefore, the sexual neutrality of BYJ's images has to be understood within the framework of soft masculinity rather than that of androgyny.

12. This expression originated from the story of a government official, Lu Tan (盧坦傳), found in the official history book of the Chinese Qing Dynasty (唐書). In Korea, the concept of 外柔內剛 has been considered to be one of the most significant aspects in the Confucian *seonbi* ideology as it represents rigid self-discipline in the cultivation of intelligence (文) and virtue (德).

13. East Asia is a sub-region of Asia that can be defined in geographical or cultural terms. Geographically, East Asia includes China, Hong Kong, Japan, Macau, Mongolia, Taiwan, and North and South Korea. Culturally, East Asia can be conceived as a "Chinese-character cultural sphere" (漢字文化圈). This term denotes a grouping of countries, regions, and people with Chinese cultural and linguistic legacies. This includes the abovementioned countries as well as Singapore and Vietnam. East Asian countries display heavy historical influences from the Chinese language, Confucianism, Mahayana Buddhism, and Taoism.

14. According to the Webster dictionary, familism is defined as "a social pattern in which the family assumes a position of ascendance over individual interests." As such, the term "familism" refers to a model of social ideology that is based on the prevalence of the family unit and which places the well-being of the family unit above the individual interests of its members. It is part of a traditional view of society that emphasizes loyalty, trust, and cooperative attitudes within the family unit, which is in opposition to the modern social ideology of individualism.

15. The Chinese term, 君子 (*junzi*) can be translated as a "wise man," a "gentleman," or a "perfect man." Literally, the term refers to a "nobleman" who has the power to control ordinary people as it implies a person who is a 有位者 (a person who is in a high controlling position) as well as a person who is a 有德者 (a person who has high morality and intelligence). The ideal of a "gentleman" or "perfect man" is that for which Confucianism exhorts all people to strive.

16. The five basic beliefs or virtues (五常) of Confucian theory are 仁 (*ren*), 義 (*yi*), 禮 (*li*), 智 (*zhi*), 信 (*xin*). They are compassion, righteousness, politeness, wisdom, and trust.

17. Here, I use the term, "Post/Colonial" to refer to the colonial and postcolonial relationship between South Korean and Japan.

18. *Joseon* can also be spelled as *Chosun*, *Choson*, and *Chosôn*, depending on different romanization methods. In this book, I use *Joseon* because I follow the "revised Romanization of Korean" which was released in July 2000. However, I retain some words and names spelled using the old romanization methods as they have been conventionally spelled as such. One example is the name of the newspaper, *Chosun Ilbo*.

19. *Kominka* is a movement that "aimed at the complete regimentation and Japanization of Japan's colonial races, and justified these goals through endless moral platitudes couched in Confucian phraseology and centered on inculcation of a sense of obligation to the Japanese emperor" (Prettie 1984: 121). There is another articulation of the term, "Japanization," which refers to the indigenization and domestication of foreign (Western) culture (Iwabuchi 2002: 9). In this chapter, however, Japanization mainly refers to the regional transcultural influences of Japan that originated from the *kominka* of the colonial era.

20. In fact, it is not very hard to find young male actors playing tough guy characters in recent South Korean films: Song Seung-Heon and Kwon Sang-Woo in *Running Wild* (*Yasu* 2006); and Jo In-Seong in *A Dirty Carnival* (*Biyeolhan Geori* 2006). Also JYPE's idol boy band, "2PM," represents tough guy images under the nickname of a "beast-like" idol band. Thus one might question this idea of disappearing macho masculinity in the South Korean popular culture industry. Nevertheless, it is significant to note the ways in which these male artists are still categorized and described as *kkonminam* stars by fans and media.

21. When *shōjo manga* first emerged in the 1960s, many of these stories dealt with girls' dreams and fantasies. Fantasy is the *shōjo manga*'s stock in trade: the more fantastic the better and portraying male homosexuality is one of the ways to reinforce female readers' fantasy (Brady quoted in Aoyama 1988: 189). Since the 1970s, the theme of sexuality, especially male homosexuality, has been incorporated into the stories of *shōjo manga* which is a subgenre of *shōjo manga*, "BL (boys' love)" or "*yaoi*" (Ito 2005). The *yaoi*

is about unrealistically pretty boys and their sexual relations. Thus, *Yaoi* has played an important role in contributing to the production of pretty boy images.

22. After President Park Jung-Hee was assassinated on October 26, 1979, it would seem that the long dark age of dictatorship (1961–1979) had come to an end and democracy had finally arrived in South Korean society. On May 18, 1980, however, there was a brutal suppression of the democratic movement in Kwangju where more than 2,000 people disappeared or were killed. According to *Asia Watch Report*, Kwangju's death statistics for May 1980 were 2,300 over the monthly average (Standish 1994: 70).

23. Many Japanese and Singaporean fans have begun to learn the Korean language to both understand their stars and appreciate South Korean popular culture. They also learn some Korean words and phrases from watching South Korean dramas or movies. Such tendency is reflected in the interviews with the fans where they use some Korean words, as is evident from Ba's comment using the Korean word, *ajumma*.

24. As evidence of BYJ's will power, many of the fans cite the fact that he had spent three months training with his personal trainer to create his new *momjjang* body.

25. Focus group interviewees also participated in the questionnaire.

Chapter 3

1. On February 16, 2008, Lotte Concert was held in Busan in South Korea to celebrate the first anniversary of the Busan-Fukuoka sister-city affiliation. This concert was co-organized by Lotte and J.Tune Entertainment. They sold concert-tour package tickets to Japanese fans in advance, where Japanese can purchase tickets for R seats, the most expensive and also the closest seats to the stage, as a part of a tour package deal (based on telephone conversation with the customer service manager of Lotte Hotel, February 13, 2008).

2. Rain's Korean name is Jung Ji-Hoon. He uses the stage name "Bi" (비), which means "rain" in Korean.

3. This number is only of those who purchased their tickets via RainSingapore.com, and does not take into account other fans who may have attended the Bangkok concert separately from the fans from RainSingapore.com.

4. The best example is the recent phenomenal success of K-pop idol girl groups, such as SNSD and Kara, in Japan since late 2010. SNSD, for example, was criticized at first due to its similarities with J-pop girl groups like Moningu Musume. However, three years after its debut, thanks to the hybridized elements, this repackaged pop product — SNSD — has conquered the originating market.

5. At the end of the year, Rain was awarded many influential South Korean Music Awards such as M.NET Male Artist Award, KMTV New Male artist, the MBC (Munhwa Broadcasting Corporation) Top 10 New Artist Award, New Artist Golden Disc Award, and SBS (Seoul Broadcasting System) New Male Performer of the Year Award (JYPE 2006).

6. At the end of 2003, many entertainment awards were presented to Rain which recognized his acting and singing abilities. Some of these awards include the "Male Performer of the

Year" from SBS, the "Top 10 Artist Award" from MBC, and the "New Actor Award" from KBS (JYPE).

7. In 2005, he achieved "the Grand Slam" in the regional MTV Awards by winning the "Favorite Artist of South Korea" award from MTV ASIA AID held in Bangkok Impact Arena (February), the "Best Buzz Asia from South Korea" award from MTV Video Music Awards Japan 2005 held in Tokyo Bay NK Hall (May), and the "Best South Korean Artist of the Year" award from MTV-CCTV Mandarin Music Honours 2005 held in Beijing (July) (W. G. Kim 2005).

8. *We Are the World* is a song written by Michael Jackson and Lionel Richie, produced and conducted by Quincy Jones, and recorded by a group of US celebrity musicians. This charity single was produced to raise funds to help famine-relief efforts in Ethiopia, which experienced unusual drought in 1984 and 1985. In January 2005, a similar fund-raising concert was held in Hong Kong. More than 150 movie stars and singers held a seven-hour charity show for the tsunami victims in southern Asia. Celebrities from Hong Kong, Taiwan, and China participated in this concert: they included Hong Kong's Andy Lau, Jacky Cheung, and Kelly Chen, Taiwan's Cheung A-Mei and China's Jet Li. At least US$11 million was collected in the two and a half hours after the "Cross-Border" concert was held at the Hong Kong Stadium (Bnetau.com.au 2005).

9. Over 12,000 tons of crude oil was spilled off the scenic Taean region on the west coast of South Korea (CNN 2007). On January 16, 2008, Rain participated in volunteer work to help clean up the oil spill, and donated US$317,000 towards the cleanup effort (M. Y. Kwon 2008).

10. I refer to the online nicknames of fan club members exactly as they have spelt them. Some nicknames have been written in lower-case, and I have kept their stylistic conventions.

11. Rain's Korean name.

12. In ancient China, there were five different classes, namely an emperor (天子), the feudal lords and kings (諸侯), the high nobility (大夫), the scholar (士), and ordinary people (庶民). Apart from the emperor and the feudal lords, who were believed to be born to be rulers as dictated by divine will, the scholar (士) and the nobility (大夫) together constituted a dominating class (士大夫) that was distinguished from the dominated class of ordinary people.

13. For example, according to *Gyeonggukdaejeon* (경국대전), the basic code of laws during the Joseon Dynasty, a man from the *sadaebu* class cannot remarry within three years of his wife's death.

14. *Samgang* consists of the following three laws: the retainer must respect the lord (군위신강, 君為臣綱); the son must respect the father (부위자강, 父為子綱); and the wife must respect the husband (부위부강, 夫為婦綱).

15. Some of the interviews were further conducted by email. I use some terms, expressions, and emoticons that the fans have used unless they create confusion.

16. In December 2007, a popular Chinese actor and singer, Huang Xiao Ming (黃曉明) released his first album *It's Ming*. After the release, there were many debates on major Chinese and South Korean websites over the similarity of his fashion, dancing style, and album jacket design to Rain's fourth album, *I'm Coming* (Asianbite 2007; DailySurprise

2007). Like Rain, Huang adopts a military look for the performances and shows his naked upper torso on his album jacket.

Chapter 4

1. On the other side of the Western fandom of South Korean genre films, it is evident that South Korean arthouse films have also been recognized by Western audiences; some well-known arthouse film directors are Hong Sang-Soo, Lee Chang-Dong, and Kim Ki-Duk. However, in this book, I will not discuss the case of arthouse cinema as I focus mainly on the online popularity of South Korean cinema, which is typified by the Western online cult fandom of South Korean genre films.

2. The expression "the time between dog and wolf" is from the South Korean television series, *Time between Dog and Wolf*. It was originally derived from the French phrase, *L'heure entre chien et loup*, which refers to the twilight hour when day is not quite night. In this chapter, this phrase is used figuratively to describe the postmodern era of cultural hybridization and multicultural flows, when Western audiences embrace *Oldboy* (and its protagonist Dae-Soo) ambivalently where they do not know whether Dae-Soo represents the primitive or the postmodern, familiarity or strangeness.

3. Park Dong-Ho, CEO of CJ Entertainment, also points out that the most significant aspect of Korean cinema in 2003 is the success of well-made films in various genres, such as Bong Joon-Ho's *Memories of Murder*, Park Chan-Wook's *Oldboy*, Im Sang-Soo's *A Good Lawyer's Wife,* and Kim Ji-Woon's *A Tale of Two Sisters* (S. W. Lee et al. 2003). Another producer, Kim Mi-Hui, clarifies this phenomenon in two words: "trend and quality" (ibid.). She points out that those well-made genre films of 2003 satisfy audiences' desire for trendy commercial films and artistic quality. Film critic Kim So-Hui defines well-made genre films as those that not only mobilize the star system and adhere to genre conventions, but also as those that contain their directors' unique style and critical consciousness. In addition, these well-made genre films are those that have gained the support of the public and are commercially successful (S. H. Kim 2004).

4. Miike Takashi is a Japanese director who is often referred to as the most controversial Asian filmmaker. Some of his films, such as *Ichi the Killer* (2001) and *Audition* (1999), have become Asian cult classics due to their explicit depictions of shockingly extreme violence and bizarre sexual perversions. Although he has produced such touching humanistic films as *The Bird People of China* (1998) and *Sabu* (2002), among Western cult audiences, he is still most well known as a master of extreme Asian cinema.

5. *The Host* opened on the largest number of screens ever for Korean films that had been released in the US up until March 2007 (E. J. Kang 2007; H. L. Kim 2007).

6. These fan-operated websites offer new sites to acquire cultural capital and contribute to the reshaping of the canon of popular culture. Some of the reviews from these sites are, however, relatively amateurish, seemingly no more than web-users' comments, and some of the so-called "online reviewers" or "online film critics" are rather unprofessional and incompetent. Therefore, I regard the comments of these minor online film reviewers as coming from ordinary site users, unless they are clearly from established film critics or reviewers from the major media.

7. Issue 39 of *Asian Cult Cinema* contains the cover story, "Explosive Korean films." Issue 28's cover story is about the horror world of Japanese director, Teruo Ishii. Issue 25 has the cover story, "Violent Pink *Eiga*," which is about Japanese soft porn movies. Each issue eagerly excavates unknown Asian films and delivers valuable information to Asian cult film fans in the US (and presumably in other Western countries). However, unlike mainstream film magazines, its style of representation is kitsch-like, crude, and coarse, helping to reinforce the notion of "Asian cult" and "extreme Asia" among Western fans.

8. The trailer can be found from http://flvs.daum.net/flvPlayer.swf?vid=Ek4L2YUKukg$ (accessed on November 5, 2009).

9. Chan's *Dumplings* features a woman who tries to stay young by consuming special dumplings composed of the bodies of aborted fetuses. In *Cut*, Park tells a gruesome story about a famous director and his pianist wife, who are held hostage by a psychopathic extra in their own home; the director must strangle a little girl or watch the psycho chop off his wife's fingers. Miike's *Box* is about a female writer who is haunted by her twin sister's accidental death.

10. In June 2005, a Korean blogger posted UGC (user-generated content) of a young woman who had refused to clean up the mess that her dog made when it defecated on the floor of a subway train. The picture of the woman was posted on a popular website without masking her face which started a nationwide witch-hunt. Within hours, she was labeled *gae-ttong-nyeo* (개 똥 녀, dog-shit girl) and pictures of her and parodies were everywhere. And within days, her identity and her past were discovered and revealed. Requests for more information about her parents and her relatives began appearing. People were able to recognize her by her dog, bag, and watch as these were clearly visible in the original picture that was posted. This incident triggered various socio-academic debates over the roles and functions of new media communication and the privacy of ordinary people.

11. Of course the US media do not publish a picture of their own president, George W. Bush, holding a hammer. One of the users of IMDb.com, Frankenstyle, wittily posted a photo of George Bush holding a hammer to satirically point out how absurd it is to find a connection between *Oldboy* and Cho.

12. The Korean word, *Ajeosshi*, normally refers to a middle-aged man. It can be translated as "Mister" or "Uncle" in English. *Ajeosshi* is the term used by Mi-Do to call Dae-Soo in the film and her use of this term demonstrates their age-gap.

Chapter 5

1. "K-pop" usually refers to South Korean popular music in the overseas market while 'K-drama' refers to South Korean television dramas. According to Carolyn Stevens, "'J-pop' is widely used by East Asian audiences to describe music from Japan overseas and has become so integrated in a wider East Asian consumer market that this terminology has recently been transformed to describe other Asian pop cultures: 'K-*poppu*' ['K-pop'] (Korean popular music and culture) is another trend seen in both Japan and other international markets" (2008: 16–17).

2. It is reported that idol groups have been occupying over 80% of the entire content of weekly music programs in the three major broadcasting companies, KBS, MBC, and SBS (J. Y. Na 2010).

3. Here, I intentionally use "queen" instead of "king" because he represents total femininity when he mimics girl groups' performances.

4. 2PM was originally a seven-member group. However, it currently consists of six members due to the sudden withdrawal of a Korean American leader, Jae-Beom, following an Internet controversy in September 2009. Jae-Beom left 2PM as well as South Korea on September 8, 2009 because of the MySpace comments he made in 2005, where he wrote: "Korea is gay … I hate Koreans …" Such comments angered many South Korean netizens who, through countless blog postings and web-forum articles, unleashed a fervent backlash against him. Only four days after his MySpace comments were first revealed, Jae-Beom said he was leaving the group and flew back to his hometown — Seattle, in the US. "According to *PD Note*, the famous current affairs program in Korea, more than 760 on- and off-line news articles were produced for the first four days, while 330 articles were intensively released only for six hours between the announcement of his leave and his actual departure" (cited in H. J. Hong 2009).

5. After presenting such a "shirt ripping" performance several times, he has obtained a nickname, "*Jjit*-Taec-Yeon." Here, "*Jjit*" is from a Korean word, *jjitda* (찢다, rip off).

6. So far, the idol star who has gone through the longest training period is Jo Kwon from 2AM. He has spent eight years for training in JYPE before 2AM's official debut in July 2008.

7. A large portion of the idol star management practices are originated from the Japanese entertainment industry. For further explanation, see *Japanese Popular Music* (Stevens 2008).

8. http://ph.answers.yahoo.com/question/index?qid=20091229031900AASBJ76.

List of Media Productions

April Snow (Oechul) Dir. Hur Jin-Ho. South Korea, 2005.

Arirang Dir. Na Un-Gyu. South Korea, 1926.

Audition (Odishon) Dir. Miike Takashi. Japan, 1999.

Babel Dir. Alejandro Gonzalez Inarritu. France, US, and Mexico, 2006.

Battle Royale (Batoru Rowaiaru) Dir. Kinji Fukasaku. Japan, 2000

Beat (Biteu) Dir. Kim Seong-Soo. South Korea, 1997.

Bichunmoo Dir. Kim Young-Joon. South Korea, 2000.

Bird People in China, The (Chugokuno Chojin) Dir. Miike Takashi. Japan, 1998.

Bitter Sweet Life, A Dir. Kim Ji-Woon. South Korea, 2005.

Black Republic (Geudeuldo Uricheoreom) Dir. Park Kwang-Soo, 1990.

Bungee Jumping of Their Own (Beonjijeompeureul Hada) Dir. Kim Dae-Seung. South Korea, 2001.

Christmas in August (Palweol-ui Keuriseumaseu) Dir. Heo Jin-Ho. South Korea, 1998.

Clockwork Orange, A Dir. Stanley Kubrick. UK, 1971.

Crouching Tiger Hidden Dragon (Wo Hu Cang Long) Dir. Ang Lee. Taiwan, Hong Kong, US, and China, 2000.

Dae-jang-geum Dir. Lee Byeong-Hoon. South Korea, 2003.

Dirty Carnival, A (Biyeolhan Geori) Dir. Yu Ha. South Korea, 2006.

Entrails of a Beautiful Woman (Bijono Harawata) Dir. Kazuo "Gaira" Komizu. Japan, 1986.

Entrails of a Virgin (Shojono Harawata) Dir. Kazuo "Gaira" Komizu. Japan, 1986.

Evil Dead Trap (Shiryono Wana) Dir. Toshiharu Ikeda. Japan, 1988.

Fight Club Dir. David Fincher. US, 1999.

Fine, Windy Day, A (Barambureo Joeunnal) Dir. Lee Jang-Ho. South Korea, 1980.

First Love (Cheotsarang) Dir. Lee Eung-Jin. South Korea, 1997.

Friend (Chingu) Dir. Gwak Gyeong-Taek. South Korea, 2001.

Full House (Pulhauseu) Dir. Pyo Min-Soo. South Korea, 2004.

Gagman (Gaegeumaen) Dir. Lee Myeong-Se. South Korea, 1989.

Ghost in the Shell (Kokaku Kidotai) Dir. Mamoru Ohii. Japan, 1995.

G.I. Joe Dir. Stephen Sommers. US, 2009.

Good Lawyer's Wife, A (Baramnan Gajok) Dir. Im Sang-Soo. South Korea, 2003.

Happy End Dir. Jeong Ji-Woo. South Korea, 1999.

Have We Really Loved? (Uriga Jeongmal Saranghaesseulkka) Dir. Park Jong. South Korea, 1999.

Hero (Ying Xiong) Dir. Zhang Yimou. Hong Kong and China, 2002.

Host, The (Gwoemul) Dir. Bong Joon-Ho. South Korea, 2006.

Hotelier (Hotellieo) Dir. Jang Yong-Woo. South Korea, 2001.

House of Flying Daggers (Shi Mian Mai Fu) Dir. Zhang Yumou. Hong Kong and China, 2004.

Ichi, the Killer (Koroshiya 1) Dir. Miike Takashi. Japan, 2001.

I'm a Cyborg, But That's OK (Saibogeujiman Gwenchana) Dir. Park Chan-Wok. South Korea, 2006.

In the Mood for Love (Fa Yeung Nin Wa) Dir. Wang Kar Wai. Hong Kong and France, 2000.

Infernal Affairs (Mou Gaan Dou) Dir. Wai-Keung Lau and Siu-Fai Mak. Hong Kong, 2002.

JSA: Joint Security Area (Gongdong Gyeongbi Guyeok: JSA) Dir. Park Chan-Wook. South Korea, 2000.

King and the Clown, The (Wang-ui Namja) Dir. Lee Joon-Ik. South Korea, 2005.

Korean Strait (Daehan Haehyeop) Dir. Park Gi-Chae. South Korea, 1943.

Laundry Warrior, The Dir. Lee Sngmoo. US and New Zealand, 2008.

Legend (Taewangsashingi) Dir. Kim Jong-Hak. South Korea, 2007.

Love Greeting (Sarang-ui Insa) Dir. Yun Seok-Ho. South Korea, 1994.

M*A*S*H Dir. Hy Averback et al. US, 1972.

Memoirs of a Geisha Dir. Rob Marshall. US, 2005.

Memories of Murder (Sarin-ui Chueok) Dir. Bong Joon-Ho. South Korea, 2003.

Musa: The Warrior (Musa) Dir. Kim Seong-Soo. South Korea, 2001.

My Sassy Girl (Yeopgijeogin Geunyeo) Dir. Gwak Jae-Yong. South Korea, 2001.

My Wife Is a Gangster (Jopok Manura) Dir. Cho Jin-Gyu. South Korea, 2001.

Never Forever Dir. Gina Kim. South Korea and US, 2007.

Ninja Assasin Dr. James McTeigue. US, 2009.

Nowhere to Hide (Injeongsajeong Bolgeoteopda) Dir. Lee Myeong-Se. South Korea, 1999.

Oldboy (Oldeu Boi) Dir. Park Chan-Woo k. South Korea, 2004.

One Fine Spring Day (Bomnareun Ganda) Dir. Heo Jin-Ho. South Korea, 2001.

Organ Dir. Kei Fujiwara. Japan, 1996.

Phantom (Yuryeong) Dir. Min Byeong-Cheon. South Korea, 1999.

Pitch Black Dir. David Twohy. Australia and US, 2000.

Ppligu Dir. Yoo Jin-Soon. South Korea, 1994.

Promise, The (Wu Ji) Dir. Chen Kaige. China, Hong Kong, Japan, and South Korea, 2005.

Pulp Fiction Dir. Quentin Tarantino. US, 1994.

Reservoir Dogs Dir. Quentin Tarantino. US, 1992.

Running Wild (Yasu) Dir. Kim Seong-Soo. South Korea, 2006.

Rush Hour 1 Dir. Brett Ratner. US, 1998.

Rush Hour 2 Dir. Brett Ratner. US, 2001.

Rush Hour 3 Dir. Brett Ratner. US, 2007.

Sabu Dir. Miike Takashi. Japan, 2002.

Sandglass (Morae Shigye) Dir. Kim Jong-Hak. South Korea, 1995.

Sang-Doo Let's Go to School (Sangduya Hakgyogaja) Dir. Lee Hyeong-Min. South Korea, 2003.

Saving Private Ryan Dir. Steven Spielberg. US, 1998.

Saw Dir. James Wan. US, 2004.

Scarface Dir. Brian De Palma. US, 1983.

Seven Dir. David Fincher. US, 1995.

Shanghai Noon Dir. Tom Dey. US, 2000.

Shiri Dir. Kang Je-Gyu. South Korea, 1999.

Silmido Dir. Kang Woo-Seok. South Korea, 2004.

Son of the General 1 (Janggun-ui Adeul 1) Dir. Im Kwon-Taek. South Korea, 1990.

Son of the General 2 (Janggun-ui Adeul 2) Dir. Im Kwon-Taek. South Korea, 1991.

Son of the General 3 (Janggun-ui Adeul 3) Dir. Im Kwon-Taek. South Korea, 1992.

*Speed Race*r Dir. Andy Wachowski, Larry Wachowski. South Korea, 2008.

Spring of the Peninsula (Bando-ui Bom) Dir. Lee Byeong-Il. South Korea, 1941.

Spring Summer Fall Winter and Spring (Bom Yeoreum Gaeul Gyeoul Geurigo Bom) Dir. Kim Ki-Duk. South Korea, 2003.

Sunny Place of the Young, A (Jeolmeuni-ui Yangji) Dir. Jin San. South Korea, 1995.

Taegukgi: The Brotherhood of War (Taegeukgi Hwinallimyeo) Dir. Kang Je-Gyu. South Korea, 2004.

Tale of Two Sisters, A (Janghwa Honglyeon) Dir. Kim Ji-Woon. South Korea, 2003.

Three Extremes (Saam Gaang Yi) Dir. Fruit Chan, Miike Takashi, and Park Chan-Wook. Hong Kong, Japan, and South Korea, 2004.

Three Extremes 2 (Saam Gaang) Dir. Peter Chan, Nonzee Nimibutr, and Kim Ji-Woon. Hong Kong, Thailand, and South Korea, 2002.

Time between Dog and Wolf (Gaewa Neukdae-ui Shigan) Dir. Kim Jin-Min. South Korea, 2007.

Titanic Dir. James Cameron. US, 1997.

Toemarok Dir. Park Gwang-Cheon. South Korea, 1998.

Transformers Dir. Michael Bay. US, 2007.

Truth about Charlie, The Dir. Jonathan Demme. US, 2002.

Untold Scandal (Seukaendeul: Joseon Namnyeo Sanglyeoljisa) Dir. Lee Jae-Yong. South Korea, 2003.

Wanderer in Winter (Gyeoul Nageune) Dir. Gwak Ji-Gyun. South Korea, 1986.

Welcome to Dongmakgol Dir. Park Gwang-Hyeon. South Korea. 2005.

What Is Love? (Sarangi Mwogille) Dir. Park Cheol. South Korea, 1991

Winter Sonata (Gyeoul Yeonga) Dir. Yun Seok-Ho. South Korea, 2002.

References

Alasuutari, Pertti. "Introduction: Three Phases of Reception Studies." *Rethinking the Media Audience: The New Agenda*. Ed. Pertti Alasuutari. London: Sage Publications, 1999.

Allen, J. Michael. "Nationalism in a Postcolonial World: The Case of Korea." *Weaving a New Tapestry: Asia in the Post-Cold World: Case Studies and General Trends*. Ed. William P. Head and Edwin G. Clausen. Westport, Conn.: Praeger, 1999.

Alter, Ethan. "*Taegukgi*: The Brotherhood of War: Review." 2005. *TV Guide*. Accessed on September 18, 2008 at http://movies.tvguide.com/tae-guk-gi-brotherhood-war/137612.

Altman, Rick. *Film/Genre*. London: BFI Publishing, 1999.

An, Ji-Seon. "이병헌, 30년 전통 일본 토크쇼 '테츠코의 방' 출연" [Lee Byung-Hun appears in the Japanese talk show "Tetsuko's Room"]. May 2, 2006. *My Daily*. Accessed on September 24, 2008 at http://news.naver.com/main/read.nhn?mode=LSD&mid=sec&sid1=106&oid=117&aid=0000046143.

Ang, Ien. *Living Room Wars: Rethinking Media Audiences for a Postmodern World*. London and New York: Routledge, 1996.

Appadurai, Arjun. "Disjuncture and Difference in the Global Cultural Economy." *Global Culture: Nationalism, Globalization and Modernity*. Ed. Mike Featherstone. London: Sage Publications, 1990.

———. *Modernity at Large*. Minneapolis, Minn.: University of Minnesota Press, 1996.

AsianBite. "Is Huang Xiaoming Plagiarizing Rain's Album?" December 19, 2007. Asianbite.com. Accessed on December 25, 2007 at http://www.asianbite.com/default.asp?display=1292.

Atkinson, Michael. "Die Hard with a Vengeance: Best Served Cold, Park Chan-Wook's Brutal Revenge Feast Comes with a Side of Live Octopus." March 15, 2005. *Village Voice*. Accessed on September 10, 2008 at http://www.villagevoice.com/2005-03-15/film/die-hard-with-a-vengeance/.

Bae, Gook-Nam. "아이돌 스타, 왜 신비감이 없을까?" [Why idol stats do not hold curious mystique anymore?]. March 7, 2010a. *My Daily*. Accessed on March 7, 2010 at http://www.mydaily.co.kr/news/read.html?newsid=201003070948301114&ext=na.

———. "짐승남 스타 신드롬, 원인과 명암?" [Beast-like-man star syndrome, reasons and results]. March 10, 2010b. *My Daily*. Accessed on March 10, 2010 at http://www.mydaily.co.kr/news/read.html?newsid=201003101049321114&ext=na.

Bae, Keun-Min and Reuben Staines. "*Hallyu* Brings New Travel Trend to Korea." February 23, 2006. *Korea Times*. Accessed on September 24, 2008 at http://news.empas.com/show.tsp/cp_kt/20060223n07087/?kw=.

Baek, Seung-Gook. "'한류'의 중심, '겨울연가'와 문화 콘텐츠" [The center of *Hallyu*, *Winter Sonata* and cultural contents]. 겨울연가: "콘텐츠와 콘텍스트 사이" [*Drama Winter Sonata between Contents and Context*]. Ed. Kim Young-Soon and Park Ji-Seon. Seoul: Dahal Media, 2005.

Baek, Won-Dam. "동아시아의 문화선택": 한류 [*The Choice of East Asia:* Hallyu]. Seoul: Pentagram, 2005.

Berry, Chris. "What's Big about the Big Film?: 'De-Westernizing' the Blockbuster in Korea and China." *Movie Blockbusters*. Ed. Julian Stringer. London: Routledge, 2003.

Beyondhollywood.com. "Did Cho Seung Hui Copied [*sic*] Park Chan-Wook's *Oldboy*?" April 19, 2007. Beyondhollywood.com. Accessed on June 1, 2007 at http://www.beyondhollywood.com/gallery/category/cho-seung-hui/.

Bhabha, Homi. *The Location of Culture*. London and New York: Routledge, 1994.

Black, Donald. "The Geometry of Terrorism." *Sociological Theory* 22.1 (2004): 14–25.

Bloody-disgusting.com. "*Oldboy* Review." August 23, 2005. Accessed on February 15, 2006 at http://www.bloody-disgusting.com/film/651.

BNET. "150 Movie Stars, Singers Hold Tsunami Fund-Raising Concert in H.K." January 10, 2005. Bnetau.com.au. Accessed on September 10, 2008 at http://findarticles.com/p/articles/mi_m0WDP/is_2005_Jan_10/ai_n8693180.

Booker, M. Keith. *Postmodern Hollywood: What's New in Film and Why It Makes Us Feel So Strange*. Westport, Conn.: Praeger, 2007.

Bradshaw, Peter. "Friday Review — To the Extreme: Film of the Week *Oldboy*." *The Guardian*. October 15, 2004, Sec. Guardian Friday: 16.

Burgess, Jean. "Hearing Ordinary Voices: Cultural Studies, Vernacular Creativity and Digital Storytelling." *Journal of Media & Culture Studies* 20.2 (2006): 201–14.

Burr, Ty. "Movie Review: Surreal *Oldboy* Thrills with Warped Fun." April 15, 2005. *Boston Globe*. Accessed on September 25, 2008 at http://www.boston.com/movies/display?display=movie&id=7630.

Butler, Judith. "Performative Acts and Gender Constitution: An Essay in Phenomenology and Feminist Theory." *Theatre Journal* 40.4 (1988): 519–31.

Byeon, Seong-Chan. "The Analogous Hollywood Line and Identity of Korean Cinema." *Inmulgwa Sasang* 32 (2004): 36–55.

Chae, Ji-Young. 일본 "한류" 소비자 연구: 한류 마니아와 일반 소비자의 소비 행태를 중심으로 [Research of the *Hallyu* consumers in Japan]. Seoul: Korea Culture & Tourism Policy Institute, 2005.

———. "때가 왔다 ... 우린 이제 '할리우드'로 간다" [The time has come ... we're now going to "Hollywood"]. November 4, 2006. *Donga Ilbo*. Accessed on September 25, 2008 at http://www.donga.com/fbin/output?n=200611040022.

Chang, Seok-Yong. 코리언 뉴웨이브의 징후를 찾아서 [*In Search of the Symptoms of Korean New Wave Cinema*]. Seoul: Hyundai Mihaksa, 2000.

Chang, Yeojean. "Students Hooked on Cell Phones." September 1, 2004. *The Korea Herald*. Accessed on September 15, 2008 at http://news.naver.com/main/read.nhn?mode=LSD&mid=sec&sid1=108&oid=044&aid=0000046140.

Ching, Leo. "Globalizing the Regional, Regionalizing the Global: Mass Culture and Asianism in the Age of Late Capital." *Public Culture* 12.1 (2000): 233–57.

Cho, Heup. "소비 주체의 시선: 남성성의 형성" [The gaze of the consuming subject: The construction of masculinity]. 한국영화 섹슈얼리티를 만나다 [*Korean Cinema Meets Sexuality*]. Ed. Yoo Jina and Cho Heup. Seoul: Saengagui Namu, 2004.

Cho, Hyeon-Woo. "'비의 노래'보다 '정지훈의 연기'가 낫다" [Jung Ji-Hoon's acting is better than Bi's singing]. October 17, 2004. *Break News.* Accessed on September 25, 2008 at http://www.breaknews.com/new/sub_read.html?uid=11530&section=section4.

Cho, Jae-Won. "배용준 입국에 공항 교통 호텔 마비상태" [Bae Yong-Joon paralyzes airport, hotel, traffic]. April 4, 2004a. *Sports Seoul.* Accessed on October 20, 2005 at http://news.naver.com/main/read.nhn?mode=LSD&mid=sec&sid1=001&oid=073&aid=0000002056&.

——. "아시아에 배용준 기금 발족" [Bae Yong-Joon fund will be launched in Asia]. April 5, 2004b. *Sports Seoul.* Accessed on September 21, 2008 at http://news.naver.com/main/read.nhn?mode=LSD&mid=sec&sid1=001&oid=073&aid=0000002152&.

Cho, Seong-Sook. "군대문화와 남성" [Military culture and men]. 남성과 한국 사회 [*Men and South Korean Society*]. Ed. Women and Korean Society Research Group. Seoul: Sahoemunhwa Yeonguso, 1997.

Cho Han, Hye-Jeong. "글로벌 지각 변동의 징후로 읽는 '한류 열풍'" [Reading "*Hallyu*" as a sign of global shift]. "한류"와 아시아의 대중문화 ["*Hallyu*" *and Asian Popular Culture*]. Seoul: Yonsei University Press, 2005.

——. 한국의 여성과 남성 [Korean Women and Men]. Seoul: Munhakgwa Jiseongsa, 1999

Choi, Heup. "'욘사마'광풍 베일을 벗긴다" [Unveil the *Yonsama* syndrome]. December 13, 2004. *Weekly Chosun Magazine.* Accessed on October 23, 2005 at http://news.naver.com/main/read.nhn?mode=LSD&mid=sec&sid1=114&oid=053&aid=0000002699.

Choi, Seung-Hyeon. "가수 비 뉴욕 공연 기획한 '배후' 박진영" [The man behind Rain's New York concert, Park Jin-Young]. February 10, 2006. *Chosun Ilbo.* Accessed on September 25, 2008 at http://www.chosun.com/culture/news/200602/200602100397.html.

Chow, Rey. "Introduction: On Chineseness as a Theoretical Problem." *Boundary 2* 25.3 (1998): 1–25. Duke University Press.

Choy, Chong Li. "History and Managerial Culture in Singapore: 'Pragmatism,' 'Openness' and 'Paternalism'." *Asia Pacific Journal of Management* 4.3 (1987): 133–43.

Chua, Beng Huat. *Communitarian Ideology and Democracy in Singapore.* Politics in Asia Series. Ed. Michael Leifer. London and New York: Routledge, 1995.

——. "Consuming Asians: Ideas and Issues." *Consumption in Asia: Lifestyles and Identities.* Ed. Chua Beng Huat. London and New York: Routledge, 2000.

——. *Life Is Not Complete without Shopping: Consumption Culture in Singapore.* Singapore: Singapore University Press, 2003.

——. "Conceptualizing an East Asian Popular Culture." *Inter-Asia Cultural Studies* 5.2 (2004): 200–221.

Cine21. "'살인의 추억', 산세바스찬 영화제 감독상 수상" [*Memories of Murder,* awarded San Sebastian Film Festival Director's Prize]. September 29, 2003. Cine21.com.

Accessed on September 12, 2004 at http://www.cine21.com/News_Report/news_view. php?mm=001001002&mag_id=21040.

——. "'올드보이', 칸 수상 ... 사실상 작품성 최고" [*Oldboy*, awarded in Cannes ... actually the best film]. May 24, 2004a. Cine21.com. Accessed on September 12, 2004 at http://www.cine21.com/Article/article_view.php?mm=001001002&article_id=24442.

——. "'태극기 휘날리며', 스크린당 주말 흥행 수입 미국 최고" [*Taegukgi* made the highest revenue per screen during the first weekend in the US]. September 8, 2004b. Cine21.com. Accessed on March 3, 2005 at http://www.cine21.com/Article/article_view.php?mm=001001001&article_id=26019.

——. "'태극기 휘날리며', 2주 연속 일본 박스오피스 4위" [*Taegukgi* has remained the 4th place in the Japanese box office for the first 2 weeks]. July 7, 2004c. Cine21.com. Accessed on March 3, 2005 at http://www.cine21.com/Article/article_view.php?mm=001001001&article_id=25076.

CNN. "South Korea Faces 'Sea of Oil'." December 9, 2007. CNN.com. Accessed on January 24, 2008 at http://edition.cnn.com/2007/WORLD/asiapcf/12/09/skorea.spill.ap/index.html.

Cogan, Brian and Gina Cogan. "Gender and Authenticity in Japanese Popular Music: 1980–2000." *Popular Music and Society* 29.1 (2006): 69–90.

Connell, R. W. *Masculinities*. St. Leonards, NSW: Allen & Unwin, 1995.

——. *The Men and the Boys*. St. Leonards, NSW: Allen & Unwin, 2000a.

——. *Understanding Men: Gender Sociology and the New International Research on Masculinities*. 2000b. Department of Sociology, University of Kansas, September 19, Clark Lecture. Accessed at http://toolkit.endabuse.org/Resources/UnderstandingMen.html.

Cornelius, David. "*Taegukgi: The Brotherhood of War*: Review." February 18, 2005. Efilmcritic.com. Accessed on September 18, 2008 at http://efilmcritic.com/review.php?movie=10669.

Corrigan, Timothy. "Film and the Culture of Cult." *The Cult Film Experience: Beyond All Reason*. Ed. J. P. Telotte. Austin: University of Texas Press, 1991.

Coyle, Jake. "VT Killer's Hammer Pose Resembles Movie." April 19, 2007a. Boston.com. Accessed on September 15, 2008 at http://www.boston.com/news/nation/articles/2007/04/19/vt_killers_hammer_pose_resembles_movie/.

——. "VT Killer's Hammer Pose Linked to South Korean Movie." April 19, 2007b. *USA Today*. Accessed on September 15, 2008 at http://www.usatoday.com/life/movies/news/2007-04-19-vt-movie-connection_N.htm.

DailySurprise. "황샤오밍, '짝퉁 비' 논란으로 한-중 팬들 시끌시끌" [Kor-Chi fans argue over Huang Xiaoming, a Rain copycat?]. December 25, 2007. Dailyseop.com. Accessed on December 25, 2007 at http://www.dailyseop.com/section/article_view.aspx?at_id=71219.

Darling-Wolf, Fabienne. "SMAP, Sex and Masculinity: Constructing the Perfect Female Fantasy in Japanese Popular Music." *Popular Music and Society* 27.3 (2004): 357–70.

Davis, Jim. "Introduction: Integrated Circuits, Circuits of Capital, and Revolutionary Change." *Cutting Edge: Technology, Information, Capitalism and Social Revolution*. Ed. Jim Davis, Thomas Hirschl, and Michael Stack. London: Verso, 1997.

Desser, David. "Hong Kong Film and the New Cinephilia." *Hong Kong Connections: Transnational Imagination in Action Cinema*. Ed. Meaghan Morris, Siu Leung Li, and Stephen Chan Ching-kiu. Durham: Duke University Press; Hong Kong: Hong Kong University Press, 2005.

Do, Soo-Yeon. "지금은 흑인음악이 대세" [The era of African American music]. November 15, 2004. *Sports Entertainment Daily*. Accessed on September 24, 2008 at http://blog.naver.com/easternox?Redirect=Log&logNo=40012374865.

Elley, Derek. "*Oldboy* Review." 2005. *Variety*. Accessed on July 2, 2007 at http://www.variety.com/404Variety.asp?requested_layout=sundance2005&debug_location=3.

Endo, Fumiko and Atsuko Matsumoto. "Currents: TV Dramas Melt Hearts, Thaw Japan-ROK Relations." *Daily Yomiuri*, December 5, 2004: 1.

Fee, Lian Kwen. "The Nation-State and the Sociology of Singapore." *Reading Culture: Textual Practices in Singapore*. Ed. Phyllis G. L. Chew and Anneliese Kramer-Dahl. Singapore: Times Academic Press, 1999.

Feldmann, Hans. "Kubrick and His Discontents." *Film Quarterly* 30.1 (1976): 12–19.

Film2.0. "'장화홍련', 드림웍스에서 리메이크" [*A Tale of Two Sisters* will be remade by Dreamworks]. June 30, 2003. Film2.0. Accessed on September 26, 2008 at http://news.naver.com/main/read.nhn?mode=LSD&mid=sec&sid1=106&oid=074&aid=0000004018.

Finke, Nikki. "Virginia Tech Murderer Mimicked Movie." April 19, 2007. Deadlinehollywooddaily.com. Accessed on September 15, 2008 at http://www.deadlinehollywooddaily.com/virginia-tech-murderer-cho-mimicked-a-movie/.

Foucault, Michel. *The History of Sexuality: Vol. 1 the Will to Knowledge*. London: Penguin, 1979.

Fraiman, Susan. *Cool Men and the Second Sex*. New York: Columbia University Press, 2003.

Freud, Sigmund. "The Uncanny." The Standard Edition of *The Complete Psychological Works of Sigmund Freud: From the History of an Infantile Neurosis*. Vol. 17. Trans. James Strachey. London: The Hogarth Press and the Institute of Psycho-Analysis, 1955.

——. *Beyond the Pleasure Principle*. New York: Norton, 1961.

Frow, John. *Time and Commodity Culture: Essays in Cultural Theory and Postmodernity*. Oxford: Clarendon Press, 1997.

Fung, Anthony. "Bridging Cyber life and Real Life: A Study of Online Communities in Hong Kong." *Critical Cyberculture Studies*. Ed. David Silver and Adrienne Massanari. New York and London: New York University Press, 2006.

Fuyuno, Ichiko. "War Torn: Soap Opera Resonates with Elderly Japanese Women." *The Wall Street Journal*, 15 September 2004: 3A.

Galloway, Patrick. *Asia Shock: Horror and Dark Cinema from Japan, Korea, Hong Kong, and Thailand*. Berkeley: Stone Bridge Press, 2006.

Gandhi, Leela. *Postcolonial Theory: A Critical Introduction*. St. Leonards, NSW: Allen & Unwin, 1998.

Garcia, Cathy Rose A. "Rain's World Premiere Tour Begins in Seoul." October 13, 2006. *The Korea Times*. Accessed on May 20, 2007 at http://times.hankooki.com/lpage/culture/200610/kt2006101017510611690.htm.

George, Cherian. *Contentious Journalism and the Internet*. Singapore: Singapore University Press, 2006.

Geum, Jang-Tae. 한국의 선비와 선비정신 [*Korea's* Seonbi *and the* Seonbi *Ideology*]. Seoul: Seoul National University Press, 2000.

Giddens, Anthony. "Comment: The 1999 Reith Lecture. New World without End." *Observer*. April 11, 1999.

Gil, Hye-Seong. "비, 한달간 '월드투어' 나선다" [Rain, going for a world tour for one month]. January 21, 2006. *Herald Kyungje*. Accessed on September 26, 2008 at http://news.naver.com/main/read.nhn?mode=LSD&mid=sec&sid1=106&oid=016&aid=0000198443.

Glassner, Barry. "Fitness and the Postmodern Self." *Journal of Health and Social Behavior* 30.2 (1989): 180–91.

Gomez-Pena, Guillermo. "The New Global Culture: Somewhere between Corporate Multiculturalism and the Mainstream Bizarre (a Border Perspective)." *The Drama Review* (Cambridge, Mass.) 45.1 (Spring 2001): 7

Gopal. "Gopal's Top 10 Movies of 2006." January 6, 2007. Beyondhollywood.com. Accessed on October 12, 2007 at http://www.beyondhollywood.com/gopals-top-10-movies-of-2006/.

Ha, Oe-Young. "교실 복도까지 CCTV, 학생 인권, 사생활은 어디로?" [CCTV at school, where are human rights and privacy of students?]. November 8, 2007. *Hankyoreh Shinmun*. Accessed on September 26, 2008 at http://www.hani.co.kr/arti/society/society_general/248746.html.

Hall, Stuart. "Encoding/Decoding." *Culture, Media, Language: Working Papers in Cultural Studies, 1972–79*. Ed. Dorothy Hobson, Stuart Hall, Andrew Lowe, and Paul Willis. London: Hutchinson, 1980.

Ham, Young-Joon. 나의 심장은 코리아로 벅차오른다: 한국, 한국인의 위대함 재발견 [*My Heart Is Filled with Korea: Rediscovery of the Greatness of Korea and the Korean*]. Seoul: Wisdom House, 2006.

Hamilton, Gary G. "Patriarchy, Patrimonialism, and Filial Piety: A Comparison of China and Western Europe." *The British Journal of Sociology* 41.1 (1990): 77–104.

Han, Ji-Sook. "시청률 조사 어떻게 할까?" [How would TV audience share be measured?] January 4, 2006. *Digital Times*. Accessed on October 2, 2008 at http://news.naver.com/main/read.nhn?mode=LSD&mid=sec&sid1=105&oid=029&aid=0000125338.

Han, Seung-Hui et al. "창궐하는 Mr. 뷰티 공화국 바야흐로 남성 소비시대" [Rampant republic of Mr. Beauty, the era of male consumption]. April 19, 2006. *Film 2.0*. Accessed on September 27, 2008 at http://news.naver.com/main/read.nhn?mode=LSD&mid=sec&sid1=106&oid=074&aid=0000014648.

Hannerz, Ulf. *Transnational Connections: Culture, People, Places.* London and New York: Routledge, 1996.

Haraway, Donna. "A Manifesto for Cyborgs: Science, Technology, and Socialist Feminism in the 1980s." *Simians, Cyborgs and Women: The Reinvention of Nature.* New York: Routledge, 1991.

Heo, In-Soon and Ham Han-Hui. "겨울연가"와 나비환타지 [Winter Sonata *and Butterfly Fantasy*]. Seoul: Sohwa, 2005.

Herald Kyungje. "배용준 인기 베컴 능가" [Bae Yong-Joon beats Beckham]. April 5, 2004. *Herald Kyungje.* Accessed on September 27, 2008 at http://news.naver.com/main/read.nhn?mode=LSD&mid=sec&sid1=106&oid=016&aid=0000131371.

Hirata, Yukie. 한국을 소비하는 일본: "한류", 여성, 드라마 [*Japan, Consuming South Korea:* Hallyu, *Women, Drama*]. Seoul: Chaeksesang, 2005.

Holcomb, Brian. "*The Host* (2006) Movie Review #2." December 1, 2006. Beyondhollywood.com. Accessed on October 12, 2007 at http://www.beyondhollywood.com/the-host-2006-movie-review-2/.

Hong, Dong-Hui. "'외국인 아이돌'의 성적표는?" [Who's the best among the foreign idols?]. February 18, 2010. *Herald Biz.* Accessed on March 4, 2010 at http://www.heraldbiz.com/SITE/data/html_dir/2010/02/18/201002180061.asp.

Hong, Hyeon-Jin. "연예기사쓰기, 참~ 쉽죠잉?" [It's so easy to write entertainment news articles, isn't it?]. September 12, 2009. *OhMyNews.* Accessed on March 3, 2010 at http://www.ohmynews.com/NWS_Web/view/at_pg.aspx?CNTN_CD=A0001276691.

Hong, Jong-Seon. "영화 "괴물" … 시사회만큼만 하면 '대박'" [*The Host* expects a big hit]. July 4, 2006. Kukinews.com. Accessed on September 26, 2008 at http://news.naver.com/main/read.nhn?mode=LSD&mid=sec&sid1=106&oid=143&aid=0000031974.

Hong, Soon-Young et al. *Korean Economy Report.* Seoul: Sam Sung Economy Research Institute, 2004.

hooks, bell. *Black Looks: Race and Representation.* Boston, MA: South End Press, 1992.

———. *We Real Cool: Black Men and Masculinity.* New York and London: Routledge, 2004.

Horrorreview.com. "Horror Bob's Top 10 Horror Films of 2005." 2005a. Horrorreview.com. Accessed on February 11, 2006 at http://www.horrorreview.com/oldtopten.html.

———. "*Oldboy* Review." 2005b. Horrorreview.com. Accessed on September 15, 2008 at http://www.horrorreview.com/2005/oldboy.html.

Hudson, Chris. "Romancing Singapore: Economies of Love in a Shrinking Population." The 15th Biennial Conference of the Asian Studies Association of Australia in Canberra. Canberra, 2004. Accessed at http://coombs.anu.edu.au/SpecialProj/ASAA/biennial-conference/2004/Hudson-C-ASAA2004.pdf.

Hwang, Ho-Taek. "일본의 '겨울연가'" [*Winter Sonata* in Japan]. June 18, 2004. *Donga Ilbo.* Accsessed on September 26, 2008 at http://news.naver.com/main/read.nhn?mode=LSD&mid=sec&sid1=104&oid=020&aid=0000245549.

Hwang, Jeong-Hyeon. "케이블 채널 속 아이돌 리얼 버라이어티" [Idol real variety shows in cable TV channels]. September 9, 2010. *Media Today*. Accessed on March 4, 2010 at http://www.mediatoday.co.kr/news/articleView.html?idxno=85882.

Hwang, Shi-Young. "More Nude Photos of Soldiers Disclosed by a Civic Group." May 30, 2005. *The Korea Herald*. Accessed on December 12, 2007 at http://news.naver.com/main/read.nhn?mode=LSD&mid=sec&sid1=108&oid=044&aid=0000051779.

IMDb.com. "*Oldboy* Rating." 2003. IMDb.com. Accessed on July 10, 2007 at http://www.imdb.com/title/tt0364569/.

——. "*The Host* Rating." 2006. IMDb.com. Accessed on July 10, 2007 at http://www.imdb.com/title/tt0468492/.

Iwabuchi, Koichi. "Uses of Japanese Popular Culture: Trans/Nationalism and Postcolonial Desire for 'Asia'." *Emergences* 11.2 (2001).

——. *Recentering Globalization: Popular Culture and Japanese Transnationalism*. Durham and London: Duke University Press, 2002a.

——. "Nostalgia for a (Different) Asian Modernity: Media Consumption of 'Asia' in Japan." *Positions: East Asia Cultures Critique* 10.3 (2002b): 547–73.

Jameson, Fredric. *Postmodernism, or, the Cultural Logic of Late Capitalism*. Durham: Duke University Press, 1991.

Jankovich, Mark. "Cult Fictions: Cult Movies, Subcultural Capital and the Production of Cultural Distinctions." *Cultural Studies* 16.2 (2002): 306–22.

Jenkins, Henry. *Textual Poachers: Television Fans & Participatory Culture*. New York: Routledge, 1992.

——. "The Cultural Logic of Media Convergence." *International Journal of Cultural Studies* 7.1 (2004): 33–43.

——. *Convergence Culture: Where Old and New Media Collide*. New York: New York University Press, 2006a.

——. *Fans, Bloggers, and Gamers: Exploring Participatory Culture*. New York: New York University Press, 2006b.

Jeong, Doo-Hui. 내 안에 살아 숨쉬는 역사 [*History, Lively Breathing in Me*]. Seoul: Cheongeoram Media, 2004.

Jeong, Myeong-Hwa. "비, 생일맞아 싱가폴 팬 항공권 선물 받아" [Rain, received a flight ticket from Singaporean fans for his b'day gift]. June 21, 2006. *Joy News*. Accessed on June 23, 2006 at http://joynews.inews24.com/php/news_view.php?g_menu=700100&g_serial=210730.

Jeong, Seong-Il, Kim So-Young, and Heo Moon-Young. "결산 한국 영화 2003: 정성일, 김소영, 허문영씨 좌담" [Korean cinema 2003: Jeong Seong-Il, Kim So-Young and Heo Mun-Young's year-end forum]. December 19, 2003. Cine21.com. Accessed on January 28, 2009 at http://www.cine21.com/News_Report/news_view.php?mm=001001001&mag_id=22380.

Jeong, Soon-Min. "뮤지컬 '대장금', '한류'열풍 이어갈까" [Will musical *Dae-jang-geum* continue the *Hallyu* phenomenon?]. May 31, 2007. *Financial News*. Accessed on

October 2, 2008 at http://www.fnnews.com/view?ra=Sent1301m_View&corp=fnnew s&arcid=0921014266&cDateYear=2007&cDateMonth=05&cDateDay=31.

Joo, Chang-Gyu. "한국 영화의 힘!: 멜로드라마적 상상력과 역사의 파토스" [The power of Korean cinema!: Melodramatic imagination and historical pathos]. 한국형 블록버스터: 아틀란티스 혹은 아메리카 [*The Korean Blockbuster: America or Atlantis*]. Ed. Kim So-Young. Seoul: Hyeonshil Munhwa Yeongu, 2001.

Jung, Sun. "The Shared Imagination of *Bishonen*, Pan-East Asian Soft Masculinity: Reading DBSK, YouTube.com and Transcultural New Media Consumption." 2009. *Intersections* at http://intersections.anu.edu.au/issue21/jung.htm.

———. "*Chogukjeok* Pan-East Asian Soft Masculinity: Reading *Boys over Flowers*, DBSK, *Coffee Prince* and Shinhwa Fan Fictions." *Complicated Currents: Media Flows, Soft Power and East Asia*. Ed. Daniel Black, Stephen Epstein, and Alison Tokita. Melbourne: Monash University e-Press, 2010.

JYPE. Rain Profile. 2006. Accessed at www.jype.com.

Kageyama, Yuri. "Love for Cute Has Japan Engrossed in Soul-Searching in Kitty, Beauty, Art." June 14, 2006. *CBS News*. Accessed on June 10, 2007 at http://www.cbsnews.com/ stories/2006/06/14/ap/business/mainD8I839SO0.shtml.

Kang, Cheol-Geun. "한류" 이야기 [*The* Hallyu *story*]. Seoul: Ih Chae, 2006.

Kang, Eun-Jin. "'괴물', 미국 개봉 한국 영화 중 최다 극장 개봉" [*The Host* opened on the largest number of screens ever for Korean films that had been released in the US]. March 2, 2007. *My Daily*. Accessed on September 15, 2008 at http://www.mydaily.co.kr/news/ read.html?newsid=200703021114171125.

Kang, Han-Seop. "한국영화 붐의 시작과 끝" [The Korean Cinema Boom, Its Beginning and the End]. *Korean Film Critiques* 15 (2003): 63–83.

———. 한국의 영화학을 만들어라 [*Create South Korean Film Theories*]. Seoul: Samuban, 2004.

Kang, Heon. "서태지, SM과 JYP 그리고 YG가 바라보는 힙합 [Hip-Hop of Seo Tae-Ji, SM, JYP and YG]. September 2005. Melon.com. Accessed on March 20, 2006 at http://www.melon.com/juice/themeZone/TheWeekSubjectReview. jsp?themeId=6&weekId=23.

Kang, Ho-Won. "중국 유명 배우 '대장금 문제 많다' … 한류 역풍 꿈틀" [Famous Chinese actor '*Dae-jang-geum* has many problems' … emerging anti-*Hallyu* movement]. October 31, 2005. *Segye Ilbo*. Accessed on October 16, 2008 at http://www.segye.com/Articles/ NEWS/ENTERTAINMENTS/Article.asp?aid=20051031000285&subctg1=&subctg 2=&DataID=200510311649000284.

Kang, Jin-Seok. "중국인이 말하는 '한류'의 도식" [The diagram of *Hallyu* from Chinese point of view: Visual effects and contemporary desires]. June 12, 2004. Gaury Cyber Study Community. Accessed on September 26, 2008 at http://blog.naver.com/uuuau?R edirect=Log&logNo=40003267896.

Kang, Joon-Man. 한국인 코드 [*The Korean Code*]. Seoul: Inmulgwa Sasangsa, 2006.

Kang, Myeong-Seok. "강명석의 TV홀릭: '풀하우스'" [Kang Myeong-Seok's TVholic: *Full House*]. August 16, 2004. *Hankook Ilbo*. Accessed on September 26, 2008 at http://

news.naver.com/main/read.nhn?mode=LSD&mid=sec&sid1=106&oid=038&a id=0000247009.

Kang, Seong-Lyul. "일제 말기 영화, 이렇게 친일로 나갔다" [At the end of the Japanese Occupation, Korean cinema had become pro-Occupation]. March 14, 2006. Culturenews.net. Accessed on February 22, 2007 at http://www.culturenews.net/read. asp?title_up_code=603&title_down_code=005&article_num=5556.

Kang, Shin-Joo. 공자 & 맹자 [*Confucius and Mencius*]. Seoul: Kimyoungsa, 2006.

Kang, Yoo-Jeong. "섹슈얼리티의 척후, 남성: 남성 소비시대 3" [A scout of sexuality, man: The era of male consumption 3]. April 19, 2006. *Film 2.0*. Accessed on March 3, 2007 at http://blog.naver.com/foxyoyo8?Redirect=Log&log No=60023717287.

Kau, Ah Keng et al. *Understanding Singaporeans: Values, Lifestyles, Aspirations and Consumption Behaviors*. New Jersey and Singapore: World Scientific, 2004.

Kehr, David. Revisiting the Korean War in a Tale of Two Brothers. September 3, 2004. NYTimes.com. Accessed on September 18, 2008 at http://movies.nytimes. com/2004/09/03/movies/03TAEG.html.

Kermode, Mark. "Heroes and Villains: Film 2004 — The Boundaries of Buck-Chasing Hollywood Have Been Redefined." December 13, 2004. *New Statesman*. Accessed on November 11, 2005 at http://www.newstatesman.com/200412130046.

Kim, Byeong-Cheol. 한국형 블록버스터의 빛과 그늘 [*Light and Shadow of the Korean Blockbuster*]. Paju: Hanguk Haksuljeongbo, 2005.

Kim, Byeong-Gyu. "'올드보이', 할리우드 리메이크된다" [*Oldboy* is going to Hollywood for a remake]. March 9, 2004. *Yonhap News*. Accessed on September 26, 2008 at http://news.naver.com/main/read.nhn?mode=LSD&mid=sec&sid1=103&oid=001&a id=0000586752.

Kim, Byung-Kook. "Electoral Politics and Economic Crisis, 1997–1998." *Consolidating Democracy in South Korea*. Ed. Larry Diamond and Kim Byung-Kook. Boulder and London: Lynne Rienner Publishers, 2000.

Kim, Cheong-Joong. "장동건, 중국 네티즌 선정 최고 '한류' CF 스타" [Jang Dong-Kun, number one *Hallyu* CF star in China]. February 11, 2007. *Segye Ilbo*. Accessed on February 3, 2008 at http://www.segye.com/Articles/News/People/Article.asp?aid=2007 0211000916&ctg1=01&ctg2=00&subctg1=01&subctg2=00&cid=0101120100000& dataid=200702111515000204.

Kim, Eun-Shil. "한국 근대화 프로젝트의 문화 논리와 가부장성" [Cultural logic and patriarchy in the Korean Modernization Project]. 우리 안의 파시즘 [*Fascism in Us*]. Ed. Im Ji-Hyeon et al. Seoul: Samin, 2000.

Kim, Gi-Gook. "'겨울연가', 빠져들기와 거리두기" [*Winter Sonata*, indulging in or keeping the distance]. "겨울연가": 콘텐츠와 콘텍스트 사이 [*Drama* "Winter Sonata" *between Contents and Context*]. Ed. Kim Young-Soon and Park Ji-Seon. Seoul: Dahal Media, 2005.

Kim, Gyeo-Ul. "'욘사마' 여행서 발간 전부터 국내외 팬 관심 폭발" ["*Yonsama*" travel book, fans show hot interest even before its release]. September 13, 2008. *Money Today*.

Accessed on September 27, 2008 at http://star.moneytoday.co.kr/view/stview.php?no=2 008091218565279030&type=1&outlink=1.

Kim, Gyeong-Wook. 블록버스터의 환상, 한국 영화의 나르시시즘 [*The Fantasy of Blockbuster, Narcissism of Korean Cinema*]. Seoul: Chaeksesang, 2002.

Kim, Ho-Il. "'괴물' 해외서 박수 사례: 칸 영화제 감독주간서 첫 선" [*The Host*, winning great applause at the Cannes Directors' Fortnight]. June 1, 2006. *Busan Ilbo*. Accessed on September 26, 2008 at http://www.busanilbo.com/news2000/html/2006/0601/0L0020060601.1043090458.html.

Kim, Hong-Goo. "동남아 '한류'의 새로운 메카: 태국의 '한류'" [The new mecca of *Hallyu* in South East Asia: *Hallyu* in Thailand]. 동아시아의 '한류' [*Hallyu in East Asia*]. Ed. Shin Yun-Hwan and Lee Han-Woo. Yongin: Jeonyewon, 2006.

Kim, Ho-Seok. "배용준 신드롬, '겨울연가', 그리고 스타 마케팅" [The Bae Yong-Joon Syndrome, *Winter Sonata* and star marketing]. "겨울연가": 콘텐츠와 콘텍스트 사이 [*Drama* Winter Sonata *between Contents and Context*]. Ed. Kim Young-Soon and Park Ji-Seon. Seoul: Dahal Media, 2005.

Kim, Hui-Jeong. "'괴물', 중국인들과 극장에서 통하다" [*The Host* attracted Chinese audiences]. March 28, 2007. Cine21.com. Accessed on August 6, 2007 at http://www.cine21.com/Article/article_view.php?mm=001002002&article_id=45475.

Kim, Hyeon-Lok. "'올드보이', 영국 개봉 아시아 영화중 최고 흥행 기록" [*Oldboy*, the best-selling Asian film in the UK market]. December 17, 2004. *Money Today*. Accessed on September 15, 2008 at http://star.moneytoday.co.kr/view/stview.php?no=20041217 08064564879&type=1&HSV1.

———. "'괴물', 미국 개봉 4주차에 흥행 가속도" [*The Host* sells even better in the 4th week in the US]. April 3, 2007. *Money Today*. Accessed on May 15, 2007 at http://star.moneytoday.co.kr/view/stview.php?no=2007040308115258494&type=1.

Kim, Hyeon-Mi. 글로벌 시대의 문화 번역 [*Cultural Interpretation in the Era of Globalization*]. Seoul: Ddo Hanaui Munhwa, 2005.

Kim, Jeong-Soo. "군사주의와 여성" [Militarism and women]. 2001. Seonggonghoe University NGO Database. Accessed on September 27, 2008 at http://www.demos.or.kr/scholar/viewbody.html?category=&code=scholarship&key=&key_re=&keyfield=&keyfield_re=&number=5603&txttype=.

Kim, Ji-Eun. "산낙지, 군만두 그리고 카메라" [Live octopus, fried dumpling and camera]. *"Oldboy" Book*. Ed. Park Chan-Wook et al. Seoul: Olive M&B, 2005.

Kim, Ji-Yeon. "무릎팍 도사 김윤진 편, 비가 일본인 역? 팬들 '들썩'" [Is Rain playing a Japanese? Fans get "angry"]. September 27, 2007. *OSEN*. Accessed on October 12, 2007 at http://news.naver.com/main/read.nhn?mode=LSD&mid=sec&sid1=106&oid=109&aid=0000089668.

———. "'대장금', 유럽까지 진출 … 총 60개국 진출 '기염'" [*Dae-jang-geum*, even sold to Europe … export to total 60 countries]. January 26, 2008. *OSEN*. Accessed on February 2, 2008 at http://www.stoo.com/news/html/000/838/885.html.

Kim, Kyung-Hyun. *The Remasculinization of Korean Cinema*. Durham and London: Duke University Press, 2004.

Kim, Sang-Ho. "월드투어 기자회견 가진 비 '쌍꺼풀 없는 눈이 무기'" [Rain, holding a press conference before his world tour "My Weapon Is a Single Eyefold]. October 11, 2006. *Sports Seoul*. Accessed on October 1, 2008 at http://www.sportsseoul.com/common/html/read.asp?ArticleID=369997.

Kim, Seon-Yeop. "귀환할 수 없는 타락천사들의 처절한 고해성사: 박찬욱 감독의 '올드보이'" [Sorrowful confession of fallen angels: Park Chan-Wook's *Oldboy*]. *Korean Film Critiques* 16 (2004): 161–67.

Kim, Seung-Gi. "'욘님' 배용준 日 정복 준비 끝" ["*Yonsama*" Bae Yong-Joon ready to conquer Japan]. March 29, 2004. *Sports Hankook*. Accessed on September 27, 2008 at http://sports.hankooki.com/lpage/entv/200403/sp2004032912013632380.htm.

Kim, Seung-Hye. 유교의 뿌리를 찾아서 [*In Search of the Root of Confucianism*]. Seoul: Jishigui Pungkyeong, 2001.

Kim, Shi-Mu. 영화 예술의 옹호 [*Defending Film Art*]. Seoul: Hyundai Mihaksa, 2001.

Kim, So-Hui. "웰 메이드" [Well-made]. January 16, 2004. Cine21.com. Accessed on September 26, 2008 at http://www.cine21.com/Magazine/mag_pub_view.php?mm=005003005&mag_id=22763.

Kim, So-Min. "스타 제조 전성시대" [The golden age of manufacturing stars]. March 15, 2006. *Hankyoreh Shinmun*. Accessed on September 26, 2008 at http://www.hani.co.kr/arti/culture/music/108979.html.

Kim, So-Young. "사라지는 남한 여성들: 한국형 블록버스터 영화의 무의식적 광학" [Disappearing South Korean women: Unconscious optics of the Korean blockbuster]. 한국형 블록버스터: 아틀란티스 혹은 아메리카 [*The Korean Blockbuster: Atlantis or America*]. Ed. Kim So-Young. Seoul: Hyeonshil Munhwa Yeongu, 2001.

———. "The Birth of Local Feminist Sphere in the Global Era: 'Trans-Cinema' and Yosongjang." *Inter-Asia Cultural Studies* 4.1 (2003): 10–24.

———. "한국 영화에 고함: 해체에 나선 남성 감독들, 장도에 나선 여성 감독들" [South Korean cinema manifesto: Male directors starting the deconstruction, female directors embarking on the ambitious journey]. January 30, 2004. Cine21.com. Accessed on September 26, 2008 at http://www.cine21.com/Article/article_view.php?mm=005001001&article_id=22867.

———. "옛 영화의 경이로운 발견" [Marvelous discovery of old movies]. March 29, 2006. Cine21.com. Accessed on September 26, 2008 at http://www.cine21.com/Article/article_view.php?mm=005004004&article_id=37469.

Kim, Tae-Eun. "'풀하우스', 필리핀 시청률 42.3%. 亞 드라마 최고" [*Full House*, audience share of 42.3% in the Philippines. The highest among Asian dramas]. May 23, 2005. *Money Today*. Accessed on October 2, 2008 at http://star.moneytoday.co.kr/view/stview.php?no=2005052314441167981&type=1&outlink=1.

Kim, Won-Gyeom. "비 MTV 그랜드 슬램 달성, '아시아 스타' 재확인" [Rain achieved grand slam in the MTV Awards, reconfirming "Asia's Star']. July 25, 2005. *Money Today*. Accessed on September 26, 2008 at http://star.moneytoday.co.kr/view/stview.php?no=2005072507324652227&type=1&outlink=1.

———.ˮ문전박대, 인정, 자신감 … 박진영의 美 도전기ˮ [JYP's challenging journey in the US]. February 7, 2006. *Money Today*. Accessed on September 26, 2008 at http://star.moneytoday.co.kr/view/star_view.php?type=1&gisa no=2006020617290606801.

———. ˮ빅뱅, 표절 의혹 제기됐던 일본 가수와 신곡 작업ˮ [Big Bang works with the Japanese artist Daishi Dance for its new songs]. May 19, 2008. *Donga Ilbo*. Accessed on September 16, 2008 at http://www.donga.com/fbin/output?n=200805190405.

Kim, Yang-Eun and Lee Young-Ran. ˮ배용준 신드롬, 그 낭만적 진실ˮ [The Bae Yong-Joon Syndrome, its romantic truth]. ˮ겨울연가ˮ: 콘텐츠와 콘텍스트 사이 [*Drama* Winter Sonata *between Contents and Context*]. Ed. Kim Young-Soon and Park Ji-Seon. Seoul: Dahal Media, 2005.

Kim, Yong-Hui. 천개의 거울 [*A Thousand Mirrors*]. Seoul: Saengagui Namu, 2003.

Kim, Young-Jin. ˮ장르 영화에 수혈하는 재간꾼들 골든보이 박찬욱의 성공이 암시하는 것ˮ [Goldenboy Park Chan-Wook]. July 16, 2004. *Film 2.0*. Accessed on September 26, 2008 at http://news.naver.com/main/read.nhn?mode=LSD&mid=sec&sid1=114& oid=074&aid=0000009845.

Kim, Young-Soon. ˮˮ겨울연가ˮ, 코드와 텍스트의 진실 게임ˮ [*Winter Sonata*, the truth between code and text]. ˮ겨울연가ˮ: 콘텐츠와 콘텍스트 사이 [*Drama* Winter Sonata *between Contents and Context*]. Ed. Kim Young-Soon and Park Ji-Seon. Seoul: Dahal Media, 2005.

Klinger, Barbara. *Beyond the Multiplex: Cinema, New Technologies, and the Home*. Berkeley, Los Angeles, and London: University of California Press, 2006.

Knowles, Harry. "Clip and Reviews of *Oldboy* from the Director of *Sympathy for Mr. Vengeance*!!!" November 23, 2003. AintItCool.com. Accessed on November 22, 2004 at http://www.aintitcool.com/display.cgi?id=16565.

———. "Anghus Loses It All for *Oldboy*, a Film of Genius, at BNAT 5." December 9, 2003. AintItCool.com. Accessed on November 22, 2004 at http://www.aintitcool.com/display. cgi?id=16640.

———. "Harry's Top Ten Films Seen in 2006!!!" January 3, 2007. AintItCool.com. Accessed on September 15, 2008 at http://www.aintitcool.com/node/31129.

Kong, Lily. "Cultural Policy in Singapore: Negotiating Economic and Socio-Cultural Agendas." *Geoforum* 31.4 (2000): 409–24.

Korean Film Council (Kofic). "2003년 한국 영화 산업 결산" [Korean film industry 2003 settlement]. December 22, 2003. Kofic.or.kr. Accessed on September 17, 2008 at http://www.kofic.or.kr/b_movdata/b_02bstatis.jsp?BOARD_ NO=10514.

———. "아시아 태평양 지역 한국 영화 진출 연구" [Korean film sales in the Asia Pacific region]. March 26, 2004. Kofic.or.kr. Accessed on September 17, 2008 at http://www. kofic.or.kr/b_movdata/b_01policy.jsp?POLICY_NO=149.

———. "2004년 한국 영화 산업 결산" [Korean film industry 2004 settlement]. January 26, 2005. Kofic.or.kr. Accessed on September 17, 2008 at http://www.kofic.or.kr/b_ movdata/b_02bstatis.jsp?BOARD_NO=10528.

——. "2005년 한국 영화 산업 결산" [Korean film industry 2005 settlement]. January 18, 2006. Kofic.or.kr. Accessed on September 17, 2008 at http://www.kofic.or.kr/b_movdata/b_02bstatis.jsp?BOARD_NO=10544.

——. "연도별 한국/외국 영화 전국 관객 수, 전국 관객 점유율, 1인당 관람 횟수" [Korean/foreign film sales, market share]. 2007a. Kofic.or.kr. Accessed on September 17, 2008 at http://www.kofic.or.kr/KOFIC/Channel?task=kofic.b_movdata.command.Industry1Retrieve4Cmd&ybook_seqno=04&ybookkind_name=연도별%20한국/외국영화%20전국%20관객수,%20전국%20관객점유율,%201인당%20관람횟수.

——. "2006년 한국 영화 산업 결산" [Korean film industry 2006 settlement]. January 18, 2007b. Kofic.or.kr. Accessed on September 17, 2008 at http://www.kofic.or.kr/b_movdata/b_02bstatis.jsp?BOARD_NO=10561.

——. "2007년 한국 영화 산업 결산" [Korean film industry 2007 settlement]. January 28, 2008. Kofic.or.kr. Accessed on September 17, 2008 at http://www.kofic.or.kr/b_movdata/b_02bstatis.jsp?BOARD_NO=22626.

Kuroiwa, Mika. "The Japanese Fandom of Bae Yong-Joon." Personal Interview (Tokyo). August 30, 2005.

Kwon, Mee-Yoo. "Rain Donates to Taean Cleanup." January 17, 2008. *The Korea Times*. Accessed on January 24, 2008 at http://www.koreatimes.co.kr/www/news/special/2008/09/178_17521.html.

Kwon, Yeon-Soo. "소비되는 '욘사마', 순수와 명품 사이" [Consumed *Yonsama*, between purity and luxurious product]. "겨울연가": 콘텐츠와 콘텍스트 사이 [*Drama* Winter Sonata *between Contents and Context*]. Ed. Kim Young-Soon and Park Ji-Seon. Seoul: Dahal Media, 2005.

Lane, Anthony. "Revenge: *The Ring Two* and *Oldboy*." March 28, 2005. *The New Yorker*. Accessed on July 30, 2005 at http://www.newyorker.com/archive/2005/03/28/050328crci_cinema.

Lau, Jenny Kwok Wah. "Hero, China's Response to Hollywood Globalization." 2005. *Jump Cut*. Accessed on September 19, 2008 http://www.ejumpcut.org/archive/jc49.2007/Lau-Hero/index.html.

Lazar, Michelle M. "For the Good of the Nation: 'Strategic Egalitarianism' in the Singapore Context." *Nations and Nationalism* 7.1 (2001): 59–74.

Lee, Chi-Dong. "Can 'The Korean Wave' Entertain Ethnic Koreans in Japan?" July 21, 2004. *Yonhap News*. Accessed on October 1, 2008 at http://www.accessmylibrary.com/coms2/summary_0286-3821783_ITM.

Lee, Dong-Hoo. "한국 트렌디 드라마의 문화적 형성" [The cultural construction of Korean trendy drama]. "한류"와 아시아의 대중문화 [Hallyu *and Asian Popular Culture*]. Seoul: Yonsei University Press, 2005.

Lee, Dong-Hyeon. "윤석호 PD, '한류 왕국' 만든다" [Producer Yun Seok-Ho, making the '*Hallyu* Kingdom']. August 17, 2004a. *Sports Hankook*. Accessed on September 27, 2008 at http://sports.hankooki.com/lpage/entv/200408/sp2004081708053458410.htm.

——. "日 통신판매 시장도 '욘사마 천하'" [*Yonsama* conquers Japan's home shopping market]. October 6, 2004b. *Sports Hankook*. Accessed on September 27, 2008 at http://sports.hankooki.com/lpage/entv/200410/sp2004100611490158390.htm.

Lee, Dong-Joon. "배용준 일본행! 베컴보다 뜨거운 환영 … 공항 마비" [Bae Yong-Joon went to Japan! Hotter welcome than Beckham … airport paralyzed]. April 4, 2004. *Ilgan Sports*. Accessed on September 27, 2008 at http://media.daum.net/entertain/others/view.html?cateid=100030&newsid=20040404021321005&p=hankookis.

Lee, Eun-Jeong. "비 태국서 '최우수 아티스트상' 수상" [Rain awarded "best artist" in Thailand]. September 19, 2005. *Yonhap News*. Accessed on October 2, 2008 at http://news.naver.com/main/read.nhn?mode=LSD&mid=sec&sid1=106&oid=001&aid=0001101790.

——. "비가 내디딘 美무대 첫발의 의미" [The meaning of Rain's first step to the US]. February 4, 2006. *Yonhap News*. Accessed on September 27, 2008 at http://app.yonhapnews.co.kr/yna/basic/article/Search/YIBW_showSearchDetailArticle.aspx?searchpart=article&searchtext=%eb%b9%84%20&%20%eb%89%b4%ec%9a%95&contents_id=AKR20060204001400005&search=1.

Lee, Geon-Ho. "비 '나는 치밀한 전략과 투자로 만들어진 강력한 문화상품'" [Rain "I am a powerful cultural product which has been created based on precise strategies and careful investments"]. January 3, 2010. *Hankyung*. March 1, 2010 at http://www.hankyung.com/news/app/newsvicw.php?aid=2010010321951.

Lee, Gil-Sang. "비 '어셔같은 가수되고 싶어'" [Rain "I want to be a singer like Usher']. April 18, 2004. *Sports Seoul*. Accessed on September 27, 2008 at http://news.naver.com/news/read.php?mode=LSD&office_id=073&article_id=0000003590&section_id=106&menu_id=106.

Lee, Gyeong-Eun. "한민족, 두 국가의 비극적 서사를 노래하라!" [One-Nation-Two-Nation-States' tragic narrative]. 한국형 블록버스터: 아틀란티스 혹은 아메리카 [*The Korean Blockbuster: Atlantis or America*]. Ed. Kim So-Young. Seoul: Hyeonshil Munhwa Yeongu, 2001.

Lee, Gyeong-Ho. "영화 흥행 톱텐에서 사라진 전설, '쉬리'" [The legend of South Korean cinema, *Shiri*, finally disappeared from the box office top ten]. September 5, 2007a. *My Daily*. Accessed on October 8, 2008 at http://www.mydaily.co.kr/news/read.html?newsid=200709050844591122&ext=na.

——. "헐리우드 왜 한국 스타를 주목할까?" [Why would Hollywood be interested in Korean stars?]. December 21, 2007b. *My Daily*. Accessed on January 4, 2008 at http://www.mydaily.co.kr/news/read.html?newsid=2007122109424011 24&ext=na.

Lee, Gyeong-Hui. "The Regional Rain Fandom." Personal Interview (Seoul). May 23, 2006.

Lee, Gyu-Rim. "비 4집 앨범 컨셉트 전격 공개 '악마를 이긴 천사'" [Rain revealed the theme of his 4th Album]. October 13, 2006a. *My Daily*. Accessed on September 12, 2007 at http://www.mydaily.co.kr/news/read.html?newsid=200610131924491130.

——. "비, 월드투어 첫공연, 만여명 대성황" [Rain's first world tour concert achieved a great success with over 10,000 fans]. December 15, 2006b. *My Daily*. Accessed on September 11, 2007 at http://www.mydaily.co.kr/news/read.html?newsid=200612152315291130.

Lee, Hui-Jin. "강타 이제 연기자로 중국 정벌" [Kang Ta, as an actor, now conquering China]. August 12, 2004. *GoNews*. Accessed on September 27, 2008 at http://gonews. freechal.com/.

Lee, Hyeong-Seok. "'한류'스타 이젠 中 영화로 대륙 정벌" [*Hallyu* stars, now conquering China through Chinese films]. August 22, 2005. *Herald Kyungje*. Accessed on September 26, 2008 at http://news.naver.com/main/read.nhn?mode=LSD&mid=sec&sid1=106& oid=016&aid=0000182636.

Lee, Hyo-Je. "한국 사회의 군사주의문화와 여성" [Militarism in South Korean society and women]. March 27, 2002. Peace Human Right Movement. Accessed on September 26, 2008 at peace.jinbo.net.

Lee, Jeong-A. "빅뱅, '이번 앨범 만족도 최고!' 한층 깊어진 음악 자신한다" [Big Bang, "We're proud of our 3rd album!" Guarantee maturer music]. August 8, 2008. *OSEN*. Accessed on September 16, 2008 at http://osen.stoo.com/news/html/001/016/984. html.

Lee, Jong-Geon. 동양 고전의 세계 [*The World of Asian Classics*]. Seoul: Gukhakjaryowon, 1999.'

Lee, Min-Ja. "청소년들을 파고드는 '한류'의 마력: 중국의 '한류'" [The magical power of *Hallyu* among the youth: *Hallyu* in China]. 동아시아의 "한류" [Hallyu *in East Asia*]. Ed. Shin Yun-Hwan and Lee Han-Woo. Yongin: Jeonyewon, 2006.

Lee, Mi-Rim. "우리사회의 건강 열풍과 웰빙" [The health and well-being phenomenon in our society]. August 29, 2005. *Kangwon Ilbo*. Accessed on September 27, 2008 at http://www.kwnews.co.kr/SearchView.asp?aid=205082800018&p=%C0%A3%BA%F9.

Lee, Moon-Hwan. "'대장금' 시청률 최고 기록 경신" [*Dae-jang-geum* broke the highest audience share record]. February 25, 2004. *Herald Kyungje*. Accessed on October 2, 2008 at http://news.naver.com/main/read.nhn?mode=LSD&mid=sec&sid1=106&oid =016&aid=0000127095.

Lee, Seong-Wook et al. "2003 한국 영화계를 돌아본다 [Korean cinema 2003]. December 12, 2003. Cine21.com. Accessed on September 26, 2008 at http://www.cine21.com/ Magazine/mag_pub_view.php?mm=005001001&mag_id=22278.

Lee, Su-Hyeon. "1년 내내 '아이돌' 그래도 좋은 이유" [Watching idols all year round, why still great?]. February 25, 2010. *Money Today*. March 4, 2010 at http://star.mt.co.kr/ view/stview.php?no=2010022420021691348&type=1&outlink=1.

Lee, Sun-Young. "Mobile Phone Users Top 40 Million." November 27, 2006. *The Korea Herald*. Accessed on September 15, 2008 at http://news.naver.com/main/read.nhn?mo de=LSD&mid=sec&sid1=108&oid=044&aid=0000061993.

Lie, Rico. *Spaces of Intercultural Communication: An Interdisciplinary Introduction to Communication, Culture, and Globalizing/Localizing Identities*. Cresskill, NJ: Hampton Press, 2003.

Light, Richard. "Sport and the Construction of Masculinity in the Japanese Education System." *Asian Masculinities: The Meaning and Practice of Manhood in China and Japan*. Ed. Kam Louie and Morris Low. London and New York: RoutledgeCurzon, 2003.

Lii, Ding-Tzann. "A Colonized Empire: Reflection on the Expansion of Hong Kong Films in Asian Countries." *Trajectories: Inter-Asia Cultural Studies*. Ed. Kuan-Hsing Chen. London and New York: Routledge, 1998.

Lin, Angel and Avin Tong. "Re-Imagining a Cosmopolitan 'Asian Us': Korean Media Flows and Imaginaries of Asian Modern Femininities." *East Asian Pop Culture: Analysing the Korean Wave*. Ed. Chua Beng Huat and Koichi Iwabuchi. Hong Kong: Hong Kong University Press, 2008.

Livingstone, Sonia. "Relationship between Media and Audiences." *Media, Ritual and Identity*. Ed. Tamar Liebes and James Curran. London and New York: Routledge, 1998.

Louie, Kam. *Theorising Chinese Masculinity: Society and Gender in China*. Cambridge: Cambridge University Press, 2002.

Louie, Rebecca. "Rain Check. A Loss Leaves Korean Pop Star Intent on Success." January 31, 2006. *New York Daily News*. Accessed on October 1, 2008 at http://www.nydailynews.com/archives/entertainment/2006/01/31/2006-01-31_rain_check__a_loss_leaves_ko.html.

Lull, James. *Media, Communication, Culture: A Global Approach*. New York: Columbia University Press, 1995.

Lyotard, Jean-Francois. *The Postmodern Condition: A Report on Knowledge*. Manchester: Manchester University Press, 1984.

Ma, Jeong-Mi. "만인의 연인, 나만의 연인" [Everybody's lover, my only lover]. "겨울연가": 콘텐츠와 콘텍스트 사이 [*Drama* Winter Sonata *between Contents and Context*]. Ed. Kim Young-Soon and Park Ji-Seon. Seoul: Dahal Media, 2005.

Martin, Hans-Peter and Harald Schumann. *The Global Trap: Globalization and the Assault on Prosperity and Democracy*. Trans. Patrick Camiller. Sydney: Pluto Press, 1996.

MBC. "영화 '괴물' 미국 상륙" [*The Host* has landed in the US]. November 2, 2006. *MBC*. Accessed on November 8, 2006 at http://news.naver.com/main/read.nhn?mode=LSD&mid=sec&sid1=001&oid=214&aid=0000022385&.

McChesney, Robert W. "The Political Economy of Global Communication." *Capitalism and the Information Age: Political Economy and the Global Communication Revolution*. Ed. Robert W. McChesney, Ellen Meiksins Wood, and John Bellamy Foster. New York: Monthly Review Press, 1998.

McGray, Douglas. "Japan's Gross National Cool." *Foreign Policy* 130 (2002): 44–54.

Meyrowitz, Joshua. *No Sense of Place: The Impact of Electronic Media on Social Behavior*. New York and Oxford: Oxford University Press, 1985.

Min, Eung-Jun et al. *Korean Film; History, Resistance, and Democratic Imagination*. Westport, Connecticut and London: Praeger, 2003.

Moon, Seok. "'괴물', 미국서 리메이크된다 [*The Host* will be remade in the US]. November 2, 2006. Cine21.com. Accessed on September 15, 2008 at http://www.cine21.com/Article/article_view.php?mm=001001001&article_id=42536.

———. "'괴물', 프랑스 '카이에 뒤 시네마' 2006년 베스트 3위" [*The Host* was selected as the third best film of 2006 by *Cahiers du Cinema*]. January 2, 2007a. Cine21.com.

Accessed on September 15, 2008 at http://www.cine21.com/Article/article_view. php?mm=001001001&article_id=43820.

——. "'괴물', 2주 연속 중국 박스 오피스 정상" [*The Host* hit the box office number one in China for the first two consecutive weeks]. March 20, 2007b. Cine21. com. Accessed on August 6, 2007b at http://www.cine21.com/Article/article_view. php?mm=001001001&article_id=45377.

Moon, Seung-Sook. "The Production and Subversion of Hegemonic Masculinity: Reconfiguring Gender Hierarchy in Contemporary South Korea." *Under Construction*. Ed. Laurell Kendall. Honolulu: University of Hawai'i Press, 2002.

Moon, Yeon-Bae. "2PM, 태국 수상과 만남 ... 6일 쇼케이스" [2PM, meets Thai prime minister ... showcase on 6]. July 6, 2009. *Asia Today*. March 6, 2010 at http://www. asiatoday.co.kr/news/view.asp?seq=264145.

Mori, Yoshitaka. "*Winter Sonata* and Cultural Practices of Active Fans in Japan: Considering Middle-Aged Women as Cultural Agents." *East Asian Pop Culture: Analysing the Korean Wave*. Ed. Chua Beng Huat and Koichi Iwabuchi. Hong Kong: Hong Kong University Press, 2008.

Moria.co.nz. "Best and Worst of 2003." 2003. Moria.co.nz. Accessed on February 11, 2006 at http://www.moria.co.nz/annuals/best03.htm.

Morley, David and Kevin Robins. *Spaces of Identity: Global Media, Electronic Landscapes, and Cultural Boundaries*. London and New York: Routledge, 1995.

Na, Ji-Yeon. "'눈은 즐겁고, 귀는 괴롭다' ... 아이돌, 과다경쟁의 두 얼굴" ['Pleasing eyes, torturing ears' ... Two faces of excessive competition among idols]. March 10, 2010. *Sports Seoul*. March 10, 2010 at http://www.sportsseoul.com/news2/entertain/ hotentertain/2010/0310/20100310101040100000000_8058733037.html.

Nam, An-Woo. "빅뱅 지드래곤, '다이시댄스와의 작업 좋았다'" [Big Bang G-Dragon, "I nagged Daishi Dance to work with him"]. August 8, 2008. *My Daily*. Accessed on September 16, 2008 at http://www.mydaily.co.kr/news/read.html?newsid=2008080810 19221139&ext=na.

Nam, Seung-Hui. 나는 미소년이 좋다 [*I Like Pretty Boys*]. Seoul: Haenaem, 2001.

Naver. "비, 생일맞아 싱가폴 팬 항공권 선물 받아" [Rain received a flight ticket from Singaporean fans for his b'day gift]. June 21, 2006. Naver.com. Accessed on July 15, 2006 at http://news.naver.com/main/read.nhn?mode=LSD&mid=sec&sid1=106&oid =111&aid=0000036913.

Ndalianis, Angela. "Stars in Our Eyes: Introduction." *Stars in Our Eyes: The Star Phenomenon in the Contemporary Era*. Ed. Angela Ndalianis and Charlotte Henry. Westport, Connecticut and London: Praeger, 2002.

Ng, Vivien W. "Ideology and Sexuality: Rape Laws in Qing China." *Journal of Asian Studies* 46.1 (1987): 57–70.

Nizza, Mike. "Updates on Virginia Tech." April 18, 2007. *The LEDE*. Accessed on May 1, 2007 at http://thelede.blogs.nytimes.com/2007/04/18/updates-on-virginia-tech/.

Nye, Joseph S. *Soft Power: The Means to Success in World Politics*. New York: PublicAffairs, 2004.

Oh, Ryong. "한국판 '조스'— '괴물', 뱅쿠버 영화제서 극찬" [Korea's *Jaws — The Host* won high praise at the Vancouver Film Festival]. October 2, 2006. *Yonhap News*. Accessed on September 15, 2008 at http://news.naver.com/main/read.nhn?mode=LSD&mid=sec&sid1=106&oid=001&aid=0001427241.

Onishi, Norimitsu. "What's Korean for 'Real Man'? Ask a Japanese Woman." December 23, 2004. *The New York Times*. Accessed on September 27, 2008 at http://www.nytimes.com/2004/12/23/international/asia/23JAPAN.html?scp=1&sq=Yonsama&st=cse.

Papastergiadis, Nikos. *The Turbulence of Migration: Globalization, Deterritorialization and Hybridity*. Cambridge: Polity Press, 2000.

Pareles, Jon. "Korean Superstar Who Smiles and Says, 'I'm Lonely'." February 4, 2006. *The New York Times*. Accessed on September 27, 2008 at http://www.nytimes.com/2006/02/04/arts/music/04rain.html?scp=1&sq=Korean%20Superstar%20Who%20Smiles%20and%20Says,%20%E2%80%98I%27m%20Lonely%E2%80%99&st=cse.

Park, Chan-Wook et al. *"Oldboy" Book*. Seoul: Olive M&B, 2005.

Park, Dong-Min. "'배용준 일본 왔다!' ... 여성팬 5000명 몰려 북새통" ["Bae Yong-Joon arrived in Japan!" ... 5,000 female fans went crazy!] April 4, 2004. *Kookmin Ilbo*. Accessed on September 27, 2008 at http://www.kukinews.com/news/article/view.asp?page=1&gCode=kmi&arcid=0919373827&code=11110000.

Park, Jae-Deok. "비, 사상 최고가에 펩시 중화권 얼굴" [Rain, new face of Pepsi in the Chinese Speaking region]. December 2, 2005. *Joy News*. Accessed on September 26, 2008 at http://news.naver.com/main/read.nhn?mode=LSD&mid=sec&sid1=106&oid=111&aid=0000023381.

———. "비, 'The Cloud' 로 지구촌 팬을 하나로" [Rain, gathering global fans together through "the Cloud"]. September 28, 2006. *Joy News*. Accessed on September 11, 2007 at http://joynews.inews24.com/php/news_view.php?g_menu=700100&g_serial=226220.

Park, Jeong-Yeon. "시청률 조사 방법" [How to measure TV audience share]. Personal interview (phone). October 2, 2008.

Park, Ji-Seon. "'겨울연가', 그 연금술적 언어" [*Winter Sonata*, the alchemical word]. "겨울연가": 콘텐츠와 콘텍스트 사이 [*Drama* Winter Sonata *between Contents and Context*]. Ed. Kim Young-Soon and Park Ji-Seon. Seoul: Dahal Media, 2005.

Park, No-Ja. 당신들의 대한민국 [*The Republic of Korea of Yours*]. Seoul: Hankyoreh Shinmun, 2001.

Park, Seon-Ae. "비의 데뷔부터 현재까지" [Rain, from his debut till today]. October 28, 2004. *Yahoo Beatbox Webzine*. Accessed on October 1, 2008 at http://blog.naver.com/ookykim?Redirect=Log&logNo=100007065775.

Park, Yong-Chae. "'욘사마 보자' 日 팬 아수라장 10명 부상" ["Let's see *Yonsama*" chaotic welcoming, 10 Japanese fans got injured]. November 26, 2004. *Kyunghyang Shinmun*. Accessed on October 1, 2008 at http://news.khan.co.kr/kh_news/khan_art_view.html?artid=200411261724531&code=940100.

Peattie, Mark R. "Japanese Attitudes toward Colonialism." *The Japanese Colonial Empire, 1895–1945*. Ed. Ramon H. Myers and Mark R. Peattie. Princeton, NJ: Princeton University Press, 1984.

Pieterse, Jan Nederveen. *Globalization and Culture: Global Melange*. Boulder, CO: Rowman & Littlefield Publishers, Inc., 2004.

Pratt, Mary Louise. *Imperial Eyes: Travel Writing and Transculturation*. London and New York: Routledge, 1992.

PuruShotam, Nirmala. "Between Compliance and Resistance: Women and the Middle-Class Way of Life in Singapore." *Gender and Power in Affluent Asia*. Ed. Krishna Sen and Maila Stivens. London and New York: Routledge, 1998.

RainSingapore.com. "The Ten Things You Must Know About Rain." September 2, 2005. Rain's Singaporean Fan Site. Accessed on September 24, 2006 at www.rainsingapore.com.

Reck, David R. "Beatles Orientalis: Influences from Asia in a Popular Song Tradition." *Asian Music* 16.1 (1985): 83–149.

Reichert, Jeff. "Fight Schlub: Park Chan-Wook's *Oldboy*." 2005. Indiewire.com. Accessed on October 1, 2008 at http://www.indiewire.com/movies/movies_050322oldboy.html.

Robertson, Roland. "Glocalization: Time-Space and Homogeneity-Heterogeneity." *Global Modernities*. Ed. Scott Lash, Mike Featherstone, and Roland Robertson. Thousand Oaks, CA: Sage Publications, 1995.

Robinson, Richard and David S. G. Goodman. "The New Rich in Asia: Economic Development, Social Status and Political Consciousness." *The New Rich in Asia: Mobile Phones, McDonalds and Middle-Class Revolution*. London and New York: Routledge, 1996.

Rodan, Garry. "Singapore in 2004: Long-Awaited Leadership Transition." *Asian Survey* 45.1 (2005): 140–45.

Rojek, Chris. *Decentring Leisure: Rethinking Leisure Theory*. London; Thousand Oaks, CA: Sage Publications, 1995.

RomancingSingapore.com. "About Us." 2006. Romancing Singapore Official Web Page. Accessed on October 1, 2008 at http://romancingsingapore.com/aboutus.php.

RottenTomatoes.com. "*Oldboy* Rating." 2005. Rottentomatoes.com. Accessed on July 11, 2007 at http://au.rottentomatoes.com/m/oldboy/.

———. "*The Host* Rating." 2007. Rottentomatoes.com. Accessed on July 11, 2007 at http://au.rottentomatoes.com/m/host/.

Ryan, Colleen. "Historical Enmities Melt as Japan Finds 'Asian Cool'." April 2, 2005. *Australian Financial Review*. Accessed on November 10, 2005 at http://afr.com/home/searchresult.aspx?page=1&count=15&keywords=Historical%20enmities%20melt%20as%20Japan%20finds%20'Asian%20cool'&=Go&date=ALL_TIME&sort=DATE_LATEST_FIRST.

Said, Edward W. *Orientalism*. London: Penguin Books, 1978.

Sankei Sports. "5000 Fans Welcome *Yonsama*." April 4, 2004. *Sankei Sports*. Accessed on October 23, 2004 at http://www.sanspo.com/geino/top/gt200406/gt2004062105.html.

Savlov, Marc. "*Taegukgi: The Brotherhood of War*: Review." September 24, 2004. AustinChronicle.com. Accessed on October 1, 2008 at http://www.austinchronicle.com/gyrobase/Calendar/Film?Film=oid%3A229793.

SBS. 2009. "한류의 위기? … 2PM에게 배워라" [*Hallyu* in crisis? Learn from 2PM]. December 24 2009. SBS Internet News Department. March 4, 2010 at http://news.sbs. co.kr/section_news/news_read.jsp?news_id=N1000688721.

Shim, Young-Hee. "Feminism and the Discourse of Sexuality in Korea: Continuities and Changes." *Human Studies* 24 (2001): 133–48.

Shim, Young-Seop. "초자아와 이드의 혈투를 담은 핏빛 일기" [A crimson diary of bloody fighting between super-ego and id]. December 24, 2003. Cine21.com. Accessed on September 30, 2008 at http://www.cine21.com/Article/article_view. php?mm=005004001&article_id=22447.

Shin, Gi-Joo. "'스캔들' 일본 개봉 성과" [Scandal, the box office result in Japan]. June 7, 2004. Film2.0. Accessed on October 1, 2008 at http://www.film2.co.kr/feature/feature_ final.asp?mkey=147702.

Shin, Gyeong-Hui. "70년대 디스코 열풍 재현해 낸 박진영" [Park Jin-Young, re-presented the 70s disco style]. 1996. *Donga Ilbo Magazine*. Accessed on October 1, 2008 at http:// www.donga.com/fbin/lets?d=9707&f=lets9707cc010.html.

Shin, Gyeong-Mi. "'한류'열풍은 '아시아 공동문화 창출'의 키워드: 일본의 '한류'" [The *Hallyu* phenomenon is a key-word to understand "creating Asia's common culture": *Hallyu* in Japan]. 동아시아의 "한류" [*Hallyu in East Asia*]. Ed. Shin Yun-Hwan and Lee Han-Woo. Yongin: Jeonyewon, 2006.

Shin, Young-Bok. 강의: 나의 동양 고전 독법 [*Lecture: My Reading of Asian Classics*]. Seoul: Dolbege, 2004.

Simpson, Mark. *Male Impersonators: Men Performing Masculinity*. London: Cassell, 1994.

——. "Meet the Metrosexual." July 22, 2002. Salon.com. Accessed on October 8, 2008 at http://dir.salon.com/story/ent/feature/2002/07/22/metrosexual/.

Siriyuvasak, Ubonrat and Shin Hyeon-Joon. "Asianizing K-Pop: Production, Consumption and Identification Patterns among Thai Youth." *Inter-Asia Cultural Studies Journal* 8.1 (2007): 109–36.

Slevin, James. *The Internet and Society*. Malden, MA: Polity Press, 2000.

Slotek, Jim. "*Taegukgi* Review: A Bond of Brothers." November 12, 2004. Canoe. ca. Accessed on October 1, 2008 at http://jam.canoe.ca/Movies/Reviews/T/ Taegukgi/2004/11/12/754450.html.

Sontag, Deborah. "The Ambassador." January 29, 2006. *The New York Times*. Accessed on October 1, 2008 at http://www.nytimes.com/2006/01/29/arts/music/29sont.html.

Sontag, Susan. "The Decay of Cinema." *The New York Times*, February 25, 1996.

Standish, Isolde. "Korean Cinema and the New Realism: Text and Context." *Colonialism and Nationalism in Asian Cinema*. Ed. Wimal Dissanayake. Bloomington and Indianapolis: Indiana University Press, 1994.

Stevens, Carolyn S. *Japanese Popular Music: Culture, Authenticity, and Power*. London and New York: Routledge, 2008.

Suk, Sarah. "S. Korean Boom Changing Japanese People's Perceptions." 2005. *Kyodo News*.

Tabata, Satoshi. "Korean Romance Excites NHK." October 2, 2003. *Daily Yomiuri*. Accessed on October 1, 2008 at http://global.factiva.com.ezproxy.lib.unimelb.edu.au/ha/default.aspx.

Tak, Jin-Hyeon. "세븐 아시아 5개국 동시 정벌 나선다" [Se7en, ready to subjugate five Asian countries]. January 12, 2006. *Sports Seoul.* Accessed on October 1, 2008 at http://news.naver.com/main/read.nhn?mode=LSD&mid=sec&sid1=106&oid=073&aid=0000015884.

Tan, Kenneth Paul. "Sexing up Singapore." *International Journal of Cultural Studies* 6.4 (2003): 403–23.

Telotte, J. P. "Beyond All Reason: The Nature of the Cult." *The Cult Film Experience: Beyond All Reason.* Ed. J. P. Telotte. Austin: University of Texas Press, 1991.

Tessei, Matsuzawa. "Street Labour Markets, Day Labourers and the Structure of Oppression." *The Japanese Trajectory: Modernization and Beyond.* Ed. Gavan McCormack and Yoshio Sugimoto. Cambridge, UK; New York: Cambridge University Press, 1988.

Thomson, Desson. "*Oldboy's* Powerful Hold." 2005. *Washington Post*, Sec. Arts & Living: WE45.

Thumem, Janet. "Miss Hepburn Is Humanized." *Feminist Review* 24 (1986): 71–102.

Toffler, Alvin. *The Third Wave.* New York: Morrow, 1980.

TwitchFilm.net. "Twitch Authors." 2007. Twitchfilm.net. Accessed on August 3, 2007 at http://twitchfilm.net/site/authors/.

Ueno, Toshiya. "Japanimation and Techno-Orientalism." *The Uncanny: Experiments in Cyborg Culture.* Ed. Bruce Grenville. Vancouver: Vancouver Art Gallery and Arsenal Pulp Press, 2001.

Vasil, Raj. *Asianising Singapore: The PAP's Management of Ethnicity.* Singapore: Heinemann Asia, 1995.

Villarreal, Phil. "South Korean Vision of Horrors of War." November 18, 2004. *Arizona Daily Star.* Accessed on October 1, 2008 at http://www.azstarnet.com/sn/printSN/48376.php.

Walsh, Brian. "The People Who Shape Our World: Rain, the Magic Feet from Korea." April 30, 2006. *Time.* Accessed on October 1, 2008 at http://www.time.com/time/magazine/article/0,9171,1187264,00.html.

Wang, Georgette et al. "The New Communications Landscape." *The New Communications Landscape: Demystifying Media Globalization.* Ed. Jan Servaes, Georgette Wang, and Anura Goonasekera. London and New York: Routledge, 2000.

Wang, Sun Hong. 중국의 어제와 오늘 [China, Yesterday and Today]. Seoul: Pyeongminsa, 2003.

Watson, Paul. "Genre Theory and Hollywood Cinema." *Introduction to Film Studies.* Ed. Jill Nelmes. London and New York: Routledge, 2007.

Welsch, Wolfgang. "Transculturality: The Puzzling Form of Cultures Today." *Spaces of Culture: City, Nation, World.* Ed. Mike Featherstone and Scott Lash. London, Thousand Oaks, CA: Sage Publications, 1999.

Were, Christian. "The Western Fandom of Asian Genre Films." Personal interview (Melbourne). January 12, 2008.

Willemen, Paul. *Looks and Frictions: Essays in Cultural Studies and Film Theories.* Bloomington and Indianapolis: Indiana University Press, 1994.

Wilson, Rob. "Korean Cinema on the Road to Globalization: Tracking Global/Local Dynamics, or Why Im Kwon-Taek Is Not Ang Lee." *Inter-Asia Cultural Studies Journal* 2.2 (2001): 307–18.

Wirelessfederation.com. "South Korea Signs Up 40 Million Mobile Users." November 27, 2006. Wireless Federation. Accessed on September 15, 2008 at http://wirelessfederation.com/news/south-korea-signs-up-40-million-mobile-users/.

Wiseman, Paul. "Korean Romantic Hero Holds Japan in Thrall; Frenzy over Heartthrob Symbolizes Changing Relations between Peoples." December 10, 2004. *USA Today*. Accessed on January 12, 2005 at http://pqasb.pqarchiver.com/USAToday/access/760396831.html?dids=760396831:760396831&FMT=ABS&FMTS=ABS:FT&date=Dec+10%2C+2004&author=Paul+Wiseman&pub=USA+TODAY&edition=&startpage=A.13&desc=Korean+romantic+hero+holds+Japan+in+thrall+%3B+Frenzy+over+heartthrob+symbolizes+changing+relations+between+peoples.

Woojungsa.com. "'우정사'에 관한 모든 것" [All About *Woojungsa*]. 1999. Woojungsa Fan Site. Accessed on January 12, 2009 at http://woojungsa.com/fhome.htm.

Yamaguchi, Mari. "All Things Korean Now Popular in Japan." November 22, 2004. Associated Press Newswires. Accessed on October 2, 2008 at http://dir.salon.com/story/ent/wire/2004/11/22/korea_japan/index.html.

Yang, Ji-Hyeon. "제 44회 뉴욕 영화제, 한국 영화로는 '해변의 여인', '괴물' 소개" [The 44th New York Film Festival, *The Host* and *Woman in the Beach* are invited]. November 7, 2006. Cine21.com. Accessed on September 15, 2008 at http://www.cine21.com/Article/article_view.php?mm=001002003&article_id=42580.

Yoo, Gang-Moon. "'야유' 퍼붓는 중국 … '반한 감정' 어디서 폭발했나" [China "boos" Korea … where "anti-Korea sentiment" began?]. August 27, 2008. *Hankyoreh Shinmun*. Accessed on October 16, 2008 at http://www.hani.co.kr/arti/international/china/306886.html.

Yoo, Sang-Cheol et al. "한류"의 비밀 [*The Secret of* Hallyu]. Seoul: Saengagui Namu, 2005.

Yoon, Go-Eun. "배용준 기부금 얼마나 되나" [How much has Bae Yong-Joon donated?]. February 22, 2005. *Yonhap News*. Accessed on October1, 2008 at http://news.naver.com/main/read.nhn?mode=LSD&mid=sec&sid1=106&oid=001&aid=0000919712.

Yoon, Gyeong-Cheol. "'대부'전세계 네티즌 선정 최고의 영화 — '올드보이' 118위" [*Godfather*, the best film of all time — *Oldboy* 118th]. July 31, 2006. *Herald Kyungje*. Accessed on October 2, 2008 at http://news.naver.com/main/read.nhn?mode=LSD&mid=sec&sid1=106&oid=112&aid=0000045279.

Yoon, Wan-Joon. "황금의 제국 페르시아 (5): 이란에 부는 한국 열풍" [The golden empire Persia (5): The Korean Wave in Iran]. April 14, 2008. *Donga Ilbo*. Accessed on October 2, 2008 at http://www.donga.com/fbin/output?n=200804140041.

Yoon, Yeo-Soo. "비, '스피드 레이서' 캐릭터 원래 국적은 일본인" [Rain, the original nationality of *Speed Racer* character was Japanese]. September 29, 2007. *Money Today*. Accessed on October 2, 2008 at http://star.moneytoday.co.kr/view/stview.php?no=2007092911043586927&type=1&outlink=1.

YTN. "'꼭 와주세요' 가수 비, 생일 선물로 항공권 받아" ["Please come to Singapore" Rain received a flight ticket for his b'day gift]. June 22, 2006. YTNstar.co.kr. Accessed on July 15, 2006 at http://www.ytnstar.co.kr/search/search_view.php?cd=0101&key=200 606220850530467&mode=&keyword=%2526quot%3B%B2%C0%2520%BF%CD %C1%D6%BC%BC%BF%E4%2526quot%3B%2520%B0%A1%BC%F6%2520% BA%F1%2C%2520%BB%FD%C0%CF%BC%B1%B9%B0%B7%CE%2520%C7 %D7%B0%F8%B1%C7%2520%B9%DE%BE%C6%2520.

Zhang, K. et al. "Changing Sexual Attitudes and Behaviour in China: Implications for the Spread of HIV and Other Sexually Transmitted Diseases." *AIDS CARE* 11.5 (1999): 581–89.

Index